Indispensable Employees

How to Hire Them
How to Keep Them

By
Martha R. A. Fields

PRESS

Franklin Lakes, NJ

INDISPENSABLE EMPLOYEES
Edited by Jodi Brandon
Typeset by John J. O'Sullivan
Cover design by Fanzone Design Solutions
Printed in the U.S.A. by Book-mart Press

To order this title, please call toll-free 1-800-CAREER-1
(NJ and Canada: 201-848-0310) to order using VISA or MasterCard,
or for further information on books from Career Press.

CAREER
PRESS

The Career Press, Inc., 3 Tice Road, PO Box 687
Franklin Lakes, NJ 07417
www.careerpress.com

Library of Congress Cataloging-in-Publication Data

Fields, Martha R. A.
   Indispensable employees : how to hire them, how to keep
them / Martha R. A. Fields.
      p. cm.
   Includes index.
   ISBN 1-56414-516-6 (pbk.)
      1. Employee retention. 2.Employees—Recruiting. 3.
Organizational change. 4. Manpower planning. I. Title.

HF5549.5.r58 F54 2001
658 .3'11—dc21

                                                          00-052991

Acknowledgments

Writing a book is a bit like having a baby. To borrow from a few cliches, with regard to this book's conception, "it took two to tango" and as the African proverb tells us, "it takes a village to raise it." Quite a few people helped me to conceive this book and a very large village helped me to raise it. My wonderful and devoted parents, Betty and Leonard Mervin, taught me that anything is possible if you believe in it and work hard to obtain it. Cira Mervin, my stepmother, reminded me along the way to remain focused and remained a support for me to "hang in there." My 10 brothers, sisters, and stepbrothers and stepsisters, as well as their spouses and children, also pitched in and some even helped with the research and various aspects of this book. Thanks Adrienne Mervin, Betty Graves, Dana Mervin, and Sharon Brown.

My immediate family, Shawna Fields, Dr. Richard K. Fields, and Michael Fields, had to live with me through this process, and they provided me with the rock-solid family foundation needed to produce this book. My precious 10-year-old Shawna Imani, whose name means "little wise one" and "faith," always gives me numerous insights into the world and she is what we have to look forward to with regard to the workforce of tomorrow.

Mrs. Gloria Battle, Joyce Frith, Martha Hofmann, Jeff Kosberg, and Penha Pereira helped me balance work life during a hectic time in my existence. Close colleagues and friends stood by my side throughout this process, and I will be forever grateful for their kind and critical words. Thanks to Dr. Barbara Addison Reid, Janine Fondon, George Kaye, Juliette Mayers, Ron Leavell (God rest his soul), Mongalam Srinivasan, Alesia Wilson, Maureen Alphonse Charles, Nina and Robert Miller Browne, and Norman Shakespeare and Carmon Cunningham of the National Black MBA Association (Boston chapter).

A CEO is only as good as his or her staff, and I feel that my success and that of this book is due in large part to the blood, sweat, and tears of the Fields Associates staff (both past and present). Although the list is long, I want to say a very special thanks to some of the people who worked tirelessly and gave of their mind, body, and soul to this project: Yolanda Brown, who has a grace and presence that inspires people to want to excel; Deane

Coady, who is a phenomenal thinker, trainer, and all-around decent person; and others who have contributed in some way to the book, including Robin Small, Mari Vazquez, Jessica Tamburrino, John Dougherty, Bettina Elliott, and Lisa Eldridge, one of the most creative persons I know. Ken Lizotte, Roberta Fitzsimmons, Juliet Brudney of *The Boston Globe,* and Sal Sagaresce were instrumental in providing the necessary guidance needed to see this book through from concept to reality.

A support mechanism of colleagues, friends, and clients is essential in the birthing process of a book. I can't thank enough the many colleagues and clients from around the country who were so willing to tell their stories and share quotes and interesting best and radical practices. Special thanks to Mary Aceto of Boston Coach, Polly Price, Carolyn Everette, Jackie Benson Jones, Jamie Hoyte of Harvard University, Marilyn Fuller of Texas Instruments, Robin Browne of the Four Seasons Hotel, Regina DeTore of Sepracor, Inc., and Judy Weil of NEHRA/ The Society of Human Resource Management.

Finally, a special thanks to the staff at Career Press who were present and center in the delivery room and have provided me the opportunity to publish what I know will be a happy, healthy book to help people recruit and retain indispensable employees in these unprecedented times.

—Martha R.A. Fields
January 2001

Contents

" The future is bright for indispensable employees with thick skins, nerves of steel, and fresh eyes.
These new-age thinkers know how to translate vision into realities, rejoice in change, and are masters at making people see the universe as their playground.
They thrive on inspiring people to achieve their maximum potential and don't hesitate to venture beyond the shores of their minds to tap uncharted oceans."

—Martha R.A. Fields

Introduction

started my career in management and human resources more than 20 years ago. Of course, I was only 10 years old then; human resources and the world were very different. There were no Americans with Disabilities Act (ADA), Family Medical Leave Act (FMLA), I-9 forms, or e-mail. Companies such as IBM practiced a "no-layoff policy." There were rotary phones, busy signals, and no voice mail. IBM Selectric typewriters and correction tape, not computers, were standard desk attire. There was no workforce flexibility. You worked from nine to five. It was a way to make a living. You had flexibility—in choosing what time to go for lunch. The flex choice options were to eat at noon or 1 p.m.

Those were the good ol' days. Managing people in today's workforce has become complex. As a vice president at a high technology firm recently told me, "It used to be all I had to do to manage people was to make sure my staff got their jobs done. Now, not only do I have to make sure they do that, but I'm playing many other roles: psychologist, parent, career coach, daycare and eldercare advisor, you name it!"

Not long ago, I was dealing with a client on a very interesting employee relations issue: workers sleeping on the job. The dilemma was that he knew certain staff were sleeping on the job, but didn't want to fire them. As the manager explained to me, "I feel torn. If my employee is breathing I want to keep him. Do you know how *long* it will take to find a replacement if I let him go? Although he sleeps on the job and I may only get six and not eight hours out of him, that's better than having no one."

Ironically, later that week, I was driving in my car and heard a radio DJ telling people about what to do if they were found sleeping on the job. His advice was to say one of two things as you emerged from dreamland: (1) "The woman at the Red Cross told me this could happen when I gave blood." (2) "Amen," followed by, "Please forgive me for saying my prayers at work." Yes, management life isn't what it used to be.

Are you fully staffed most of the time? Do you have few or no problems finding and keeping talented and competent staff? Do you have too many unfilled jobs and not enough qualified candidates? Are too many good staff leaving for better jobs elsewhere? Are your human resources profession-als and managers running out of innovative retention strategies and ap-proaches to fill your rapidly growing number of vacant positions? Does your organization want a more diverse workforce, but isn't able to locate or keep qualified women, immigrants, and people of color?

If you answered yes to any of these questions, read on. You will find *Indispensable Employees: How to Hire Them, How to Keep Them* a useful guide to help you solve your labor shortage.

Welcome to the age of indispensable employees (IEs), and say goodbye to the era of the disposable workforce. Many of the organizations that "downsized," "right-sized," and "gave people the ax" in the late 1980s to mid-1990s now dangle massive carrots before hard-to-hire applicants hoping to lure them inside their walls. The most staggering of these carrots in-clude all-expenses paid vacations, BMWs, wardrobe allowances, and even $100K signing bonuses.

Why the dramatic turnaround? Simply put, there's a gigantic labor short-age today that the Department of Labor predicts will be with us at least through the year 2006. In such times, Corporate America needs to wake itself up. Unfortunately, many organizations, large and small, know that some-thing is wrong, but they don't know what it is or how they can fix it. This book will show you how to:

- Maximize your recruitment and retention dollars by imple-menting the Fields Associates, Inc. model of retention *and* recruitment.
- Utilize techniques of best-practice organizations and adapt or adopt them to your company's style.

- Decrease costly turnover.
- Maximize recruitment efforts by turning employees and managers into goodwill ambassadors and headhunters.
- Employ new approaches to recruit and retain:
  - Generation Xers.
  - Baby Boomers.
  - Matures.
  - People of color (Asians, African Americans, Latinos, and Native Americans).
  - Foreign nationals/immigrants.
  - Individuals with disabilities.
  - Women.
  - White males.
- Discourage key talent from being lured away by competitors.
- Understand what top experts and organizations are saying about how to solve labor shortages, as well as what are some of the best, interesting, and radical practices organizations are using to lure and retain indispensable employees.

Indispensable Employees: How to Hire Them, How to Keep Them is built on my 23 years of management experience combined with a management consulting practice that has guided Fortune 500 companies, Ivy League schools, and nonprofit organizations to measurable, impressive results. The inventive strategies found in these pages will help you compete in the talent war contests of today's unmercifully competitive labor market.

My company works frequently with the world's top organizations regarding issues of management consulting, recruitment, retention, diversity/globalization, and management and executive training/development/ coaching.

Often, people are looking for us to give them one pill that will solve all of their management, human resources, and organizational pains and woes. Unfortunately, there is no panacea. In fact, after reading this book, I hope you'll reach the conclusion that both short-term and long-range solutions must be utilized to solve your labor shortage. You will also see that many of these approaches take more than a quarter to implement (the quarter reference is to both money and time). They also require a gargantuan amount of blood, sweat, tears, patience, and perseverance.

This book first focuses on understanding the context and what has happened in the workplace, in society, and in your organization. That requires us to look at recruitment and retention issues from different—even revolutionary and radical—lenses. People often are in a hurry and want to gloss over, delete, or skip understanding the context. The reasons and variables that contribute to *why* we are doing what we are doing are of utmost importance.

It is my belief that to hire and keep IEs, you must first understand the context or the why, and then move to the "how." I urge you to "hang in there" and carefully read the first few chapters of this book. Once you realize why it is important, I guarantee you that you'll be more than open to issues explored in the second half of the book—the "how-to-do-it" chapters. Throughout the book, you'll find included:

- Forms and action plan exercises to help you analyze and/ or implement the material covered in the chapter.
- The best, interesting, and radical practices that organizations are utilizing to reel in IEs and keep them there.
- Company spotlights, which highlight the practices of organizations that have taken steps to address recruitment and retention issues.

Regardless of your organization's size and budget, many of the best, interesting, or radical approaches outlined can be adapted or adopted. Keep an open mind as you read about some of the conservative and traditional, as well as the wild and crazy, things organizations regardless of size are doing.

For this book, I've interviewed numerous experts and human resources and management professionals, as well as everyday people who are just trying to make a living. You'll see that an eclectic array of industries are represented, because it is my belief that we can all learn from people within our industries, and there is also much to be gained by focusing our brain cells to listen to what organizations that are different from our own are doing. Small and large companies are featured. Everyone is experiencing challenges. Large companies can learn volumes about this issue from smaller ones and vice versa. Remember, these are unprecedented times in which we are living. Never has the job market been so illusive. We are pioneers to some extent as we chart our course and create new templates for getting work done in our organizations.

Following is a list of organizations that I've interviewed and are included in this book. They are large and small, some with names that are familiar to our eyes and ears; others you've perhaps never heard of. Both for-profit and nonprofit organizations in a variety of industries are represented. As you will see, many of them were candid and open about the challenges and opportunities associated with recruiting and retaining IEs. My thanks to all of them for their willingness to share their experiences so others can benefit from their sage advice. The companies in this book include:

- Allegiant Media.
- Bentley College.
- BostonCoach—a Fidelity Investments Company.
- Butler Home Products, Inc.
- *DiversityInc.com.*
- Ezenia! Inc.
- Evergreen Investments.
- Fidelity Investments.
- Fitzgerald, Stevens and Ford.
- Fleet Financial.
- The Four Seasons Hotel—Boston.
- Giga Information Group.
- The Gillette Company.
- Government Accounting Office.
- Harvard University.
- Lesley University.
- Lockheed Martin.
- The Massachusetts Institute of Technology.
- The National Black MBA Association.
- The New England Aquarium.
- Operation A.B.L.E of Greater Boston.
- Partners HealthCare System.
- The Partnership.
- Sepracor, Inc.
- State Street Corporation.
- Texas Instruments.
- Timberland.
- Tufts Health Plan.
- Union Hospital.
- Unity First/Unity Online.
- U.S. Armed Forces.

Straight from the expert's lips:

"Retention is a function of how people feel while they are at work. Do they feel valued? Do they feel empowered? Do they feel challenged? Do they feel acknowledged and appreciated? Do they feel like they belong? Do they feel proud about the work and the company?

"Employees' feelings, or lack thereof, form their thoughts about the organization. The manager's role has the greatest impact on the environments in which people work and how they feel. It is quite simple: People will stay in an organization where the climate/environment allows them to feel good about being there.

"Managers who have 'emotional intelligence' about how people are reacting to the climate are critical to retaining employees: being hypersensitive to the subtle changes of the climate and ensuring that there is the right amount of comfort and challenge; the optimal amount of content and context; and the perfect balance of form and void.

"So ask, how does it feel to be here? The answer to that question can give great insight for opportunities to create a more productive workplace."

—Alesia Wilson,
Director of Management Development, Fidelity Investments

Startup exercise

As you start to learn about how to hire and retain IEs, reflect on the following questions. (You may even want to jot down your responses.)

1. How long have you been employed in the workforce?
2. What is one significant change that you've seen during that time in:

a) Society?

b) The workplace?

Read on to further explore how the unprecedented changes in society and the workplace have and will impact upon your ability to find and keep indispensable employees.

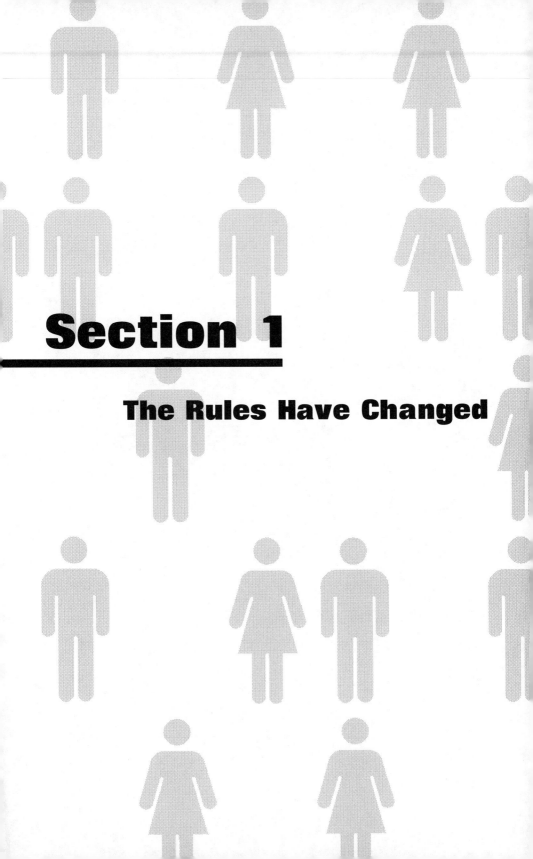

Section 1

The Rules Have Changed

Chapter 1

From Disposable to Indispensable Employees: The 1980s to the 2000s

An old Bob Dylan song told us, "The times are a changing." I can't think of a more appropriate statement to describe today's workplace. Reflect on your answers to the exercise in the Introduction. The changes in the workplace, in society, and in organizations over the past few years have been massive. In fact, we have not seen such monumental changes in the workplace since the Industrial Revolution.

Today, people often use the word "revolutionary" to describe the unprecedented changes taking place in society and the workplace in this new technology age. Think for a moment about the word *revolutionary*. What happens during a revolution? Some people are discontent and feel fear and chaos; others are invigorated and excited as new leaders emerge and a different and fresh way of thinking, doing, acting, and being emerges. Danger and opportunity abound. Does this sound familiar? Isn't that what many workplaces today are touching, feeling, and tasting like during these revolutionary times?

Our unprecedented times call for new and yet-to-be-discovered approaches to address issues related to recruiting and retaining staff. The massive changes within society, the workplace, and organizations have caused the rules of the workplace to change.

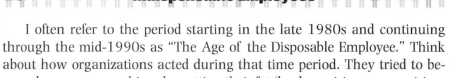

I often refer to the period starting in the late 1980s and continuing through the mid-1990s as "The Age of the Disposable Employee." Think about how organizations acted during that time period. They tried to become lean, mean machines by cutting their fat (by downsizing, reorganizing, and ostracizing their employees). By the mid-1990s, America was back on top of the global marketplace, and many organizations seemed to realize their goals: Revenues increased, and so did stock prices.

What many managers didn't bargain for was how great a job they had done in rebuilding America, but how poor a job they had done in preparing our current and future workforce's skills for the challenges that came with improved technology—namely, more jobs that required higher technological skills than in the past. As the year 2000 approached, employers were suddenly in for an enormous Y2K, new millennium surprise. However, if they really thought about it, they would have seen it gaining momentum for a number of years. The end of the Age of the Disposable Employee had arrived.

The ranks of workers with the right technological and managerial stuff to survive and thrive shrank and those "with the goods" started to flex their workforce muscle and demand some heretofore unthinkable things if they were to be recruited and retained in an organization. In other words, the movement has switched from the Age of the Disposable Employee to that of the Indispensable Employee.

What American managers didn't plan for, however, was the impending labor shortage and the "skills gap"—that is, the difference between the technical proficiency necessary in the workforce, and the labor force's actual general lack of know-how and skills. Additionally, economic growth was expected to remain ahead of population growth. Simply put, there were and would be many more jobs available than qualified and technically proficient workers to fill them.

Let's examine further how workers have gone from being disposable to indispensable.

Wave goodbye to "my way or the highway" management

If there is one thing that you take away from this book, it is to recognize that it is no longer a buyer's market.

The early 1980s were prosperous times. Baby Boomers had blossomed into mature adults and were spending their future earnings away.

Workplace Changes

Late 1980s to Mid-1990s

- "Age of the Disposable Employee"
- "Right-sized, downsized, ostracized, re-engineered, gave people the ax, lean and mean machines

Now

- "Survivor's Syndrome"
- "Age of the Indispensable Employee"

(As we will learn later, this would later haunt them. Many of them hadn't saved enough money to retire and would therefore have to stay employed in the workforce longer to make ends meet and pay for their astronomical healthcare benefits.) Many organizations had little need to focus on issues of retention, because the job market was robust with workers. A popular management mantra was, "If you don't like the way I'm doing things, take the highway and leave. I'll just call the next person waiting in the wings to gladly take your job."

As economic times soured during the late 1980s to mid-1990s, management sharpened its axes and started disposing and laying off people in record numbers.

From the late 1980s through the early 1990s, organizations throughout the United States entered into a battle for their corporate lives. Sales and the economy plummeted in the United States. American businesses were flocking to Japan to learn about how they did things. They even learned how to manage from American-imported gurus such as Deming.

American business leaders, however, had temporarily lost the battle to capture the business world, but were unrelenting and not ready to throw in the towel and lose the war. The Jack Welches (as you may recall, some referred to him as "neutron Jack Welch" back then) and the Lee Iacoccas fought back. As in Greek mythology, they were determined to resurrect their organizations from the ashes, put quality into their work, and make their organizations number one again. Tightening their organizational belts to become lean, mean organizational machines, they slashed, burned, and churned management positions so that flattened hierarchies became the "in thing."

As with Sylvester Stallone's Rambo character, they were relentless in their pursuit to win the war, not the battle. By the mid-1990s, the fruits of their labor bore the sweet fruit they had been waiting to taste. Gradually stock prices rose. Alan Greenspan and the Feds helped Corporate America to refuel the economy. America was well on its way to an unprecedented period of economic growth and prosperity as it entered the new millennium. The Asian tigers also were in for a rude awakening as Singapore unleashed a domino effect throughout the Asian Pacific Rim and the world when its monetary system collapsed.

America got through the battle *and* the war and emerged as a world business leader. The toll it exacted on its employees, however, was enormous.

The survivor's syndrome

By the mid- to late 1990s, America was back on top of the world. The impact that the war and the "Age of the Disposable Employee" exacted was huge.

After corporations had finished slashing, burning, flattening hierarchies, and re-engineering, there emerged strong, financially sound institutions. The people within them, however, didn't fare as well. After the dust from the corporate "Rambo grenades" settled, what organizations were left with were employees who suffered from what researchers have termed the survivor's syndrome.

Knowledgeable people who have conducted research on employees experiencing the trauma of the Age of the Disposable Employee period report that many staff suffered from the "survivor's syndrome." What were some of the characteristics exhibited by employees who had lived through these trying times? It's not a pretty picture. Researchers tell us that "survivor's syndrome employees" experienced the same type of characteristics that people have when they've been through major traumatic experiences. When they say major, they mean gargantuan—think plane crashes, the Holocaust, and earthquakes and other significant natural disasters. Sounds serious? It is.

Just when organizations were back on their feet, doing well, and in need of employees who could help them move agendas further, boost sales, and assist in building the future, they were stuck with these oftentimes needy survivor's syndrome employees. Such employees were frequently risk-adverse and conflicted. They were happy to survive the blade of the layoff ax, but they were concerned about their friends who had to take lower-paying jobs, had to go on unemployment, or were about to lose their homes.

As economic times improved by the late 1990s and as survivor's syndrome employees recovered from their condition, some extremely interesting dynamics took place in the workplace.

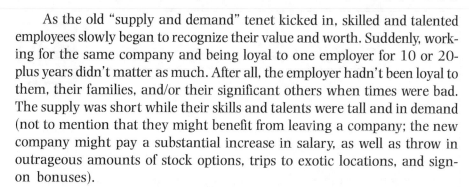

As the old "supply and demand" tenet kicked in, skilled and talented employees slowly began to recognize their value and worth. Suddenly, working for the same company and being loyal to one employer for 10 or 20-plus years didn't matter as much. After all, the employer hadn't been loyal to them, their families, and/or their significant others when times were bad. The supply was short while their skills and talents were tall and in demand (not to mention that they might benefit from leaving a company; the new company might pay a substantial increase in salary, as well as throw in outrageous amounts of stock options, trips to exotic locations, and sign-on bonuses).

As organizations have continued to merge, be acquired, or go out of business because they are no longer viable in today's economy, many find that they are still faced with handling survivor syndrome employees. Unfortunately, because of a strong economy (unlike the weak one in the late 1980s and early 1990s), employers are having a more difficult time holding on to valuable talent, who are just not patient enough for a company to "get its act together and back on its feet." The life brought about by outrageous salaries and perks is just too alluring.

Moving from the 1980s through the 1990s and into the 2000s, we are reminded more than ever about Bob Dylan's prophetic statement: "The times are a changing," or Donna Summers' "She works hard for the money so you better treat her right" disco anthem. In a few short decades, Gen Xers have graduated from their latchkey status and have entered the workforce. By the new millennium, the war for talent was in full swing.

Mixed messages

If having to change your management style from "my way or the highway" to treating employees like professional athletes (that is, giving them outlandish perks to win the talent wars) was not enough, today's managers must also manage in a workplace that is filled with mixed messages.

Think of the years when we've had a booming economy and low unemployment. Mergers and acquisitions abound, as do layoffs caused by organizations folding in the e-commerce–driven world. Despite the stories of 20-somethings becoming instant millionaires as dotcom companies went public, not everyone in society prospered. Unemployment rates among urban minority youth, individuals with disabilities, and older workers remained high.

Mergers and acquisitions, particularly of organizations that were fierce competitors then joined in holy matrimony, continue to boggle the mind as

Straight from the expert's lips:

"The most effective retention strategy I know is to make sure that employees feel valued for their individual contributions to the mission and success of the organization. In other words, they understand—because they are told and because the reward mechanisms reinforce the message—that they bring unique capabilities to their jobs. They matter; they make a difference."

—*Laura Avakian, Vice President for Human Resources, Massachusetts Institute of Technology (M.I.T.)*

well as managers who struggle to manage during and after them. Creating a new corporate culture, rather than a blended one, is often a tall order—and one that may take years to accomplish, assuming that it *can* be accomplished. Managers must therefore work even harder to keep valuable talent and IEs from abandoning ship.

In addition to facing these challenges, today's employees are handling a multitude of issues—some of which are workplace-related, and others that are personal life issues and changes that society has imposed. It's no wonder that so many of us are tired at the end of the day!

Is the labor shortage here to stay?

So you're thinking that from the 1980s to the 2000s, the labor market has gone from feast to famine. Does that leave open the door for another reversal of fortune? Can this blip on the labor market screen continue for any respectable period of time? Here is the million dollar question every employer must now face: Is the labor shortage here to stay? The answer is quite clear: The Bureau of Labor Statistics predicts that current labor shortages will continue until at least 2006. It is my belief that these are the good ol' days, and that our talent shortage may even continue beyond 2006.

Action plan exercise

Use this exercise to help you better understand where your organization stands with regard to some of the topics discussed in this chapter.

What implications does the information you've learned have for recruiting and retaining IEs?

- Mixed messages.
- The end of disposable employees.
- Workplace changes.
- How to wave goodbye to "my way or the highway" management.
- Continued labor shortages at least until 2006.

Once you've examined these issues, think about any action plan items you need to implement in order to recruit and retain IEs.

Chapter 2

How the Workplace Has Changed

"There will never be job security. You will be employed by us as long as you add value to the organization, and you are continuously responsible for finding ways to add value. In return, you have the right to demand interesting and important work, the freedom and resources to perform it well, pay that reflects your contribution, and the experience and training needed to be employable here or elsewhere."
—*Fortune*, June 13, 1994

n the late 1990s, information technology (IT) positions were the hardest to fill. Today, countless other positions are keeping managers and human resources professionals up all night. Sleep-deprived managers have begun asking, *What type of signing bonus, salary scale, flexible schedule, or other benefits will it take to keep our positions filled?*

Surprisingly, it doesn't necessarily take dollar signs to keep employees happy. A fabulous book entitled *1001 Ways to Reward Employees*, by Bob Nelson, states that numerous studies indicate that the number one employee motivator is praise for a job well done. Because it's no longer a "buyer's" or "employer's market," where a recruiter or a hiring manager can pick and choose from among stacks of resumes, organizations must begin taking such findings seriously. Simply put: Employees rule.

You don't have to be a rocket scientist or brain surgeon, or have earned your millions by joining a dotcom company before it went public, to know that the rules of the game in the workplace have changed since the 1980s.

The June 13, 1994 article in *Fortune* that is cited at the beginning of this chapter articulated so well how the workforce was changing and the context for the new employee/employer relationship.

In addition to the employee/employer relationship changing after the trauma of the late 1980s and 1990s, other significant changes have affected the demographics of our society and workforce. To better understand the profile of an IE, we must understand some key demographic changes. Before reading on, take a moment to complete the quiz that follows concerning the changing workforce. You might be surprised by the answers.

Workforce Demographics Quiz

1. The age of the U.S. workforce can be broken down as:

___% Matures (born between 1920 and 1945)

___% Baby Boomers (born between 1946 and 1964)

___% Generation Xers (born between 1965 and 1981)

(Source: *Rocking the Ages: The Yankelovich Report* (adapted))

2. The Bureau of Labor Statistics (BLS) predicts the workforce will grow by ___ percent per year between 1996 and 2005.

a) 30

b) 10

c) 1

(Source: *Workforce 2020*, Hudson Institute)

3. According to *Pension, Retirement and Eldercare*, the average retirement age will soon be___.

a) 60

b) 70+

c) 80

(Source: *Pension, Retirement and Eldercare*)

4. What three states will account for more than 45 percent of the nation's total population growth between 1995 and 2025?

1. _____

2. _____

3. _____

(Source: *Workforce 2020*, Hudson Institute)

5. Race in the United States can be broken down as follows:

___% Whites/Caucasians

___% Blacks/African Americans

___% Latinos/Hispanics

___% Asians

___% Native Americans

(Source: *Newsweek*, November 2, 1998)

6. The "Workforce 2000" study by the Hudson Institute predicted that by the year 2000, 85 percent of the new additions to the workforce were_____:

a) women, immigrants, and people of color (minorities)

b) white males

c) people with disabilities

(Source: *Workforce 2020*, Hudson Institute)

7. According to the BLS (1997), the three fastest employment growth industries between 1996 and 2006 will be (select three):

a) management and public relations

b) watches, clocks, and parts

c) footwear, except rubber and plastic

d) computer and data processing services

e) health services

(Source: Bureau of Labor Statistics)

Workforce Demographics Quiz Answer Key

1. **21%** Matures
   53% Baby Boomers
   26% Generation Xers
2. c
3. b
4. **California, Florida,** and **Texas**
5. **73%** Whites/Caucasians
   12% Blacks/African Americans
   11% Latinos/Hispanics
   3% Asians
   1% Native Americans
6. a
7. a, d, and e

Workforce demographics explained

Now that you've taken the quiz and checked your answers against the real answers, did anything surprise you?

Many people seemed astonished by the 1-percent annual labor force growth through 2006 as projected by the Bureau of Labor Statistics. Think about that: Only 1 percent of people entering the workforce each year are new employees. The other 99 percent are already employed. Moreover, 85 percent of this labor force growth are women, immigrants, and people of color.

Why is the labor force growth so low? From 1964 to 1990, the birthrate in the United States was significantly lower than it was prior to 1964. The birth rate dipped precipitously, hitting a real low in the 1980s, resulting in thousands of fewer babies born each year for 26 years, hence producing the labor shortage we are experiencing today. There are significantly fewer young people entering the workforce today. In fact, Baby Boomers (born between 1946 and 1964) make up 53 percent of the workforce, Matures (born between 1909 and 1945) 21 percent, and Generation Xers (born between 1965 and 1981) 26 percent.

What does this mean in terms of the age of our workforce? Today 74 percent of workers are older than 35. Our workforce is aging, with fewer younger people available in the foreseeable future to reverse this aging workforce trend.

Population changes

	1900	2000	2050
Whites	81%	73%	53%
African Americans	19%	12%	14%
Latinos	n/a	11%	24%
Asians	n/a	3%	8%
Native Americans	n/a	1%	1%

(Source: *Newsweek*, November 2, 1998)

Now let's look at the changing demographics in terms of race. Which races are growing the fastest? Asians (from 3 percent to 8 percent by the year 2050) and Latinos (from 11 percent to 24 percent by 2050). Latinos will soon surpass African Americans to become the largest minority group in the United States by 2050.

What implications do these demographic changes have for your organization in terms of staff recruitment and retention? What changes does your organization need to consider to meet the needs of an older, more racially and culturally diverse workforce? Are your benefits attractive to older workers? Have you considered such benefits as eldercare? Is your organization's management well versed and skilled in managing diversity?

These are some of the key questions you must answer in order to meet the needs of a workforce that looks quite different today (and will tomorrow) than it did even five years ago. Let's look further at how the rules of the workplace have changed and how this impacts on your ability to recruit and retain IEs.

The game plans and rules regarding lifelong employment with one employer have changed dramatically. Most employees can no longer look forward to receiving a gold watch or company rocking chair for lifelong service. Cradle-to-grave employment is indeed a retro memory.

Some experts predict that employees may have as many as six careers and 15 different jobs in a career lifetime. This means that IEs need to constantly update their skills, learn new ones, and be flexible. IEs have to work independently, but also be good team players. Above all, they are responsible for the direction their careers and working lives take. Everywhere employees are taking control of their careers and workforce destinies by viewing themselves as a profitable corporation. They've mutated themselves a into a company (Me, Inc.) that looks out for their interests. Here are some ways the rules of the work game have changed:

OLD GAME	NEW RULES
Cradle-to-grave employment.	You're on your own. Six careers and 15 jobs in a lifetime.
Set for life once you received your degrees.	Lifelong learning is the name of the game.
Dealing with people locally.	Dealing with people locally and in faraway places.
"My team is the people I work with in my department."	"My team is the people in my department. But I also work on multidisciplinary teams throughout the company and with outside consultants."
"My company planned my career for me, told me when and how I would get promoted, then made career opportunities happen for me."	"I must chart my own destiny. My organization can't necessarily promise me job security or career advancement." "I must form Me, Inc. so that I can be gainfully employed in the future in my own organization, or elsewhere."

What is an indispensable employee?

Today's employee is looking rather battered with all these changes to contend with. What exactly is an indispensable employee? Consider these characteristics of IEs:

- Understands the organization's mission and vision, embodies it, and believes in it.
- Meets goals, personal and organizational.
- Views problems as challenges to be solved.
- Works hard and is flexible.
- Has an innovative and responsible way of doing the job.
- Possesses knowledge and skills that cannot easily be replaced.

Straight from the expert's lips:

"The old rules are gone. Organizations that do not really value employees as an asset as integral as real estate and finances are destined to see themselves fall off the competitive curve."

—*George Kaye,*
Dean, Lesley University School of Management

- Works well within the culture; chemistry and fit are a match.
- Knows that the cost to replace her is very high, monetarily and knowledge-wise.
- Retains basic knowledge level but learns continuously.
- Has strong work ethics and is committed to the values of the organization because they are in line with his or her personal value system and philosophy.
- Mutates regularly; is comfortable with chaos, ambiguity, and change in the workplace and personal life.
- Knows how to balance work and life through plate spinning (see Chapter 17 for more information).

Given how difficult it is to find and keep an employee, it's no wonder management holds on to certain employees who are seriously underperforming. Managers say, "At least they're still breathing. Isn't a warm body better than no body?" But what happens when we learn about "bad apples" in the organization?

- It can demoralize others.
- It can drag down the good performers.
- Distrust festers.
- Good staff may leave.
- Responding to change may not happen.

Guess what employees talk about at the water cooler and at home at the dinner table? Their managers. *"Why doesn't he or she do something about so and so, who's dragging the rest of us down?"* Not everyone is an indispensable employee, and managers would be wise to, as the old Kenny

Rogers song goes, "Know when to hold 'em, know when to fold 'em, know when to walk away, know when to run" from staff who tarnish the environment of your IEs.

What employers are looking for in indispensable employees

Although this book focuses more from an employer's perspective on what they need to do to hire and keep indispensable employees, the question is often raised: What must employees do to become indispensable? Many employers are looking for IEs who:

- Work effectively in teams/have excellent interpersonal and communication skills.
- Have an excellent customer service attitude.
- Network and help capture business.
- Are computer-literate.
- Practice continuous lifelong learning.
- Keep up with trends in business, industry, and field/ profession.
- Are multiskilled, are flexible, can take on extra work, and do not have a "that's not in my job description" attitude.
- Deal effectively with the global marketplace and diverse customers and employees.
- Add value, do more with less, and help to increase revenue, customer satisfaction, and quality.
- Strive for excellence and seek continuous improvement.
- Understand their business, the industry, and how their job fits into the strategic direction of the organization.
- Can be flexible, live with chaos and ambiguity, and even work as contingency workers (consultants, part-times, temporary help, etc.).
- Are not overly dependent on job security and career advancement opportunities.

Where is the job growth?

To better understand where the job growth is for your IEs refer to the chart on page 35.

The 10 occupations
with the fastest growth from 1996-2006

Occupation	Employment*		Change,1996-2006*	
	1996	2006	Number	%
Database administrators, computer support specialists, and all other computer scientists	212	461	249	118
Computer engineers	216	451	235	109
Systems analysts	506	1,025	520	103
Personal and home care aides	202	374	171	85
Physical and corrective therapy assistants and aides	84	151	66	79
Home health aides	495	873	378	76
Medical assistants	225	391	166	74
Desktop publishing specialists	30	53	22	74
Physical therapists	115	196	81	71
Occupational therapy assistants and aides	16	26	11	69

*Numbers in thousands of jobs.
Source: OOHInfo, Bureau of Labor Statistics, *OOHInfo@bls.gov*,
September 8, 1998

Play to win and keep
indispensable employees

One of my staff consultants recently overheard a conversation between two women while shopping in a department store. It went something like this:

"I heard she makes her salespeople write a daily report stating whether or not they made their target goals," said one woman. "And, if they didn't, they have to write a report about what went wrong and how they're going to fix it."

"Oh God, I'd hate that," the other woman responded.

"Me too! A lot of them just quit, like *that*," she said, snapping her fingers. "Why would anybody want to stay when they can just walk out the door and find a better job?"

Sound familiar? If employees don't like their organizations' managers, practices, policies, salaries, benefits, and so forth, they can—and will— leave. So equipping managers and human resources professionals with the do's, taboos, and how-to's of managing a talented, competent, and diverse workforce has never been more important. A model to link recruitment and retention efforts is a must. In the pages that follow, we'll explore one model that can help you solve your labor shortage and recruit and retain IEs.

Chapter 3

The Fields Associates, Inc. Recruitment and Retention Model

As major employers are feeling the chilling effects of the labor shortage, innovative organizations that don't want to be caught on the wrong side of this issue must start to make significant changes to how they recruit *and* retain a competent and diverse workforce. These two issues can't be separated as they have in the past; they must be looked at as a joined-at-the-hip package deal.

Principles to live by

Now that we've explored why we must change with the times, it's time for the meaty how-to's of recruitment and retention that form the overall Fields Associates, Inc. (FA) Recruitment and Retention Model for solving the labor shortage. We will begin by examining the FA principles of recruitment and retention.

Principle #1

Organizations must candidly examine the effectiveness of their traditional external recruitment strategies and, in many cases, adapt and/or adopt new ones that are appropriate for the times.

> **Quiz**
>
> Is your company currently utilizing antiquated approaches to recruitment? If you're not sure, here's a simple test to find out:
>
> 1. Are your hiring managers typically panicking and frantically trying to fill vacancies whenever they arise?
> Check one: ☐ yes ☐ no
> 2. Do your hiring managers routinely consider only applicants "looking for work" (those who can start immediately)?
> Check one: ☐ yes ☐ no
>
> If you answered yes to either of the questions, your company is likely to be in a lot of trouble. It's definitely time for an overhaul. Become proactive now by learning how to *anticipate* job needs well ahead of time. This capacity is crucial to successfully navigating current labor shortages.

Principle #2

Organizations need to focus on internal recruitment strategies as much or possibly more than traditional external recruitment initiatives so that a ready supply of internal workers is available to fill crucial positions.

Internal recruitment measures range from employee referrals, goodwill ambassador programs, and mentoring programs to internal job fairs to identify and utilize the talents of existing staff. Promoting qualified internal applicants is good for your organization's morale and is usually far more cost-effective than attracting and training new recruits.

When external recruitment is necessary, a personal referral from a respected employee is often a safer bet than hiring someone from more depersonalized sources. After all, networking with people who are employed is the number one way individuals find jobs. Employees don't want to recommend someone who will ultimately make them look bad.

Principle #3

Organizations should view external and internal recruitment plus retention as a "package deal" and recognize that the best form of recruitment is retention.

Usually retention initiatives are considered separate from recruitment efforts. In today's market, they are inextricably bound. As we will see in later chapters, the best form of recruitment *is* retention.

Think about it this way: Right now your organization may be spending lots of time and money trying to court top prospects into the door. Hundreds of thousands of dollars may be doled to executive recruiters.

But how will you retain these new superstars when your competitors begin dangling even bigger carrots their way? Given the many delicious choices luring great employees in both robust and weak economies, all of your managers need to think ahead about what it takes to retain employees immediately after the recruitment process, not just what it takes to attract them.

Keeping what you've read in mind, it's time to probe deeper into the Fields Associates, Inc. Recruitment and Retention Model and examine the big picture. After reading on, you'll begin to see that it's not as bad as it seems.

An overview

The Fields Associates, Inc. (FA) Recruitment and Retention Model is based upon the notion that in order for organizations to conquer their labor shortage dilemmas they must view their recruitment and retention efforts together as a "package deal." At the same time that a person is recruited into the organization, managers must also think about what they need to do to retain that individual.

As illustrated in the following graphic, the FA Model identifies three key areas that organizations must consider when crafting their strategy and they are all linked: external recruitment efforts, internal recruitment programs, and retention initiatives.

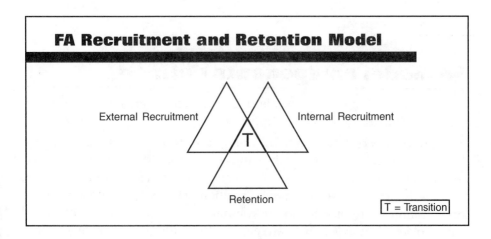

FA Recruitment and Retention Model

External Recruitment / Internal Recruitment

T

Retention

T = Transition

Transitions affecting recruitment and retention efforts

Why must we reexamine our traditional approaches to recruitment and retention? As we've discussed, times have changed. A variety of transitions has affected society and the way we do business and subsequently our approach to luring and keeping talent.

The "T" in the middle of the model stands for **transition**. What worked in the past may not be enough to satisfy the workforce needs of today's changing organizations. To effectively recruit this tight labor market, instead of cultivating *applicant pools,* employees need to market their organization to *vast seas* of passive candidates.

Various transitions affect recruiting and retention efforts. These conditions are fueling organizations to update now-antiquated recruitment and retention methods. Some of these are:

- Mergers and acquisitions.
- Cross-training.
- Redeployment/retraining.
- Outplacement and layoffs.
- Technology changes and productivity improvements.
- Terminations for cause.
- Changing workforce relations.
- Telecommuting.
- Contingency workers.
- Outsourcing.
- Retirement.
- Customer-driven changes.

FA model components defined

To hire and keep indispensable employees, employers must craft strategies that address three major components.

External recruitment activities are those that the organization utilizes to recruit talent from outside of the organization. They include marketing and advertising efforts that set the organization apart from the competition, as well as promotional and public relations events that underscore the organization's commitment to the community, employees, customers, and shareholders. These activities are designed to build the organization's image as "an employer of substance and choice." By this I mean that the organization must utilize both brand and image marketing so potential candidates know:

- What the organization stands for from an employee's perspective.
- What distinguishes the organization from the competition—in other words, why it is an employer of substance and choice.
- That the organization isn't merely bragging about what it can offer (that is, great benefits, flexibility, diversity, family-friendly environment, etc.) but that it can live up to its bravado.

Internal recruitment efforts occur within the organization and assist the institution with recruiting staff from within. Another facet of internal recruitment is utilizing current employees to bring in outside talent. Central to this notion is turning employees into goodwill ambassadors to get the word out about the employer as an employer of substance and choice. With the tight labor market and only 1-percent workforce growth in coming years, the employees you currently have are, basically, what you have to work with in the future.

Internal recruitment efforts also involve cultivating the talents, skills, and competencies of staff already on board so that they can become a possible recruitment source to fill vacant positions. "Growing your own employees" through mentorships, educational opportunities, succession planning, and redeployment of workers will increasingly become a major recruitment source.

Retention initiatives are often thought of as separate from recruitment. However, they are inextricably tied. An organization may have the most elaborate and sophisticated recruitment program around, but if the environment is inhospitable once individuals are hired, given the choices that indispensable employees have in this labor market, managers will soon find themselves looking for another replacement and also seeing the huge impact that turnover has to the bottom line.

•••

As the Fields Associates, Inc. model depicts, external recruitment, internal recruitment, and retention must be joined at the hip and viewed as a package deal. In other words, at the same time you are hiring an indispensable employee, you should be thinking about what you must do to keep him.

External recruitment efforts

As we learned in our demographic quiz, most people are not looking for jobs (at least not on the surface). Unemployment rates have been at an all-time low. In many areas of the country in the past few years, they are less than 5 percent (a figure some economists say is the magic number that constitutes full employment). Despite these statistics, when jobs become vacant, many organizations continue to focus their recruitment strategies on locating people who are looking for jobs.

One reason that many organizations are having problems solving the labor shortage is that they are missing the proverbial boat by utilizing traditional recruitment tactics to quell some unprecedented labor seas. For more than 20 years, I've either worked as a human resources executive or consulted to others. From this experience, let me share with you a typical scenario that occurs regularly at too many organizations:

A job becomes vacant as an employee leaves to seek greener pastures elsewhere. The manager inevitably becomes quasi-panicked, wondering how the work will get done without this body around. The manager runs to human resources and demands that human resources pull out all the stops to get his or her position filled tomorrow. More often than not, the manager will demand that an ad be placed in a local or national paper or on the Internet so they can "find someone who is looking for a job." Sometimes this approach will do the trick and candidates are generated to fill the vacant position. Recently, however, this strategy isn't hitting the bull's eye. Why? Because it's based on one very wrong premise for the labor market conditions that currently exist in most areas of this country: Most people aren't looking for jobs.

Many organizations don't realize it, but they have an antiquated approach to recruitment. All too often, a main strategy employed by human resources professionals and hiring managers to fill vacant positions is to search for individuals who are "looking for work" and are readily available to start immediately.

One has to wonder if organizations have stopped to ask one important question: How many people are out there who fit that criteria? If they did, they'd very quickly implement the following approach.

To start, human resources professionals and hiring managers need to take a look at unemployment statistics, both nationally and locally. What they'll find is that most people aren't looking for jobs. As we've discussed, the unemployment rate in the United States has basically hovered at less than 5 percent for some time now. In many metropolitan communities, it ranges from between 3 to 4 percent.

To delve further into those numbers, employers must also analyze what types of people are included in those unemployment rates. Unfortunately, those numbers tell a not-so-wonderful picture. Included in these numbers are the ranks of the chronically unemployed, people who don't even want to work again, and individuals with skills that are obsolete.

Human resources employees and managers must understand that recruitment is a continuous process. Organizations must constantly be looking for talent, much in the same way that athletic talent scouts are always looking for the latest hot draft pick, and college recruitment officials are on the lookout for promising students. (See Chapter 4 to understand how organizations can utilize the recruitment techniques of a variety of industries.)

This continuous recruitment process is, in many cases, counter to how organizations currently operate. Usually the approach is much more reactionary and not at all proactive; a job is open before a recruiter starts to hunt for bodies to fill it.

Because most people are employed and not actively looking for work (although a lot would consider a new job or career opportunity if the right one presented itself), the trick is to not only look at attracting "active" job seekers, but to entice the "passive" ones. Organizations' external recruitment activities must become less about recruitment and more about marketing the organization as an employer of substance and choice.

In addition to brand and image marketing structured to get the word out about the organization as an employer of substance and choice, organizations, through community outreach efforts, must also develop ways to partner with their community so that they can be a source for job applicants and customers. In return, the company works within the communities to strengthen them.

How-to's of external recruitment

To improve your external recruitment activities, make sure you:

- Market your organization as an employer of substance and choice, especially to passive job seekers.
- Use multicultural marketing techniques and marketing segmentation to recruit a diverse and competent workforce.
- Cultivate community resources.
- Develop your employee demographic profile.

- Create a proactive recruitment plan. (In other words, look for passive job candidates as well as active job seekers.)

Here is some more detail regarding each of the external recruitment how-to's:

Market your organization as an employer of substance and choice.

In today's competitive marketplace jungle, where it often feels like each organizational animal is on the prey, you have to find a way to distinguish yourself from the competition. You must constantly market yourself as an employer of substance and choice. What sets you apart from the rest? Why should people consider you as an employer? Given the fierce competition for top talent, you *must* distinguish yourself from the pack.

Use multicultural marketing techniques and market segmentation to recruit a diverse workforce.

If your recruitment strategy isn't tailored to diverse segments of the labor force, you won't be successful. In today's job market, one size doesn't fit all—or even most. You most often craft approaches to attract targeted employee markets such as Generation Xers, Baby Boomers, Matures, people of color, and so forth. (See Chapter 6 for more information on multicultural marketing.)

Cultivate community resources.

What are you doing to cultivate stronger relationships with the community you serve? It makes good business sense to help strengthen the communities in which you reside and/or do business. These communities can be a source of employers and customers.

Develop your employee demographic profile.

In order to know what and who you need to recruit, you must understand the current demographics of your current employee population. In Chapter 5 you'll learn how to detail your demographic profile (age, sex, race, geographic location, etc.). You can then analyze whether or not you need to change that profile or think about how to better serve what you already have.

Create a proactive recruitment plan.

Develop a plan that can measure your external recruitment efforts. Use the information gathered to discover what draws people into your organization. Stop looking only for active job candidates. Get on the radar screen of passive job seekers.

A proactive, continuous recruitment plan

Armed with the knowledge of the specifics of your labor shortage, you will need to develop a proactive recruitment strategy. By creating this plan, you will receive answers to the following questions:

- What have been your previous recruitment efforts?
- Where have your recruitment dollars been focused?
- Which of these efforts have been most successful?
- What traditional and nontraditional approaches might help you to find competent and diverse staff?
- Are your recruitment approaches active or passive?

Creating a continuous recruitment program, where you are constantly searching for top talent, is one secret for solving your labor shortage. To do this, people have to know what and who you are targeting.

A good recruitment plan identifies ways to target candidates constantly, not only when positions become vacated. Components of this plan may include:

- School-to-career initiatives. What is your organization doing to partner with educational institutions as a means of helping you to cultivate young, talented energy so they could be potential employees later?
- Strategies to cultivate community outreach programs.
- Programs to locate hard-to-find minority candidates and other diverse individuals (women, persons with disabilities, etc.).
- Multicultural marketing and market segmentation techniques.
- Innovative techniques to increase candidate pools.
- Ways to reduce and/or stabilize recruitment advertising search firm budgets.
- Approaches to marketing the organization as an employer of substance and choice.
- Techniques to turn employees/managers into headhunters.
- Employee alumni relations programs.
- Measures to evaluate the proactive recruitment plan.

Reduce and/or stabilize your recruitment advertising and search firm budgets

Of course your recruitment advertising and search firm budgets are off the charts. But stop and think. Are you spending those dollars effectively? Let's talk about what can be done to stabilize and/or reduce them while increasing your effectiveness to fill jobs.

Recently, one of my clients asked me to troubleshoot his organization's recruitment plan. When I analyzed the budget, I discovered that the organization was spending close to a million dollars a year placing help wanted ads in a single newspaper. In the past, this might have been a sound decision. After all, this massive circulation daily has an employment section known for years as "the one to look at" when you're searching for a job. Still, my client's ads generated only 14 percent of new hires.

Why is there such a small return? Today most people are already employed and not actively searching for a job. The labor shortage has shuffled all those candidates who were pounding the pavement throughout the late 1980s and mid-1990s into cubicles. Those who are actively "looking" increasingly use the Internet and other alternative sources. Also, immigrants and people of color (a large percentage of the new entrants into the workforce) are more likely to read publications and turn to other sources such as TV and radio. These mediums target their specific needs and interest more than mainstream, wide-circulation publications.

All of these factors have left many organizations wandering aimlessly, still trying to extract job candidates from "the streets."

If you're spending a phenomenal amount of money and still not getting enough candidates to fill all of your open positions, you may need to take a different approach. In Chapter 4, we will explore how organizations can tap into the passive job seekers. You will learn some new methods that will over time increase your candidate pools and reduce and/or stabilize your recruitment advertising and/or search firm budgets.

Internal recruitment defined

All too often organizations look to the outside when jobs are open. This is a missed opportunity. Internal recruitment efforts are those that occur inside of the institution and assist the organization with recruiting and retaining staff. Central to this notion is utilizing employees (as goodwill ambassadors) as the number one way to get out information about your company. Satisfied employees will get the word out about the employer as an employer of substance and choice.

Internal recruitment efforts also involve utilizing the talents of staff already on board by seeing them as a possible source to fill vacant positions.

Think about it: If you go to a career counselor or outplacement expert and ask him or her what the number one way to get a job is, any one of those people will answer the question the same way. They'll tell you that time and again studies have shown that networking is the number one way people get jobs.

As the conversation would progress, this person would recommend that you network with everyone that you know—don't rule out barbers and hairdressers, bartenders, plumbers, anyone. He or she would probably also advise you to *definitely* network with people who are employed. Why? Because they can provide you with invaluable information about an organization and your job search. People who are employed will fill you in on the organization and tell you whether the potential company in which you could go to work:

- Is a good company that cares about people and pays well.
- Trusts its employees.
- Is full of good or bad managers. (They'd also tell you other biased information about your prospective new boss; is he or she a good boss or a real jerk?)
- Has decent benefits, salaries, and career advancement opportunities.
- Is doing okay financially. Is it here to stay?

In other words, tapping into your employees may be the number one way to solve your labor shortage. Turn your employees and managers into headhunters and talent scouts.

How to turn your employees into goodwill ambassadors

The tragic truth is that many organizations spend a pitiful amount of time cultivating the number-one source (their employees) for getting the word out about their jobs. Not all organizations consider how they can rally the troops to help them tackle critical labor shortages through such incentives as employee referral bonuses. Furthermore, they have minimal enticements or incentives for employees to refer their compadres, family, and friends through cash-incentive employee referral programs.

In order to "grow their own employees," they may need to start the process much sooner than when a position becomes available. Staff may

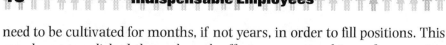

need to be cultivated for months, if not years, in order to fill positions. This may be accomplished through such efforts as mentorship and succession planning programs.

How-to's of internal recruitment

You can improve your organization's internal recruitment capabilities through a variety of efforts. These include:

- Turning your employees into goodwill ambassadors. Your employees can be your best source to get your jobs filled as they serve as your goodwill ambassadors! (Some approaches to get your staff to help you fill jobs are found in Chapter 11.)
- Labor market forecasting. In order to be less reactive and more proactive, you need to know what you have and what you'll need as far as staff. (You can figure this out in Chapter 5.)
- Mentorship and succession planning programs. (Programs to help you grow your own employees are explained in Chapter 12.)
- Crafting career development/planning programs. Help people craft their careers elsewhere in your organization. Why? In many instances it will help to retain them. If employees feel they are growing in their job and learning, why would they need to go elsewhere? If the employee, because of your efforts, is ready to move on, why not try to find him or her a more fulfilling position—preferably somewhere else within your organization. In Chapter 12, I'll show you some career development approaches organizations are using that are attractive to IEs.
- Offering human resources services. Help your human resources department *and* managers improve customer service to internal clients and job seekers. (See Chapter 9 for help.)

The recruitment process

The hiring process consists of more than just plowing through a stack of resumes to "weed out" the undesirables. Each time a position becomes vacant, take a few minutes to evaluate your overall approach to filling it by following these steps:

1. Job application.
2. Job posting.

3. Job review with manager.
4. Applicant sourcing.
5. Human resources screening/interview.
6. Department interview.
7. Manager and human resources department discussion.
8. Reference check.
9. Salary determination.
10. Job offer and acceptance.
11. Post-employment information gathered.
12. Offer letter and other data mailed to new hire.
13. Orientation.

Steps to consider before interviewing candidates

Consider these steps each time you begin the process of hiring an indispensable employee.

Review the job description, duties, roles, and responsibilities.

When replacing a position, utilize the time before recruiting for it to reconsider exactly what you want the position to entail. Ask yourself these questions:

- Have any of the job responsibilities changed?
- Are there more effective and productive ways to get job duties accomplished?
- Should any of the job responsibilities be done by another person or in another way (such as through automation)?

Also, make sure that the business need for the job is clear.

Decide whether or not the job should be posted.

Organizational job posting requirements vary. In some organizations, all jobs must be posted. In others, only jobs at a certain level are posted. Many organizations choose to post jobs for a variety of reasons, including:

- To ensure that there is equal opportunity access to knowledge about jobs and careers.
- To allow internal candidates the opportunity to bid for a position before an external search is launched.

If you decide not to post a job, be ready to explain your rationale for not doing so or you risk sometimes serious employee relations issues. This becomes particularly important when an external candidate is brought in and internal employees feel that they were qualified for the job and not given the opportunity to bid for it.

Review the particulars of the job.

Be sure that recruiters and others involved in the hiring process are aware of the essential functions of the job.

Identify who will be involved in the interview process.

Define their role and to what extent they will be part of the final hiring decision. (This includes search committees and employees.)

Determine applicant sourcing.

Anticipate who will find qualified employees, and where they will find them.

Determine how the screening, interviewing, and referral of candidates will take place.

Do you want to see all resumes, or only those which have been screened?

Determine the best times to schedule interviews.

If multiple people are involved in the interview process, what is the sequence in which people will interview the candidate? When will this take place?

Issues to consider during the interview process

1. What interview questions will be asked? Remember to be uniform; ask applicants the same questions so you'll be able to compare bananas to bananas when you've interviewed all of the applicants.
2. How will the interview be structured?
3. How can the job be marketed so as to attract IEs? What are the high and low points of the job and organization?

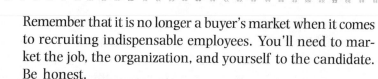
Remember that it is no longer a buyer's market when it comes to recruiting indispensable employees. You'll need to market the job, the organization, and yourself to the candidate. Be honest.

4. What will determine if a candidate is selected for the next round of interviews or becomes the final candidate?

5. Who will determine final candidates for the position, and how will the finalists (and those who have been rejected) be notified? This includes:
    *   Who will conduct the reference checks?
    *   How many reference checks will be made?
    *   What type of questions will be asked of references?

6. How will the final salary determination be made, and who will negotiate the salary, benefits, and perks with the candidate? Determine a salary range and decide with others involved in the recruitment process (such as human resources, a search committee, etc.) the parameters for increasing salary offers.

7. What post-employment information must be gathered? Consider timing for special circumstances, such as physicals, drug tests, criminal record checks, licensure and educational verifications, and so forth.

8. Who will make sure that the offer letter is sent? Also, what information regarding starting employment does it need to contain?

9. What type of orientation program is needed to acquaint the new hire with the department, organization, and job? How will it be structured, who will conduct it, and when must it begin and end?

Company Spotlight:

The Four Seasons Hotel, Boston

For years my organization has held events at the Four Seasons Hotel in Boston. I've been perennially impressed with how pleasant the staff throughout the hotel are and how happy they seem to be in their jobs. What has really impressed me is the fact that they are always raving about the place and how well they feel they are respected and treated by members of management, including their general manager, Mr. Robin Browne. I became impressed with the staff's unbelievable, impeccable service and the fact that so many of them that I have come to know over the years didn't leave the organization, but were promoted and transferred to areas where they could continue to grow.

I hear a lot of employers and executives talking about what's wrong with their organization, but seldom do I see employees like those at The Four Seasons Hotel, who speak positively and seem to really believe so highly in their employer. I decided to get to the bottom of what was making them seem so happy. I asked for an interview with Mr. Robin Browne, General Manager. I asked him about his extraordinary staff and their loyalty, commitment, and overall positive outlook about their place of employment.

Robin Browne is general manager of Boston's Four Seasons Hotel. He is responsible for a staff of 600 people and an annual revenue of more than $60 million. When the company was founded, the chairman, CEO, and founder was determined to establish an enduring work culture and ethic. The cornerstone of the company is ethics. This may sound commonplace, but it works for the Four Seasons. Robin has worked at the Four Seasons for more than 20 years. He is a relative newcomer, as their senior manager's average length of service is 25 years. The Four Seasons' culture is built upon the notion of laying down the golden rule and expecting everyone to live by it to the best of their abilities. The orientation process is "one of the most important things we do to ensure new people uphold the organization's culture once they are hired," Robin Browne states. When Mr. Browne interviews people and looks at who to hire, he goes by his sheer gut reaction to a candidate. He looks for whether he or she could share in the organization's values of self-motivation and respect for the human race. Forget the resume and background; he peers into the candidate's soul and sees if he or she has the ability to be self-motivated and give to the organization and the culture as they give back to the employee.

How does he go about interviewing people? Mr. Browne explains that there are no tick boxes, personality tests, and the like. "We just don't do those things," he explains. Applicants interview with a department head or assistant department head, and the quite-lengthy interview process doesn't end there. Candidates may be interviewed by a division head, resident manager, or Mr. Browne's assistant. Eventually, they meet with Mr. Browne. Robin Browne screens everyone personally. Robin states that he can tell within the first two minutes whether or not a person has what it takes to be a part of the Four Seasons' culture. At the end of the interview, Robin can tell whether the interviewee is good with people, is motivated, and is a self-starter.

What about turnover? The organization's annual turnover rate is 20 percent, low for the industry. Out of 600 employees, then, 120 people turn over per year. The company tracks turnover and knows the difference between good or bad turnover. Thirty to 40 people per year are "planned turnover." These are people who are graduating from some of the area's top colleges, such as Simmons and Harvard. Four Seasons Hotels does a huge amount of transfers and promotions from within. In 1999, about 37 people transferred to other Four Seasons Hotels, and there are as many as 120 promotions in a year.

The hotel's 1999 turnover rate was its lowest rate in 15 years. In the hospitality and hotel environment, that rate is almost unheard of. Mr. Browne is a big believer in employee referral. Rather than run ads in newspapers that can cost thousands of dollars and might barely be read, Four Seasons Hotels relies on its employees. Employees receive $500 to $1000 in cash bonuses as an incentive to refer new employees.

Half of the employees have been with the company for more than five years. The culture works overtime to treat its guests *and* its employees well. For example, the employee cafeteria serves 600 people, and employees eat some of the same gastronomical delights served to customers for free. "We don't have a different approach to treating employees," Robin Browne explains. "They get the same level of respect and intensity [that] we give to our guests."

The Four Seasons Hotels has been recognized for its workplace excellence. It is a frequent flyer on Fortune's 100 Best Companies to Work For list. Managers are encouraged to attend two to five days of management skills training seminars.

What about people who leave? Robin Browne receives exit interview data and people are brutally honest. Information from the exit interviews is given back to ex-employee's managers. To summarize Robin Browne's and the Four Seasons recruitment and retention philosophy: "If people are good and honest, give them all the room in the world. Look for the good in everyone."

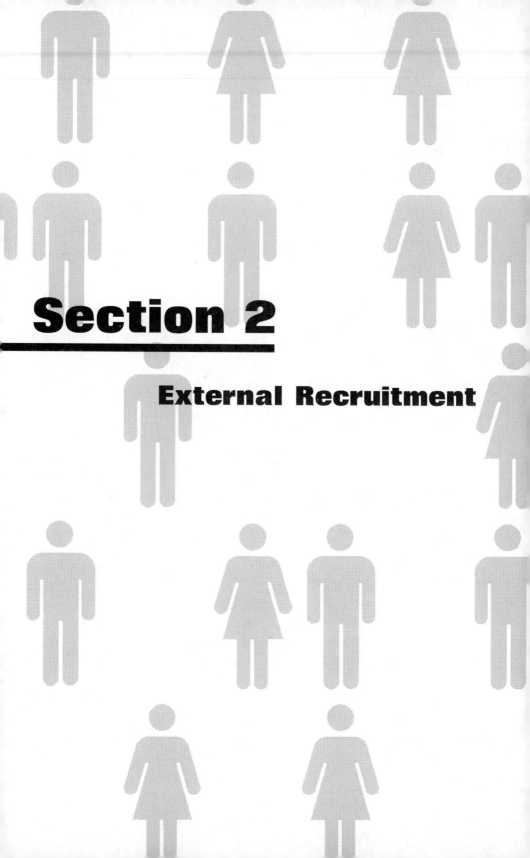

Section 2

External Recruitment

Chapter 4

Stop Looking Only for Active Job Candidates

Even if human resources wanted to fill a position immediately, 99 percent of the time they can't. By the way, you can best believe that the recruiter doesn't want the job to be open any longer than the manager does. She wants to fill that position because there is another huge pile just waiting for her attention.

Let's review again why the recruiter probably can't fill the position immediately:

With low unemployment rates and fewer skilled people to select from, few people are readily available, as they are already gainfully employed. The exceptions are the rare cases where someone is between jobs because of a merger and acquisition, temporary assignment ending, or layoff.

Even if you find someone who is ready and eager to change jobs, if the person is gainfully employed, they generally can't start working immediately because they have to give an adequate termination notice period to their current employer.

The termination notice period

Sometimes managers—in their desperation to fill a job—may not think twice about asking the soon-to-be new employee if he or she will skip on the notice period to their current employer and just start right away.

A word to the wise is in store here. Think about this: If a soon-to-be new employee is willing to leave one job quickly and burn bridges with a current employer, who probably won't have enough time to replace him quickly without a lot of pain, don't you think that employee might someday do the same to you?

Conversely, the employee who has been pressured to not give his current employer adequate notice so he can get started in the new company right away should think about this as well. Couldn't that same manager who is forced to cut costs and make staff/personnel changes some day (likely when he's least expecting it) put the employee out of a job with little or no notice and not even think thrice about it?

What is adequate notice?

In some cases, companies have policies as to how much notice must be given for a voluntary termination. As a rule of thumb, allow at least a two-week notice period for nonexempt (hourly, paid) positions and four weeks for exempt (professional and management) positions. Some organizations stipulate that the notification should be the same amount of time as the annual vacation period.

Reel in passive job seekers

Because most people are not actively looking, but might consider a change if the "right opportunity or challenge" presented itself, one approach that organizations can use to recruit indispensable employees is to stop looking only for active job seekers. Start to seek out passive job seekers. These are people who are gainfully employed and not necessarily looking at the moment. But they could change their mind at any time.

What does this mean exactly? I'm not suggesting that you raid other companies to fill jobs. Remember the old adage "what goes around comes around." That rings true when companies make it part of their recruitment strategy to openly raid others.

Raiding talent is not what we're talking about here, but rather creating avenues whereby you get on the radar screen of passive job seekers so they become familiarized over time with your organization and its career opportunities. The key words here are "become familiarized over time with your organization." At some point, the passive job seeker may be ready for a new challenge. If you are on his or her map, the process of courting him or her becomes much easier.

The Armed Forces model: A lesson from Uncle Sam

The Armed Forces are motivated by the same recruitment challenges faced by Corporate America: the ongoing challenge to meet recruitment targets (but sometimes falling short on their efforts). Unlike many of their corporate counterparts, though, the Armed Forces have learned to constantly reinvent themselves and upgrade their recruitment tactics to keep up with the times.

When it comes to recruiting, Corporate America has much to learn from the Armed Forces, whose recruitment strategies are both proactive and continuous. Aren't the Marines, for example, always "looking for a few good men?" And the Army has long recognized the importance of profiling enlistment candidates and capitalizing on the data when scouting out new recruits.

The Armed Services are the hands-on frontrunners when it comes to crafting hiring slogans (think about "Be all that you can be"). Now such hiring slogans have begun coming into vogue with many successful organizations—with tremendous results—but decades behind the Services' use of them.

And when it comes to high-tech recruitment techniques, the Army uses CD-ROMs and a dynamic, personalized Web site that many private companies can only dream about. How can Corporate America learn from all this? By becoming aware of where it goes wrong and where the Army goes "right," for starters.

Mirroring Corporate America, the Army significantly downsized during the 1990s, referring to this shrinkage, brought about by Defense Department budget cuts, as "The Big Draw Down." At the same time, new recruits declined as well, in part due to changes in Baby Boomer parental attitudes ("You've enlisted in what? I marched in antimilitary demonstrations in the 1970s!"), all-too-frequent negative publicity, and a strong economy with many job opportunities.

However, the recruitment process of all the Armed Services (Army, Navy, Air Force, Marines, and Coast Guard) remains both continuous and extremely proactive. Even when they have been under fire for not meeting their hiring goals (as happened in previous years), they don't give up. Their tactic is to go back to the drawing board, reassess what's not working, and reinvent themselves so they fit into the marketplace. They are extremely

effective—so much so, in fact, that they frequently woo job candidates who would otherwise end up in Corporate America. Once recruits are done with their stint in the Armed Forces, some end up in Corporate America.

Fortunately, many of the Armed Forces' successful recruitment strategies can easily be translated into successful private sector strategies, if only companies would listen. For example: Can you name the location of at least one Armed Forces recruitment station near where you live or work? How many times have you personally seen one of their ads on television or heard one on the radio? Think about it for a minute. I'll bet you have a location in mind and remember seeing or hearing an ad.

In addition to specific strategies, most of us are also aware that the Marines have for a long while been "looking for a few good men." Though such sexist language may turn some people off, the principle of using an advertising slogan that says what their target market is nonetheless works wonders.

How about the Army's slogan? *Be all that you can be.* It's outstanding! Who could argue with a tagline like that? Notice, however, how the tagline has evolved. At one time it was: "Be all that you can be. Find your future in the Army." It appears that the slogan has mutated with the times. The Army wants people to be all they can be, but not necessarily stay there to find their future. Two to four years will do just fine. In 2001, after recruitment targets were not met, the Army reinvented itself once again, this time with a "hip," Generation X–like slogan proclaiming that recruits could become "an Army of one!"

Most corporate recruitment strategies, on the other hand, go the other way. They're passive, low-key, sober, and expectant. Generally they do not *go after* job candidates, assuming instead that candidates will be eager to come after them. It used to be that way, this is true. But it's not that way anymore.

The hiring process: Two methods

Let's look at how the process tends to work in both cases, contrasting Corporate America practices with those of the Armed Services. In most organizations, it works this way:

A position becomes available. The manager of a department approaches the company's HR department and wants the job to be filled *now*. The manager also demands that an ad be placed in the town's top newspaper. The HR recruiter calls the local newspaper (or its advertising firm) and places an ad. Responding candidates' resumes are sifted and interviewees are called in. Hopefully the position is filled within a reasonable amount of time. Increasingly this time frame extends for months because most people aren't immediately available to work (because they are gainfully employed).

In the Armed Forces, though, things move more quickly and aggressively: A prospective candidate can literally walk in off the street, because recruiting officers are officed in every other city and town. Recruiters for the Armed Services are always available during standard business hours. If a potential recruit phones during these hours instead of visiting, she'll speak to a real, live person—not a job-line or an HR employee's voice mail. By the way, the Armed Forces are constantly recruiting, not just when a job becomes available.

When job candidates walk in to a company's human resources department off the street how are they treated? Does "Fill out this application" or "Just send us your resume and we'll call you if your resume goes with what we need" ring any bells? Might such questions aptly describe the way your organization and others you have known treat potential new hires? Perhaps, as so many others do, your organization sends a "Don't call us, we'll call you" message. If it does, your company definitely has a few adjustments to make, especially if it is to compete for today's best talent. Don't let this frustrate you, of course; such "recruitment" practices are not by any means unique.

Most corporations institutionalize many obstacles when it comes to making themselves accessible to potential employees. Of course, I'm not suggesting human resources departments should open themselves up to every Dawn, Ahmed, and Larry who shows up on their doorstep with a crisp new resume in hand. However, organizations today need to become more user-friendly with regard to prospective employees. After all, would your company's sales operatives ever consider sending a walk-in prospective customer back out into the street empty-handed, instructing, "Mail us your request for one of our products and we'll let you know"? Yet that's exactly what many organizations do. (For more about how to strengthen human resources and management services, see Chapter 9.)

Now think next about the rest of the process: After inviting those select few in for an interview, and then ultimately choosing the best man or woman for the job, what happens to the candidates who were the second, third, and fourth pick in the final rounds? Does your organization keep in touch with them? What about candidates who received an offer from you but declined?

Unfortunately, many times such candidates slip away without so much as a fare-thee-well. Out of sight, out of mind, companies seem to feel.

How does the Army operate? The same way? Not on your life! Instead, the U.S. Army keeps in touch for a while. Although each Army recruiter retains his or her own style, most flag whatever occupations or benefits seem to interest the interviewed candidates, and then, about three months after the contact (so as not to appear too pushy), most recruiters send a personalized follow-up note, or even an applicable brochure or update. Only when the candidate returns a definite and final, "Uh-uh, no way," does this correspondence end.

A field test

I got so intrigued when I started comparing these two recruiting approaches that I decided to conduct a field test to see how they stacked up against each other. I had my "sleuth," Lisa Eldridge, a senior consultant from my firm, pose as a potential recruit for both a Greater Boston Army Recruitment Station and for Capital One, a consumer and retail lender. I wanted to see how Lisa's direct experience with the Army would compare with one of the best in Corporate America.

Here's what happened:

The Army

Lisa phoned the recruiting station and a pleasant-mannered sergeant named Charles Tomberlin answered. Lisa pretended she was a recent high school graduate who was very undecided about what she wanted to do next. Sergeant Tomberlin listened attentively, then invited her to come in for a visit. "I can show you many options based on your areas of interest," he explained. Tomberlin also offered to answer any questions Lisa might have right then and there over the phone, spending as much time with her as she wished.

He also offered to "qualify" her over the phone, something human resources folks refer to as screening. To do so, he explained, he would ask Lisa some basic questions. He warned that some of the questions might seem a little personal, but that he would always explain the reasons each such "personal" question was being asked.

After answering Sergeant Tomberlin's list of questions, Lisa was informed that she did indeed qualify. As a convenience to her, he also mentioned a recruiting station that was closer to her geographically and told her that she could go there if it was more convenient. He even gave her a name to ask for and described the friendly characteristics of the recruiter he named. Then he described in detail what the visit would be like for Lisa, all the while talking as though he had nothing better to do but answer every question she had.

At the end of the conversation, Lisa felt she'd made a personal connection with Sergeant Tomberlin. Though this had only been an exercise to test out how consistent the Army's practice of its recruiting methods was with its theories, Sergeant Tomberlin and the U.S. Army passed with flying colors.

Capital One

When Lisa called, she encountered a voice message referring her to an automated job line. She also had the option of transferring to a receptionist by pressing "0," which is what she did.

After a little prodding, Lisa convinced the receptionist to put her through to a human resources representative who, although very pleasant, was not a decision-maker. This HR rep assured Lisa that if she used the company's "phone application" process, a recruiter would get back to her shortly after.

This time an automated, radio announcer–sounding phone robot handled Lisa's qualifying/screening process. After prompting Lisa through a series of questions, many somewhat uncomfortable, as the Army's had been (for example "What is the longest period of time you ever worked at a job?" and "How would your supervisor rate you for dependability compared to other people?"), she was invited to come and pay a visit.

At the Richmond site, she was told she would take several qualifying tests (similar to the Army's process). But unlike with the Army, she could not come by any time, at her own convenience. In this case, she had to choose from a list of "test dates."

The next morning a human resources representative from the company called Lisa, as the HR rep had said. But this person didn't appear to be a decision-maker either. Sergeant Tomberlin, in contrast, had the authority to decide Lisa's fate all by himself. In this case, she would be meeting with someone who had a final say.

The HR rep very cordially thanked Lisa for applying for a job at Capital One, and then attempted to verify the testing date Lisa had entered. Because "something had come up," Lisa explained that she would not be able to keep that particular date after all. Suddenly there was a prolonged, awkward silence. The HR rep somewhat mechanically informed Lisa she would have to reactivate her application once she had decided on a new test date.

So far, which reception would appeal to you? All things being equal, do you suppose you'd go with the Army or with Capital One at this point?

But there's more. What about perks? Each organization wisely insisted on sharing with Lisa what it had to offer her.

The Army had been engaged in this activity from the very beginning, advertising its benefits on TV and in print ads before Lisa had ever picked up the phone. Army benefits were even plastered all over recruiting station windows so that candidates typically knew much about what they were getting into before even stepping inside a recruitment station's door. In fact, such a thorough job has been done by the Armed Services over the years that most of us can today name at least a few perks enlistees will receive even without peeking at an official list. For example, how many of the following look familiar to you?

Army benefits

- College tuition assistance (up to $50,000).
- Free housing.
- Automatic enrollment in selected universities.
- 30 vacation days annually.
- All-expenses-paid travel.
- First-time sign-up bonuses ranging from $2,000 to $12,000.

The magic words

Let's return to Lisa's phone conversation with Sergeant Tomberlin. "Call me Charles, if that feels more comfortable," the good sergeant told her after a while. He then got down to business, casting his line with some tasty bait: bonuses up to $12,000. Depending on her assigned position, Lisa could potentially receive an additional $6,000 bonus if she came on board within the next two weeks.

Tomberlin also informed her that she would probably be able to choose where she was stationed, including overseas destinations. This time he had uttered truly magic words, as Lisa loves to travel. When she responded enthusiastically to the overseas bait, Charles began reeling her in.

He shared with her how much he'd enjoyed being stationed in Germany, assuring her that she'd probably be able to travel a great deal. "Most all the people I've known in the service who wanted to travel overseas have been able to," he told her. Despite this being only an exercise, Lisa was tempted to sign up right then and there!

On the other hand, Capital One's automated voice system informed Lisa early on that the company ranked among the top 10 credit card issuers and that *Fortune* magazine had tagged it, in a recent issue, "One of the Best

Companies in America to Work For." The smooth, electronic voice then reeled off the company's own enticing benefits: three weeks of vacation after the first year, a "generous" 401K match, tuition reimbursement, and much more. But though the marketing and sales spiel was right on target, the artificial voice seemed no match for Tomberlin's warm, human enthusiasm and personalized conversation style.

And the winner is...

Overall, the Army seemed to have the strongest methods and the most enticing perks. Certainly, most American companies are missing the boat by not applying their recruitment designs.

Despite losing by a nose to Sergeant Tomberlin, Capital One seemed to be doing a fantastic job, too, especially when compared with the rest of Corporate America. As have many savvy organizations, it's been spending much time and energy the last couple of years jazzing up its perks and ensuring its HR interface is employee-friendly. Capital One's operation has even built a multimillion-dollar amenities building that boasts a fully equipped gym (with personal trainers available) as well as stores, a dry cleaner, and other services.

Why so much good stuff? Capital One is one of many credit card call center competitors located within a 10-mile radius. Like the Army, it's got to compete.

You can compete

Are you a tiny (by comparison) organization that can't afford such multimillion dollar complexes? Relax. Even small companies can compete by delivering positive, "low-cost-or-no-cost" perks and rewards. Studies have shown that workers tend to appreciate sincere gestures, such as simple praise for a job done well (which may be the highest ranking employee motivator of all), more than higher-priced carrots. Here are a couple more ideas that should give you a sense of what I mean:

- The vice president of engineering at a high technology company called Ezenia! required his managers to submit a list of recent department achievements, including praise for specific individuals' achievements, for publication in the company newsletter.
- Capital One has a few "low-cost-or-no-cost" motivators tucked up its large corporate sleeve, one of which is called Happy Hour. During Happy Hour, bar food (such as chicken

wings and chips and salsa) is placed in every corner. The lights are dimmed and a disco ball spins in the lobby. Each sale that a telesalesperson made earns that person a raffle ticket. Happy Hour lasts for three hours and at the end of each hour a name is drawn. Prizes vary from an extra vacation day to dinner and a movie for two. Although employees reported that the event leads to "intangibles" for them, such as a morale boost, the company reports a direct correlation between the event and "tangibles," such as increased sales performance.

Know your employee profile

Can you describe the traits of your typical employee and the reasons he or she may have been attracted to your organization in the first place? Not many managers, executives, and HR pros in organizations can recite these on the spot.

The Army can do it, though, and does so routinely. Between 50 and 65 percent of their new recruits, they've determined, come from local high schools and colleges. They've also established a "potential recruit profile" that includes such categories as:

- Students who are undecided about their future.
- Students who have just dropped out of college.
- Students who need to repay student loans.
- Students who are college-bound and in need of financial assistance.
- People who have been out of school for six months or more and haven't been able to find an occupation that satisfies them.
- People tired of the "paper chase."
- Reserve Officer Training Corps (ROTC) members.
- Current Junior Reserve Officer Training Corps (JROTC) members.

Though most corporate marketing departments worth their salt maintain detailed profiles of company customers, few HR and/or marketing departments have so identified employees. Yet the Army has enjoyed great success from this procedure for decades and reveals that profiling employees isn't all that different from profiling customers—nor all that difficult. It makes sense to take some time and think about your employee demographic profile.

Interesting practice: Harvard leads the way

Want to see a great example of a recruitment brochure in the non-military sector of our society? Look no further than Harvard University. Sporting a picturesque, aerial view of the Ivy League campus, Harvard's folder-styled recruitment brochure is impressive. One of the brochure's headers/logos reads, "Creative Freedom...the freedom to be your best." In another section, the employment environment is described as one with "small, collaborative work groups, each with its own personality and goals." Translation? Harvard is not a big, impersonal institution where an individual employee will get lost, but rather a community of employees broken down into nurturing pockets. Harvard's benefits, the brochure prominently explains, include a generous vacation allotment, reduced-fee Harvard courses, wellness programs, and a university-funded retirement plan. Finally, potential employees are even invited to "stop by."

Recruitment brochures

In terms of other inventive recruitment methods, the Army also routinely prints full-color recruitment brochures that are terrific examples of multicultural and segment marketing. (See Chapter 6 for more information on multicultural marketing.) The people featured in these brochures reflect a diversity in the Armed Forces that many American companies wish they had. The Army's brochures are even geared to appeal to specific segments of the population, such as women, people of color, potential enlistees who have families, or persons seeking specialized training. There's even a brochure designed to recruit people into the Army band! You certainly can't get much more diverse than that.

Turning employees into headhunters

The Army rewards qualified enlistees with a promotion in rank, including a pay raise, when they meet certain referral goals. The Army also rewards enlistees who provide referrals with gifts such as specialized jackets.

Although corporate employee incentive programs have been around for years, many of them need to be updated. Deloitte & Touche has done just that in the past. The company has offered referral fees as high as $10,000 for hard-to-fill positions. On top of its usual cash awards, during its fiscal year, it has created a "Promotional Period." During this period, the first 10 people to make five employee referrals leading to a new hire win a trip for two to Europe. Additionally, Deloitte & Touche holds a drawing for everyone who has made a referral. The grand prize is a Corvette. The "consolation prize" is a Jeep Wrangler or $15,000!

Even after dolling out all these goodies, the company can still save money. For example, if one of Deloitte & Touche's new hires is a $100,000 salaried IT person, the company may have saved as much as $27,000. How? If the average Information Technology new hire's annual salary is $100,000, and the mid-range headhunter/search and placement firm charges a placement fee of 30 to 35 percent of the IT person's annual salary, then the hiring organization pays that headhunting firm a whopping *$30,000* to *$35,000* commission. And it's not unusual for other fees, such as phone calls and travel, to be added to this figure. Many organizations pay these kinds of fees and more because they cannot produce enough candidates of their own on short notice.

What could your organization do with $30,000 to $35,000 added to its recruitment budget? Plenty. Most of the alternative recruitment strategies are more fun than you could even envision. They're limited only by your human resources and management teams' imaginations.

Even $10,000 isn't much to pay for a new hire compared to $30,000, is it? To your employees, though, $10,000 translates into a partial down payment on a home or car or the vacation of a lifetime. Imagine racking up five or six employee referral bonuses in a year. Wouldn't *you* be inspired? If you create an employee incentive program or upgrade your existing one, you'll not only save your company money, you'll also spread good will.

An added bonus of employee referral

Employee referral programs make great sense for less tangible reasons as well. Employees who refer a friend or relative to a company most likely know your candidate personally. They also know your organization's needs. Therefore, those referred could be a better fit than someone just walking in off the street, answering an ad, or being recruited by an outside search consultant. Deloitte & Touche found that referred employees stay with the company 33 percent longer than non-referred employees. After reviewing hiring data, Tracey Staley, Director of Staffing for Lockheed Martin, told us she found similar results.

Promoting your organization's allure

If I told you that my company was willing to give you on-the-job training, educational assistance, adventure, and free travel, would you be intrigued? I bet you would. These are just a few of the carrots that draw people to the Army—and you can be sure that the Army knows it.

How can your company go about understanding and promoting your organization's "allure?" Here are a few ideas culled from our client files.

First, survey your present employee population. In an anonymous format, ask specific questions about why your workers chose your organization. For example, was it your organization's:

- Relaxed atmosphere and dress code?
- Compensation package?
- Location?
- Established reputation?
- Flexible schedule?
- Corporate culture?

Maybe it was some other factor, such as being part of a startup company. Find out all you can about why your employees made their final decision to accept your job offer. (See Chapter 10 for some help with asking those questions.)

Next, discover which elements of your organization turn people off. Also, ask what your people feel can be done to turn them back on. This useful data helps immeasurably when the time comes for examining your retention rates.

Why not also survey those candidates who declined your job offers? Why did they ultimately choose to go elsewhere? Was it location? Compensation? Something else? This kind of information will also tell you legions about changes you need to make and new directions you might want to take.

Balancing work, life, and family services

Some organizations provide outstanding services to their employees. The Armed Services provides quality-of-life services to the whole family. Just consider this list of programs offered in the past by the Armed Services:

- Counseling services for both recruits and their families, including individual, marital, family, parental, grief, financial, and occupational counseling.

- Deployment support to assist enlistees and their families in successfully coping with the challenges caused by prolonged separations.
- Spouse Employment Assistance Program services, including help with launching a career search or locating meaningful volunteer opportunities.

Many people in the private sector are drawn to progressive organizations willing to help them balance their work, family, and personal lives. Some employees have even demonstrated a willingness to take a pay cut in return for these amenities (which they often consider necessities). In turn, cutting-edge organizations have discovered that face time doesn't necessarily correlate with productivity. That said, once word spreads that an organization has exceptional life-balance policies and programs in place, they tend not, in these times, to suffer from any shortage of resumes.

Support systems in place for employees in such organizations may include:

- Flexible benefits.
- Childcare and eldercare resource information.
- Earned time.
- Employee assistance programs.
- Wellness programs.
- On-site childcare centers.

High-tech recruitment methods

Remember the recruitment station that was more centrally located than Sergeant Tomberlin's was to Lisa? She went there for a visit, during which she found herself more than impressed by an interactive CD-ROM that began by greeting her by name: "Eldridge," it hailed, "picture yourself in the Army."

Next, the CD-ROM offered her a variety of subject areas to click on, including:

- Education.
- Adventure.
- Money.
- Training-skills development.
- Service to country.

Clicking on Adventure first, Lisa was not disappointed. Images and verbal descriptions of one exotic location after another appeared on the screen.

People in action, interesting job tasks, fun locales. A persuasive narrator guided her journeys along.

Because of such high-tech personalization, two things happened:

1. By allowing Lisa to pick the sequence, the recruiter could learn what most appealed to her—and what his selling points should be.

2. Lisa could picture for herself what it would actually be like to be in the Army.

The good effects didn't stop there. Various clicks awaited her, ready to go with answers to all of her questions: benefits, further opportunities, additional options, everything.

Beyond CD-ROMs, the Army has also set up its Web site, *www.goarmy* with links to *www.army.mil.* When Lisa opened *www.goarmy,* money didn't just talk, it blared: "$6,000 bonus just to join the Army? Click Here."

Below the $6,000 heading, three men toted schoolbooks. She clicked the link and a message read, "Report by September 30th to meet eligibility requirements." Another read, "May be combined with any other bonus." How's that for dangling a gigantic carrot?

The site also provided endless information about the enlistment process, occupational specialties, and more benefits. It even asked Lisa if she wanted to take a tour inside a tank!

Then Lisa surfed over to *www.army.mil* and found herself facing a kind of newsletter/press release/goodwill section. That day's headlines were "Secretary of Army Helps Launch New School Year" and "Kosovo Community Project Shows Ethnic Groups Can Work Together."

Making it easy

When Lisa compared Capital One's Web site to the Army's, she was pleasantly surprised. The private company's Web site was equally appealing. Capital One's benefits, referred to as the Advantage One Plan, were touted all over the place. One caption read "Our benefit package is found at few, if any other companies."

Unlike many corporations' employment Web sites, Capital One's job bank was easy to maneuver. Lisa discovered that she could send in her resume/application via fax, e-mail, or regular mail. Capital One even detailed what its interviewing process and various employment tests would be like. When Lisa clicked on "Meet Our Associates," a diverse range of employees offered majestic quotes that hit all the selling points. These employees ranged from collegiate-faced neophytes to a vice president. All in all, it was an impressive showing and definitely worth the trip.

A Web site as a recruitment tool

Using a Web site as a recruitment tool is almost imperative for organizations these days. Well-done sites do more than just list job openings. They also reflect corporate image and culture, as well as display your recruitment slogans, benefits, upcoming career fairs, and any other selling points that make your organization unique.

Numerous employment Web sites even allow applicants to e-mail their resumes or fill out electronic applications. Many sites also provide U.S. and world maps. Users can click on the area where they'd like to work and access regional employment information, including job postings and application information.

School-to-career initiatives

The Army starts seeking prospective recruits while they're still in high school. A Boston area Army recruiter, for example, advises the five recruiters he manages to go out and build relationships with local high school students. Wearing their uniforms, Army staffers volunteer to cover detention classes for the schools and to be substitute teachers. They also work with teenagers who have gotten themselves into trouble. The idea isn't to approach students directly and say, "Do you want to join the Army?" but to make themselves available and known so that students will come to them.

Some high schools even allow the Armed Services to offer elective leadership classes, referred to as the Junior Reserve Officer Training Corps (JROTC). Although the JROTC program is designed primarily to assist students in the development of leadership skills, this program serves as a recruitment tool as well. Then, at the college level, students have the option of joining a ROTC program.

Are the Armed Forces alone in developing effective career initiatives? Not at all. Many organizations have created their own models and have much to teach the rest of Corporate America. Basketball camp models developed by Nike and Adidas are amazingly effective school-to-career/advertising campaigns, but with a twist. (You'll read about them later in this chapter.)

How to market continuously

As we learned in the previous chapter, organizations that are constantly looking for talent and are more proactive then reactive in their approach stand a better chance at winning today's war for talent.

The million-dollar question is: Just how do you continuously market to passive and active job candidates? We've already explored one interesting model. Now let's take a look at models from some sources who are also about recruiting people. Let's see how these four models might be adapted or adopted to recruit indispensable employees:

- Fund-raiser's (development) model.
- Athletic talent scout model.
- College recruitment model.
- Executive search firm model.

The fund-raiser's model: prospecting for gold

Fund-raisers (or development people) are the ultimate recruiters. Think about it. They have to be extra good at what they do: to convince people to part with their money for a particular cause. In many cases the people they recruit are bombarded by requests to contribute to one company rather than (or in addition to) another. To secure a commitment from a donor may take months (or even years) to do, but a savvy fund-raiser who has targeted a good catch is patient in his or her pursuit.

What's the fund-raiser's motto? Prospect, network, prospect. Fund-raisers make it their business to know who has the time, interest, and cash flow to further their causes. Many times a potential prospect (donor) is "mined" for months or even years. Both patient and consistent, these artful networkers know that their hard work could eventually pay off. Thus they are constantly employing approaches to recruit: sending multiple mailers, hosting fund-raising events (many of them glamorous), and often kicking off sophisticated public relations campaigns.

Good fund-raisers conduct thorough research on prospects. They may be aware of the idiosyncrasies of the individual, who their friends are, and what type of causes they have contributed to in the past.

Creating lists of potential passive candidates can be a useful exercise. Ask yourself who the people are you'd like to entice into your organization. What are their career and personal idiosyncrasies? Are there ways that you might begin to show them how they could be a good match with your organization?

Recruiters must "mine" potential employees the same way fund-raisers do potential donors. Who should organizations be mining?

- People recently promoted and featured in newspapers and trade publications.
- Past employees who left on good terms.
- Candidates who were second and third picks during previous searches.
- Candidates who turned down job offers.
- Students who've successfully completed summer jobs, internships, co-ops, or any other school-to-career initiatives.
- Employee referrals.
- Individuals who have previously attended job fairs or applied for positions.

The athletic talent scout model: sign 'em up

Talent war competition has heated up, and all too often employees view themselves as free agents. Their talents are not necessarily retained by the highest bidder when it comes to salary, but rather by the bidder that can tailor a package of salary, benefits, worklife flexibility, and perks that address WIFM (What's in It For Me?). The perks of the job have in some cases become extreme. Take, for example, a Georgia-based company that the *Wall Street Journal* (Sept. 15, 1998) reported was giving away leased BMWs to new hires.

A friend of mine in the outplacement business told me about a high technology firm that was starting out engineers with a salary of $80,000 and throwing in a sign-on bonus of $100,000. By the way, that wasn't the entire compensation package. Stock options, relocation costs, and other perks were added to seal the deal.

That is all fine and good, you may be thinking, *but my company isn't signing people up for million-dollar contracts (at least not at the moment) and can't afford fancy cars as perks. Where does that leave us? In the dust?*

The answer is a resounding not so. Treating employees as stars, however, can be done very cost-effectively. Consider these ideas:

- From the start of the recruitment process, make all job applicants feel like kings and queens. Make sure the receptionist or person in charge of greeting the job applicants in human resources *and* at the hiring manager's office is cordial, pleasant, and welcoming. Too often, job applicants are met with a "don't call us, we'll call you" attitude.

- Consider delivering candy, roses/flowers, helium-filled balloons, or tickets to a hot concert or play to an applicant. You've never heard of anyone doing that? All the more reason to do so. Show candidates that they're special—and so is your organization. What company has ever treated them so well? Have any other companies pursuing them done anything to show how much they *really* want them?

The college recruitment model: giving it the ol' college try

How do colleges charm potential students? Let me count the ways. During the fall, admissions officers travel near and far, visiting as many high schools as possible. During these high school visits, admissions officers interface with students and guidance counselors, showing their pearlies, painting glorious verbal pictures about campus and academic life, answering questions, and distributing an array of eye-catching catalogs. At night they set up booths at local college fairs hoping to talk with juniors and seniors about their future plans.

You can bet that before these conversations end, a student with potential will be asked if she would like to fill out a contact card. Contact cards lead to databases; databases lead to more glossy brochures, including open house invitations. Open house visits hopefully lead to love at first sight. Who needs to say more? The University of Maine at Farmington even has a live on-line chat option on its Web site, allowing potential students to chat electronically with UMF students.

As are Army recruiters, admissions officers are more than happy to speak with parents and families. Quite often parents are influential in helping a potential employee develop an opinion about a company and/or make a final decision about whether or not he'll be happy at XYZ Company. During open houses, many colleges have upperclassmen leading campus tours and giving testimonials about their school. Meetings with potential faculty advisors are often available to provide the potential students with specific career assistance, including how the school's programs could position them for optimal career success.

Lessons to be learned from college recruitment efforts

Once again we are presented with the continuous nature in which college recruiters operate. They are constantly scouring for top talented recruits. The extent to which some colleges employ administrative personnel and faculty in the recruitment process is something corporate recruiters can learn from.

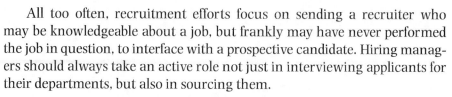

All too often, recruitment efforts focus on sending a recruiter who may be knowledgeable about a job, but frankly may have never performed the job in question, to interface with a prospective candidate. Hiring managers should always take an active role not just in interviewing applicants for their departments, but also in sourcing them.

A hiring manager's attendance at professional association meetings, where he or she can talk with candidates about the company and open positions, is extremely helpful in the recruitment process.

More and more organizations encourage hiring managers and senior management to participate as faculty members at colleges, particularly those with students who could become potential employees and/or interns during the summer or throughout the years.

A family friend recently relayed an interesting story about her, son who attends a prestigious school in the Washington, D.C. area. One of his professors also works for a major employer in the area. After the midterm exam, the top students in the class received calls from the company in which the professor works. The caller asked students about their summer work plans and invited them to lunch or dinner with a recruiter.

The executive search firm model: finding ways to schmooze

One way that executive recruiters keep tabs on who's who is to attend (and in some cases actively participate in) professional organizations and social, civic, and business and community events. They make the rounds and may even provide corporate sponsorships that underscore their visibility in a given market and provide them with entry to collect the business cards from individuals who attend the event. Networking with the right people is an essential part of the executive recruiter's job. Here are some things we can learn from executive recruiters:

Plan a yearly calendar of events to attend within your community. Consider sponsorships for some events, particularly those that will showcase you as an employer of substance and choice and/or give you an opportunity to build relationships with people who could become potential employees and/or friends of your company who can help get the word and positive messages out about your great organization.

Set a monthly dollar limit for hiring managers and recruiters to spend on cultivating relationships with potential candidates or passive employees whom you want to impress. Consider the traditional approaches of taking people out to fancy restaurants and sporting events, but also consider doing more far-fetched things such as offering concert tickets to the prospective candidate. Please note, if you try this approach, be sure to keep up with what groups are truly "hot" and awesome at that time as it changes quickly and without notice.

Routinely survey the marketplace and know in which organizations good talent is residing and why it is staying there. Once you're research is complete, think about what you can do to lure them to your front door, or at least close enough to where they can take a look at what you're about as an employer.

Databases

Executive search firms and fund-raisers build comprehensive databases that capture activities utilized to cultivate and attract prospects. A database is only useful if it is current. Decide on individuals and groups you want to prospect, and then keep your database updated. A useful trick is to do electronic or snail mail marketing quarterly or up to six times a year. That way addresses can be updated and you'll never be off the prospect's radar screen for very long.

Consider keeping fresh databases for:

- Exemplary past employees (they may decide to return someday).
- Students and interns.
- Individuals who've applied to jobs on-line and in person.
- Candidates who were a second or third pick in a job search.

The talent war evolution

A Gen Xer that I know has been extremely successful on the career-hopper boat. In two years, she's changed jobs three times (each with a different company) and in doing so has increased her salary by 100 percent.

Many Baby Boomer managers I know often complain that the workforce isn't what it use to be: "I would have never thought about negotiating salaries like these kids do. Even if the total compensation package is outstanding and they know it, they still want to negotiate. It's like a given with a lot of them."

Where does this leave us? If some employees are acting like they are part of the NBA or some other professional sport, should we consider turning ourselves into talent scouts to pursue them? Maybe. Consider the approach some companies, such as Nike and Adidas, have taken to cultivate top talent in their early years. There are some lessons to be learned here.

In July 1998, *60 Minutes* aired a segment detailing how Nike and Adidas developed a school-to-career program with a twist. Essentially, these two sporting-goods giants created basketball camps for aspiring NBA players, many as young as 10, 11, and 12 years old.

Nike and Adidas both equip their prospective NBA drafts in shoes and clothes bearing their logos. When these hotshots go back to their neighborhoods, who is watching and admiring them? You guessed it: their peers. And which shoes will these peers want to wear? Right again.

Adidas scored really big from this endeavor: One of its graduates is NBA sensation Kobe Bryant, who has appeared on the Web site for live chats.

In December 2000, Venus Williams signed a $40-million contract with Reebok, the largest endorsement ever for a female athlete. IN an interview on December 21, 2000 on *Today,* she revealed that her loyalties to Reebok run deep: She'd worked with them since she was 11 years old!

Think about the implications of this approach: It's basically a win/win situation. The kids and schools get support for these companies, and these sports company giants have access to talent they've cultivated for years. When stardom hits and it's time to sign contracts to endorse certain sports company products, one would think that it might be a little tough *not* to remember how a large company with deep pockets helped you get your start and helped you to "just do it."

Company Spotlight:
Texas Instruments

Here's what Marilyn Fuller, Materials and Controls Manager of Diversity Development and Employment at Texas Instruments, Inc., had to say about the varied recruitment and retention approaches that this top company utilizes.

"Texas Instruments (TI) recognizes that a diverse empowered workforce is a means for achieving a sustained competitive business advantage. Because of this, TI has taken great strides in recent years toward not only embracing diversity, but weaving it throughout the fabric of the corporation."

Here are some of the recruitment efforts TI is committed to:

- Including women and minority candidates for every external opening.
- Including candidates who may not precisely "fit the mold."
- Partnering with agencies that specialize in diversity recruitment.
- Actively seeking women and minority junior military officers (JMOs) leaving military service.
- Focusing 70 percent of its college recruiting efforts toward women and minority students.
- Offering internships and co-ops to high-potential women and minority students.
- Using a "Buddy System" where a contact of the same race/gender is provided as support throughout the recruitment process.
- Implementing "Speed Hiring" as a process to increase acceptances to its job offers knowing that top talent is only available for 10 days or less.
- An employee referral program pays $3,000 to $5,000 for engineering and technical candidates.
- Compensating managers and recognizing them for their diversity recruiting efforts.

As far as retention efforts go, Fuller says: "Practices in place are both formal and informal mentoring; early identification of leadership potential; formal succession planning; accelerated management development programs for identified women/minority employees; executive MBA programs/graduate school paid for by TI; individual development plans; high visibility assignments, special projects, flexible work arrangements; innovative recognition process for high potential employees; international assignments; identification process for high potential employees; [and] managers are encouraged to shake 'the status quo.'"

Chapter 5

Employee Demographics: Know What You Have *and* What You Need

ho was it that said, "If you fail to plan, you plan to fail?" Many human resources professionals and managers are overloaded with unfilled jobs and can't bear the thought of taking time out of a chaotic schedule to plan. As painful as it may seem, the fact remains that performing a needs assessment and doing some market research *must* be done to improve an organization's success at recruiting and retaining indispensable employees.

When it comes to the numbers, it never ceases to amaze me how very little many organizations know about their employee population and its demographic profile. A business would never think about offering a new product line or service to its customers without doing some serious research about the people who would potentially utilize the product or service. Before cranking out anything, the business would run the numbers and do some research about the purchase potential of the product or service. When market researchers and number-crunchers put their minds to it, it's simply miraculous what they can tell you about a consumer: age, name, rank, serial number, why he or she would or wouldn't buy the product, how often he or she would use the product, and so on.

Why is it that many organizations spend so much time understanding their consumers, yet when it comes to their employees, even the most basic demographic information about this group is often lacking. You might be thinking, *I don't exactly get the message that's trying to be conveyed here.* Let me illustrate further. Take a moment and right off the top of your brain answer the questions on the facing page about the demographic profile of your organization or department.

How well did you do on this spontaneous quiz? If you couldn't answer a lot of the questions, hadn't ever really thought about the answers, and/or didn't fair as well as you would have liked, don't worry. You're not alone. Many people unfortunately haven't taken the time to gather and digest this type of basic data on their most important resource: their human capital.

Think, however, about the implications of not doing this. It's pretty scary. How do you really know what benefits you should be offering to those indispensable employees if you can't say whether or not they are young, Gen Xers, Baby Boomers, or Matures (older workers)?

If 90 percent of your employee population is younger than 30 and single, is it really worth spending money and time enriching the family health insurance benefits? Say you want to add more diversity to your population, and 95 percent of staff are recruited from and live in two sections of the city where less than 1 percent of its population are Blacks, Latinos, and Asians. Do you think you'll increase those diversity numbers by not looking in other communities with higher concentrations of people of color? If you don't know the races of your population and the locations from which they are currently recruited, you may never get to the point of improving your organization's diversity.

Know what you've got to find out what you'll need

Until you know what type of employees you currently have and what skills and competencies they possess, you can't possibly know where you're headed in the future with regard to your labor needs. In the pages that follow you will learn about how to determine your employee demographic profile *and* forecast future labor needs.

Employee Demographic Profile Quiz

Employee population

_____ % Matures (ages 55-80)
_____ % Baby Boomers (ages 37-54)
_____ % Generation Xers (ages 19-36)

Average age of workers

_____

Marital status

_____% married with no children   _____% married with dependents
_____% single with no children   _____% single with dependents
_____% domestic partners   _____% domestic partner with
                                              dependents

Gender

_____% women
_____% men

What are the top five cities and towns in which your employees live?

1._____   4._____
2._____   5._____
3._____

(You get brownie points if you can break these down into percentages.)

Educational Levels

_____% completed high school
_____% completed college
_____% completed advanced degree

Length of Service

_____ Less than years   _____ Six to 10 years
_____ Three to five years   _____ 11-plus years

Race

_____% White   _____% Native American
_____% African American/Black   _____% Other
_____% Latino   _____% Mixed Racially

Employee demographic profile

What distinguishes you from the competition? You probably know the answer to this question when it comes to your customers, but what about when it comes to your employees?

Don't be ashamed if you don't know. As mentioned previously, many employers can't readily answer these questions. In this labor market, though, you want to get a handle on these issues. Doing so will enable you to craft benefits, recruitment strategies, training programs, and compensation packages that will set you apart from the rest.

Developing demographic profiles

One of the first things you must do is develop an employee demographic profile (age, sex, race, where they live, etc.), and then look at whether or not you need to change that profile or think how to better serve the people you have.

Retaining current staff is as important as recruiting new staff. Once you have information on your employees' demographics, you can make more informed decisions about how to serve your current employee population with regard to:

- Benefits.
- Compensation.
- Incentives.
- Marketing.
- Advertising.
- Communications.
- Social enterprise (responsibility) efforts.
- Training and advancement initiatives.

Current workforce demographics identified

Make sure that the following demographic information is routinely updated on the employee population:

Total number of employees (specify bodies or full-time equivalents).

- Age.
- Gender.
- Racial composition (overall and by job categories, such as middle and senior management; professional staff; technical staff; and hourly employees).
- Ethnicity.
- Geographical residence.

- Marital status (if available).
- Education levels.

Other demographics you may want to collect include:

- Racial and gender composition of board and vendors.
- Turnover rates.
- Post-hiring experience survey results of candidates and managers.
- Affirmative Action statistics.

Look inward to tackle turnover

Turnover can be defined as "the flow of people in and out of active employment. Quite often people forget that turnover costs include those associated with the person leaving *as well as* those with the new hire.

Creating an employee demographic profile and analyzing turnover can tell you volumes about who you currently have on staff, what keeps them there, and why they leave. This analysis will help you to fine-tune your recruitment, retention, and employee marketing strategies.

Dissatisfied employees who are considering leaving can be very taxing. Low morale is often contagious and can lead to:

- Low productivity and morale.
- Employee theft or sabotage.
- An unwillingness to recommend your organization to prospective employees and customers.

When it comes to keeping your employees, take a hint from salespeople who know that it is six to seven times easier to keep a satisfied customer than it is to recruit a new one.

Nurturing and growing your current staff is far more cost-effective than attracting and training new recruits.

Exit interviews

Despite a company's best efforts, some staff members will leave. Understanding why they leave is essential to preventing further turnover. Many times, turnover occurs because of a poor job match or an unsatisfactory work environment. Well-executed exit interviews not only reveal what needs to be changed, but what is working as well. They also may provide insights into curbing turnover by giving you data of colleagues who may also be preparing to leave.

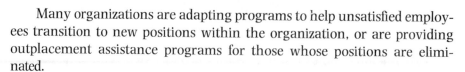

Many organizations are adapting programs to help unsatisfied employees transition to new positions within the organization, or are providing outplacement assistance programs for those whose positions are eliminated.

Ensuring that employees leave on good terms is important, as current and past employees can be excellent goodwill ambassadors for future staff and customers.

Not all turnover is bad

Believe it or not, all turnover is not bad. In fact, it can be very positive. In some cases it may be inevitable, even desirable, that a person leaves your organization. Think about the high-revenue producer who is just phenomenal with customers and rakes in the dough, but is a bear to all of her colleagues. Turnover has skyrocketed in her department, because not one of her colleagues can stand to be around her for longer than five seconds. Many people have left the organization mumbling something about why management doesn't wake up and do something. Is it because they're afraid of losing the revenue and don't care about how the people who work with her feel? If management woke up, what it might discover is that the revenue produced by the high-rolling, bad team player has to be offset by the astronomical turnover costs of the other good people leaving.

As skill sets change and employees no longer possess the competencies needed to do the job, turnover may also need to occur. As we will learn later, the two most important and memorable employee interactions are what happens when an employee enters an organization and what takes place when he or she leaves. Smart organizations that are interested in recruiting and retaining IEs understand this phenomenon all too well. They structure the entrance and exit processes so the door can always be left open and people feel more than good about how they were treated during their tenure.

Plan an employee's exit process carefully, especially when a layoff occurs. Horror stories about how staff are treated spread quickly when a long-term, well-liked, and respected employee is called to HR and told it is his last day. With tears in his eyes and a lump in the throat, he is escorted by security to his cubicle to collect only his personal belongings and then led to the front door and asked not to come back on the premises except to see human resources. Those types of turnover stories live a very long shelf life on the grapevine of any company, and some people delight in relating them over and over to anyone in or outside the company who's willing to listen.

The keys to turnover are to recognize when you want and need it and to manage the process effectively. With some jobs, for example, such as those in the advertising industry or in research, clients dictate when work begins and ends. Once the project is completed, if a grant isn't renewed or a client doesn't sign on for another advertising campaign, the job must be eliminated because the revenue is no longer there to support it.

When turnover blindsides you and an unsuspected employee decides to leave, you need to seriously dissect the root causes behind the exodus. Exit interviews can be helpful in this regard. If problems are revealed during the exit interview process, don't be slow to address them—especially if there are things causing the morale of others to rot. Time is definitely of the essence. Often it only takes one brave soul to break out. That sometimes encourages the domino effect to be activated, as other staff become inspired to also do something about their own bad work situations and walk out of your door into the open arms of a competitor.

The cost of turnover

In the June 1, 1998 issue of *Forbes* magazine, Kaye Morgan of MRI, a recruitment firm, stated, "In some fields right now, it would cost $60,000 to hire a middle-level manager....That's a lot of money if the person is going to leave 14 months later."

Some turnover costs include:

- The hiring manager's time (to sift through resumes, meet with recruits, interview candidates, discuss pay and start date, orient employees, etc.).
- Overtime and temporary-help costs for staff who must take on additional work.
- The recruiter and HR staff's time (to source and find candidates, screen them, meet with the hiring manager, interview candidates, check references, negotiate salary, get past employment information, conduct new-hire orientation, and do paperwork).
- The search committee's time (if utilized).

There are also hidden costs when it comes to turnover. These include:

- Unemployment insurance.
- Lawsuits and discrimination claims.
- Lost business due to insufficient staffing levels.
- A decrease in morale and productivity.
- A negative impact on customer service.

What experts say about turnover costs

Finding a definitive answer on what turnover really costs is difficult. Experts have different opinions on what the true cost of turnover is to the bottom line. They do, however, agree on one thing: Turnover costs organizations mega bucks, and there are many "hidden" costs that all too often CEOs, CFOs, and HR pros miss when they are laying off people and hoping for cost savings as a result of their actions. They often take little action to analyze what it really cost to replace an indispensable employee.

More care definitely needs to be given by the finance people, senior management, and human resources when looking at turnover costs. Approaches to better retain the *right* staff must be developed. Such an action will undoubtedly translate in a positive way to the bottom line. John Challenger, CEO of outplacement firm Challenger, Gray and Christmas, said in the May 29, 2000 issue of *Fortune*, "When you consider lost productivity and replacement costs, a single defection can cost a company between $50,000 and $100,000. It gets even worse if you lost top talent, with their vast sources of intellectual capital gleamed over years at the company."

What's really behind the numbers

If you think that the cost to replace an employee who leaves is only the money needed to cover the person's salary, think again. Turnover costs are astronomical and include costs associated with the person leaving *and* those related to bringing in and orienting the new hire. You owe it to yourself to be disciplined and take the time to calculate the *real* cost of an indispensable employee leaving.

What follows is the Fields Associates, Inc. Turnover Costs Worksheet, which you can use to tabulate what you spend for replacing an employee who leaves your organization (especially those who are IEs.) You may want to produce reports on a weekly, monthly, or quarterly basis that are shared with senior managers and hiring managers so they better understand where turnover is occurring and how much it is costing them. Once this is done, go beyond the numbers and craft tactics to tackle the turnover by creating an action plan to address policies, programs, procedures, benefits, and management issues needed to retain indispensable employees.

Turnover Costs Worksheet

1. Advertising costs: $_____
   - Newspaper.
   - Internet.
   - Journal.
   - Job fairs.
   - Other (please specify). _____

2. Employee referral fees/sign-on bonus. $_____

3. Agency or search firm fees. $_____

4. Screening/sourcing (activities used to locate suitable candidates for an applicant pool). $_____
   - Time spent posting job and discussing job qualifications with recruiter and hiring manager.
   - Screening/review of resume.
   - Telephone screening time.
   - Search committee time.
   - Time spent contacting applicants to interview in HR and/or with hiring manager.
   - Other time spent screening applicant (please explain) .

   _____

5. a. Interviewing: $_____
      (Remember to include cost of total time spent for each set of interviews conducted.)
      - Human resources/recruiter.
      - Manager.
      - Search Committee.
      - Others (please specify). _____
   b. Interview preparation and analysis time spent:
   c. Any costs spent entertaining the candidate (food, air travel, entertainment, time spent with the spouse or significant other).

6. Selecting the final candidate. $_____
   a. Time spent analyzing interviews conducted, reviewing candidate's credentials, and selecting final candidates.
   b. Reference checks.
   c. Other employment screenings/tests conducted (e.g., health screenings, drugs and alcohol screenings, criminal background checks, honesty, personality test, etc.).

    d. Checks conducted on applicants credentials (e.g., education, licenses, certificates, degrees, training).

    e. Salary negotiation.

    f. Visa/green card verification.

    g. Costs associated with drafting of employment contracts and/or golden parachute/severance pay arrangements.

7. Post-employment activities. $_____

    a. Gathering of post-employment information (date of birth, medical information, etc.).

    b. Establishing start date/logistics regarding office space, telephone, computer, etc.

    c. Relocation considerations (domestic or international).

    d. Orientation: $_____

       • Establishing date.

       • Time spent attending company-wide and/or departmental orientation.

       • Benefits administration (time to sign person up for benefits).

       • New-hire paperwork processing time (both for new employee to complete and HR/hiring manager to complete).

    e. Training time for replacement. (Consider that on average a person in a salaried (nonexempt) may take three to six months to learn a job and one in a professional, technical, or managerial job (exempt) may take up to a year to adjust.) $_____

8. Legal/litigation costs if employee sues or files a discrimination claim. $_____
(This includes attorney fees, as well as HR and hiring manager time, time spent in preparing for the case, etc.)

9. Unemployment insurance claims. $_____
(Depending on the circumstances and state laws, this may apply even if the employee leaves voluntarily.)

10. Lost business, contractors, vendors, and customers. $_____

11. Work not performed or business not accepted due to low staffing as a result of person leaving. $_____

12. Overtime costs for staff taking on additional work. $_____

13. Temporary help, consulting, or other outside labor costs needed to supplement staffing until a replacement is found. $_____

14. Low productivity, low morale, and unproductive work time by employees discussing the "ain't it awful" circumstances surrounding the employee's departure. $_____

15. Turnover due to the domino effect as other staff leave as a result of the person's departure. $_____

16. Increased wage costs due to salary adjustments given to get other staff to stay. $_____

17. Outplacement costs or costs associated with any employment termination contracts or severance payment arrangements or contracts. $_____

18. Benefits administration cost for terminated employee (such as COBRA, processing of 401K or 403B rollovers, etc.). $_____

Run the turnover numbers

Once you've run the turnover numbers, in the vast majority of cases, you'll conclude that it truly is cheaper to keep the IEs you have. Instead of racking up turnover costs and high fees from search firms that can cost you 30 to 35 percent annual compensation or more, why not take some preventative measures and utilize that money to strengthen your employees and cultivate them for jobs? Another way to look at it is to think about how much money your organization would save if it reduces turnover. How much more could you offer staff if you did a better job at retaining them? (In Chapter 12, I'll offer some ways to retain your employees by creating internal candidate pools that are ready, willing, and able to assume future jobs that you have available.)

Mastering labor forecasting

Remember when, for a hot second in the mid-1980s, some industries (such as healthcare) experienced by today's standards a mini-labor shortage and were trying to find ways to get ahead or stay on top of the talent drain game by doing what was called "manpower planning?" Of course, few people would be so politically incorrect these days and exclude women from the terminology, but the concepts that people used then are ones that we need to revisit today.

As previously discussed, before you can predict what you need, you must know what you have. Understanding the demographic profile, the turnover rates, and the stories behind them will greatly assist you in that endeavor. With those issues settled, another way to find and keep indispensable employees it to look at exactly what type of IEs you will need in the short- and long-term in order to keep your company profitable. This is where labor forecasting can help. (We've updated the "retro" concept of manpower planning to fit new millennium thinking.)

It may sound tedious, but labor forecasting, derived from information collected during a needs assessment, *can* make life easier. Both short-term (six months to a year) and long-range (two or more years) views are needed. To prepare a labor forecast plan of action, you will need to concentrate on answering these basic questions:

- What jobs will be needed in the future?
- What skills will be needed to perform these jobs?
- Where will the talent come from? (Internal sources? External sources?)
- When will these jobs be needed?
- What outreach efforts will be undertaken?
- What are some multifaceted approaches that can be used to fill jobs?
- What type and how many workers will be needed in one year? Three years? Five years?

Tracking where your new hires come from is crucial, especially when trying out new techniques and deciding whether or not to use long-favored methods to predict staffing needs. As we've discussed, employers must understand the demographics of their present employee population—that is, where their employees live, their ages, sex, race, etc. In other words, who has the organization been attracting and who does it want to attract—both now and in the future? Your organization would conduct a thorough market analysis before launching a new product line, so it makes sense to do the same thoughtful analysis when hiring staff.

Issues surrounding labor forecasting

When thinking about your labor needs, consider where the slow- and fast-growth jobs are—and in what parts of the country and the world these jobs will be located. To help you in that regard, consider the following information:

- According to the Bureau of Labor Statistics (BLS), the two fastest-growing industries from 1996 to 2006 in terms of employment were/will be computer and data processing (108 percent) and health services (68 percent).
- Of the 30 fastest-growing jobs, according to the BLS 1996–2006 Employment Projections, 50 percent of them are in the healthcare industry.
- According to *American Demographics* (May 1998), people who can assist with increasing computerization (database administrators, systems analysts, and desktop publishers) and those who can assist with new medical technology (medical aides, nurses, and home care workers) will also be in demand.
- Of the 50 counties in the United States with the highest expected job growth, 28 are in the South, 16 are in the West, 6 are in the Midwest, and none are in the East (according to *American Demographics*, May 1998).
- Also according to *American Demographics* (May 1998), U.S. jobs will increase by 12.7 percent between 1998 and 2010 (to almost 172 million jobs), and U.S. employment growth will remain ahead of population growth at 10.2 percent between 1998 and 2010.
- The BLS predicts that the majority of job growth will occur in the services industry, at least until 2006. The services industry includes business services (computer programmers and temporary help); personal services (hair stylists and dry cleaners); engineering and management services (architects and accountants); and employees at health clubs, hospitals, and hotels.
- Slow-growth jobs include those that are clerical (due in rise to automation) as well as manufacturing and laborer jobs, according to the BLS 1996-2006 Employment Projections. Fast-growth jobs include professional/technical specialties, service workers, managerial and administrative positions, and marketing and sales.
- According to *Workforce 2020,* some of the fastest-growing jobs, such as software and Web site development, did not exist before 1987.

The Fields Associates, Inc. Forecasting Labor Needs Form

Use this form to help you forecast your short- and long-term labor needs. To make the process go more smoothly, keep a copy of your demographic employee profile handy to refer to. (You'll remember this information from the quiz on page 83 of this chapter.)

STEP 1

Break down your total number of employees into the following categories:

- Full-time.
- Part-time.
- Temporary.
- On-call.
- Consultants.
- Other (Please specify).

Next, break down the organization's racial composition as follows:

	Middle Mgt.	Senior Mgt.	Supervisors	Professional and Technical	Non-Exempt Employees
% White					
% Black					
% Latino					
% Asian					
% Other					
% Mixed					

Note: Pay special attention to demographics of senior and middle management and professional and technical positions for people of color and women.

Next, calculate your turnover rates from the last three years.

With all of this information in hand, answer the following questions:

1. What is our current turnover rate?
2. Which areas are underrepresented? (Affirmative Action Plans may be used.)

3. How will we communicate this information to hiring managers, executives and other key stakeholders? (List stakeholders.)

4. What are the specific multicultural marketing, market segmentation, or traditional recruitment techniques that we will use to attract the following groups:
   - Women.
   - Matures (born between 1920 and 1945).
   - Baby Boomers (born between 1946 and 1964).
   - Generation Xers (born between 1965 and 1981).
   - People of color.
   - Other ethnic groups (please list).
   - Individuals with disabilities.
   - White males.

STEP 2

List your major job groups and provide an assessment for each regarding:

- The extent to which current employees possess the skills needed to perform jobs capably, both now and in the future.
- Whether or not the skills for each job will change over the next one to five years.
- What new skills will be needed.
- Which staff have those necessary skills.
- Any efforts that can be used to improve staff skills so that they will be ready to assume their job in the future. These efforts can include:
  - Internal training.
  - External training (college, vocational training, adult educations, etc.).
  - Internships.
  - Succession planning programs.
  - Mentorship programs (formal and informal).
  - Job shadowing.
  - Rotational assignments.
  - School-to-career initiatives.

Be sure to note which future skill(s) each effort targets, as well as which staff members can help with which programs.

Now answer the following questions, based upon this information.

- Based upon the analysis of the current population and future labor force needs, determine organizational deficiencies and what is needed to reach future goals. In other words, decide what must be done to bridge the gap between where you are and where you want to be.

- Take a short-range view (one to two years) and develop a labor forecasting plan to address these questions:
  - What jobs will be needed in the short-range future (one to three years)?
  - What skills will be needed to perform these jobs?
  - What internal sources can be used to recruit staff? External sources?
  - When will these jobs be needed?
  - What community outreach efforts are needed?

- Take a long-range view (three to five years) and develop a labor forecasting plan to address these questions:
  - What jobs are needed in the long-range (three to five years) future?
  - What skills will be needed to perform these jobs?
  - What internal sources can be used to recruit staff? External sources?
  - When will these jobs be needed?
  - What community outreach efforts are needed?

- What external relationships can be used to cultivate a diverse and qualified supply of workers? List possible strategies/plans that involve the following:
  - School-to-career initiatives.
  - Elementary and high schools.
  - Job fairs.
  - Colleges.
  - Religious settings (churches, mosques, synagogues, etc.).
  - Vocational/technical schools.
  - Community partnerships.
  - Work with community agencies.
  - Specialized search firms.
  - Employee referrals.
  - Customer/vendor referrals.
  - Other efforts (please specify).

- What internal mechanisms will be established to "grow our own employees"? (Decide which of these apply to your needs and think about how each can be developed and implemented.) Consider the following:
  - Succession planning programs/identify high potentials.
  - Formal mentor programs.
  - Management career development programs for non-supervisors/aspiring leaders.
  - Job shadowing.
  - Internships.
  - In-house skills development programs.
  - External courses (specify educational institution).
  - Tuition reimbursement.
  - Management development programs.
  - Other efforts (please specify).
- Which individuals are potential leaders and/or can perform higher-level functions?
- How will we communicate this labor forecasting plan to managers and employees and elicit their support to help with recruitment efforts?
- What strategies will we utilize to decrease turnover and address the issues that staff have revealed as they leave? What is our timetable for implementing these strategies?
- Who will be involved (staff, managers, and executives) in the implementation of the plan to decrease turnover?
- How and when will we measure the effectiveness of this plan? (List specific details.)
- What financial resources are needed to implement items identified with the labor forecasting plan?
- Who (which individuals) will need to review and/or "buy into" this plan?
- Which sources will we use to find candidates? These include:
  - Search firms.
  - Traditional minority and women's colleges.
  - Professional associations.
  - Job fairs.
  - The Internet.

- Community agencies /community outreach efforts.
- Religious institutions.
- Youth programs.
- Other efforts (please list).

Chapter 6

Creating a Brand Image as an Employer of Substance and Choice

As discussed in Chapter 5, often organizations are not as clear as they perhaps should be on the demographic profile of their employee population. Now that you've thought about the type of people you attract to your organization, seek to understand what it is that attracted them to you—and what it will take to make them stay put.

In other words, what special something does your organization possess that makes you an employer of substance and choice? Or, as marketers might put it, what is your brand image?

Most organizations can talk about their brand image as it relates to customers. Few, however, think of it in terms of their employees. What makes a customer become enamored with your organization may or may not be what makes and keeps an employee coming back to take on more work every week.

You need, then, two brand images: one for your customers and one for your employees.

Employer of substance and choice defined

The phrase "employer of substance and choice" has come to be defined as an employer that is highly regarded by a targeted population of employees because it offers great opportunities, rewards, compensation, etc. that are in line with that niche market's personal and professional value systems. In other words, the employer becomes so attractive to people that they choose to work for that employer rather than a competitor.

Everywhere organizations are seeking to find and create a "differentiator," something a little more special than anyone else has, and they are tattooing themselves as an employer of substance and choice.

As you engage in this branding and tattoo process, it is important to keep in mind two things:

1. As with a real tattoo, the brand that you choose to display to the outside world can be permanent. This is wonderful news for the company that has created a positive brand and really practices what it espouses. It is, however, devastating and has negative long-range implications for the company that creates a brand and can't live up to it. For example, brands that are crafted to make the company appear to be flexible and family-friendly come unraveled if employees ask for but aren't given the flexibility to manage childcare or eldercare issues.

2. Live up to your bragging, or don't brag. A company that markets itself as embracing diversity, for example, but does not have any people of color in its senior ranks or on its board may find the tables turned if that issue ever surfaces publicly. If you brag, live up to it. That is why we talk about organizations needing to become an employer of substance *and* choice.

Designing a good employer of substance and choice campaign includes creating a slogan. For one of its campaigns, McDonald's chose the slogan "a job that can take you anywhere." Every company should settle on a slogan that encompasses what the whole organization stands for and what it can offer applicants. Additionally, marketers would never consider throwing away precious marketing or advertising money on customers who are not part of their target market or not potential purchasers of their goods or services. Do your homework to define who would want to be a part of your winning team.

A further look at the McDonald's job advertising campaign

One summer my family and I were driving home from a very relaxing Cape Cod vacation when my daughter spotted a McDonald's and asked if

McDonald's:
"A job that can take you anywhere."

- "A job that can take you anywhere."
- "Future software engineer."
- "Future teacher of the year."
- "Future CPA."
- "Future McDonald's restaurant owner."
- "Whether you're new to the workforce or returning to it, McDonald's jobs give you valuable work skills. Skills with momentum. Skills that give you a running start on your future, no matter what that may be."
- "If you're interested in a job that can take you anywhere, talk to a management team member today."

we could stop for a Happy Meal. As we munched on burgers, my eyes glanced at a tent card on our table. Still trying to balance work life and keep my relaxing vacation in mind, my management consulting instincts couldn't help but analyze the tent card in terms of what McDonald's was trying to say to the masses (myself included) who would be chowing down on burgers and fries. What did the company want to convey about working at McDonald's and why I should consider a job stint there?

The ad campaign was so powerful that I was sucked right into reading the tent card, and it spoke volumes about the employer of substance and choice image McDonald's was portraying. After digesting the information, I reached this conclusion: If I was in the job market for a position at a company like McDonald's, I believe I would have considered applying that day.

The previous box shows what the tent card said. Think about the powerful messages that McDonald's was sending to passive candidates about why it is an employer of substance and choice. Also think about things that distinguish your organization from the competition and can be used as part of your recruitment strategy. Then compose a marketing slogan that could be used as a recruitment tool for your organization.

Four distinct employer brands

The McKinsey Report 2000 outlines four distinct employer brands. The first is *prestige*. "If you work for this company you can work anywhere."

Examples of companies that are household names, offer prestige, and could fit into this category include McKinsey, Cisco Systems, and Harvard University.

The second brand is *a cause*. "You will make a difference in the world." Companies that espouse this brand are Oxfam America, The Peace Corps, and the EPA.

Brand three is *high risk but big reward potential*. "You can make it 'big' here!" Internet companies prior to going public are a prime example of this brand.

The fourth distinct employer brand is *true balance of work and personal life*. "Work here and you can still have a life!" A perfect example is SAS Systems in Maryland, which in the past has locked its doors every night at 6 p.m.

Ask yourself what you really have to offer regarding the following:

- Compensation/benefits.
- Training/advancement.
- Flexibility.
- Balancing work with life.

What, then, must you do to reveal the uniqueness of your organization? Begin by thinking about the following dimensions, and then brainstorm around ways your organization can differentiate itself in regards to the competition:

- Mission.
- Vision.
- Values.
- Benefits.
- Corporate culture.
- Working environment.
- Management style.

Put your image into action

In this competitive marketplace, recruitment must take on more of a sales and marketing flavor. An organization is in real trouble if prospective employees are made to feel that they should be honored to have the privilege of interviewing at XYZ Company. From the moment a candidate has the first contact with your company, all the signs and vibes he or she receives should read: "We want you to consider us. We're a terrific place to work."

Issues to consider

1. Complete your employee demographic profile (see Chapter 5). This will help you figure out the type of people you are already attracting. The exercise will assist you in answering the questions of what to look for both in terms of new employees and those you will need to retain. It may also help you focus on who else you need to attract (aside from those who are currently on your radar screen).

2. What does your niche market like and dislike about your organization from an employee's perspective? What is your image in the mind of others?

   Knowing what type of people you do and don't attract is one indicator of the type of people who could be successful in your organization. A second issue you need to consider is what the market is telling you about what it likes and dislikes about you as an employer. Don't assume you know what people want. Ask them. You need to listen to the voices of a cross section of people, including:

   • Current employees (including new hires and employees with a long service record).
   • Past employees (including retirees).
   • Vendors, consultants, and third parties who conduct business with your organization.
   • Shareholders.
   • Community agencies, organizations, leaders, and residents.
   • Industry leaders.

3. Test out what key stakeholder groups feel is your organizations image/brand. What do you stand for as an employer in the eyes of others? To listen to these voices, you don't necessarily have to reinvent the wheel. Think about those vehicles you already have in place that offer data and insights into what you're doing right as an employer and those areas upon which you need to improve. Consider these pre-existing vehicles:

   • Turnover reports. What are the underlying causes? Are they being addressed?
   • Exit interview data. What drives people away? What did they like and dislike about their working experience? Are there any trends that could indicate what is working for

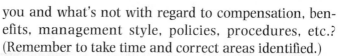

you and what's not with regard to compensation, benefits, management style, policies, procedures, etc.? (Remember to take time and correct areas identified.)

- Customer surveys.
- Information collected from evaluation forms (at company-sponsored events, seminars, training activities, etc.).
- Feedback from performance appraisals and employee self-evaluation appraisals.
- Employee survey results.
- Suggestion box information collected.

4. Live up to bragging rights. Make sure that whatever things you say you're about match up with the indispensable employees you're interested in attracting and keeping. You may have positioned yourself as an employer of substance and choice that stands for flexibility. Create a family-friendly environment, then, and a benefits package geared towards Baby Boomers in their 40s and 50s with lots of family-centered perks. After looking at what you'll need in the next three years, say you find that you want to also attract more 20- and 30-somethings. You've hit a major stumbling block, because your benefits aren't in line with the population you want. Some changes may be in order to position your organization as an employer of substance and choice with this group.

5. Benchmark. Where do you stand with regard to the competition? To know this, there are a few things you must get a handle on:
   - How are you defining the competition when it comes to hiring and keeping indispensable employees? Is there a major competing company or industry? (Remember that you may lose people to others outside your industry, so also think of the competition in broad industry and non-industry terms.)
   - What size are your competitors? Even if you are a large Fortune 100 company, your competition may include small companies as well as other Fortune 100 companies. Keep in mind that most businesses in the United States have 500 or less employees. The global nature of organizations may cause you to view overseas competitors.

- What does the competition have to offer that is the same, different, better, or worse than what you offer? (Benchmarking—gathering best practice information— will help you to answer this question.)

6. Mutate regularly. Create and share your employer of substance and choice statement with others and mutate it regularly as times change. Once you've done your homework and realized what you stand for as an employer of substance and choice (and you know it will stand up to the bragging rights test), develop an employer of substance and choice statement. You might also want to work with your internal and/or external marketing experts to craft a catchy statement that encapsulates what you stand for, something that will remain tattooed in the minds of active and passive job seekers as well as your own indispensable employees. Think of the Army's "Be all that you can be." Doesn't that say it all to the niche market of young people the Army recruits?

●●●

Remember not to rest on your laurels. You must mutate that statement so it doesn't become stale or doesn't reflect the organization as it changes. Do you recall when the Army's slogan was: "Be all that you can be. Find your future in the Army"? After the downsizing activities of the 1980s and 1990s, the slogan changed. The Army did a smart thing and mutated the statement by keeping what applied. The outcome was the fresh, but familiar and catchy phrase "Be all that you can be." In 2001, Army commercials talk about being "an Army of one." Try your hand at creating what you stand for as an employer of substance and choice by completing the exercise that follows.

Employer of substance and choice exercise

Complete the following exercise to help you focus your thinking about what makes you an employer of substance and choice.

1. What is our employee demographic profile?
2. What are people telling us about what they like and dislike about our organization from an employee's perspective? Consider this data if it exists:
   - Demographic profiles of current employees (including new hires and longtime employees), past employees (including retirees), customers, vendors, consultants, third

parties who conduct business with your organization, shareholders, community agencies, organizations, and industry overseers.

- Turnover reports, exit interview data, customer surveys, information collected from evaluations at company-sponsored events, feedback from performance appraisals and self-evaluation appraisals, employee attitude survey results, and suggestion box information collected.

3. What is our image in the mind of people both within and outside the organization?

4. Does our image match up with the indispensable employees we are trying to attract and keep? How? (Or why not?)

5. Do the following match up with our employer of substance and choice image? If no, what can we do to improve them?
   - Benefits.
   - Compensation.
   - Management style.
   - Work environment.
   - Work ethic.

6. Who are the competitors, and where do we stand in relation to them? (Consider domestic and international competitors, those from inside and outside the industry, and those of similar and different sizes.)

7. From an employee's perspective, what are the positives about our organization? (Consider benefits, working environment, training and advancement opportunities, work/life and flexibility policies, HR practices, management style, etc.)

8. As an employer, how are we different from/better than the competition?

9. What needs to be improved to enhance our standing as an employer of substance and choice?

10. What is our employer of substance and choice statement?

11. To receive input, with whom will this statement be shared?

Marketing slogan exercise

Compose a marketing slogan that can be used as a recruitment tool for your organization. Think about the qualities that distinguish your organization from the competition.

One size doesn't fit all—or even most

It was only several years ago that I learned how much people in human resources, management, and marketing stand to gain if they work together. I had been asked by Janine Fondon, a colleague who is an expert in the marketing and communications field, to serve on a committee of the Ad Club of Boston. (Ad Clubs are professional organizations for people primarily in the advertising, communications, marketing, and public relations fields.)

This committee of the Ad Club had been formed to put together a diversity resource guide that would be utilized by professionals to increase the diversity within their organizations and advertising agencies. I was the only human resources and management person on the committee, and I learned volumes from that experience about what marketing is all about.

One of the first things that I discovered was that there is a difference between marketing and advertising. The executive director of the Ad Club Foundation, Juliette Mayers, helped to dispel my lack of knowledge of the differences between some of these often-confused fields (advertising, PR, publicity, promotions, and marketing).

The second lesson I absorbed was how sophisticated marketing people are when it comes to defining their target market. After a little research into the target market's wants and needs, they can design products and campaigns that get people to purchase things. After listening to the members of the committee, I began to think to myself, *Why is it that we aren't using some of these marketing tricks of the trade, which are used to lure customers into organizations, to recruit people into our organizations?*

Just as my thinking started to swerve in this direction, another interesting life lesson came my way. My company began to work on a project for a large retail food chain. At the time of our engagement, this organization was launching a new service to customers that would allow them to use a card that would provide them with discounts on certain items every time they shopped. As a person who always cut coupons but never remembered to bring them to the store with me, I thought that this was a great idea.

I also learned something else that totally amazed me: The same card that was allowing me to get these fantastic discounts every time I shopped was really more than just a discount card. It provided my client with invaluable information about me, the consumer, that it could utilize to improve its sales and target marketing efforts to me.

Here's how my card *really* works: Every time I purchase something from that supermarket and utilize my discount card, it records everything that I purchase. In essence, that supermarket, over time, can compile a customer profile based upon the items that I purchased.

That profile tells the store how many times I purchase even the most mundane of items. Based upon my profile and spending habits, the store can utilize the information to, you guessed it, get me to buy even more. This is because the store has researched me and knows my spending habits.

After the Ad Club experience and the revelation produced by my work with the supermarket, my brain started to work overtime thinking about the implications of the tools that marketing and advertising people utilize for recruiting and retaining customers, and how those very tools might also be employed to attract and maintain employees into an organization.

Tips for attracting indispensable employees

1. Many recruitment efforts are based primarily upon advertising (in print, on the Web, on TV, or on the radio). Although those can be effective ways to get the word out to everyone, when recruiting for a job, you should consider who you want to attract and whether you want to broadcast your message to the masses or target your approach to a specific group.

2. Consider a comprehensive recruitment strategy that utilizes a variety of marketing, advertising, public relations, promotions, and multicultural marketing approaches throughout the year. Keep in mind that, given the labor market, you need to be recruiting active *and* passive candidates. Passive candidates can really be turned off by hard-sell tactics that try to lure them into your organization. A kinder, gentler approach may just be right.

   To achieve this, remember the Armed Forces approach from Chapter 4. It is long-term and geared to a niche market. "Be all that you can be" was a staple of radio and TV advertising for years.

   Think about doing more longer-term promotions and public relations. Place articles about your star indispensable employee in his or her community/town newspapers, for example. Appealing to the passive and active candidate market requires that your comprehensive recruitment mix include the following:

- Print (newspapers, magazines).
- Direct mail.
- Radio.
- Television.
- The Internet.
- Public relations.
- Sponsorships.
- Outdoor/transit (billboards).

3. If your organization attends certain community and civic events, take out sponsorships and let your advertising for the event reflect what you stand for as an employer of substance and choice—even if it is not an employment-related event or job fair. Unfortunately, these efforts often aren't coordinated, and your multidisciplinary staff who do work for your organization in the community (such as public affairs, marketing, human resources, and community affairs) aren't always working together. Too often, individuals in these departments aren't aware of the efforts of others outside of their departments. The outcome here is a missed opportunity for everyone involved. Take some time within your organization to survey these areas and find out what type of activities each has on the calendar for the year. Are there ways the departments can collaborate and thus present a united front about careers in your company at these events or to community organizations and leaders?

    For example, each year a Community Affairs Department may sponsor a large event that thousands of the people in the community traditionally attend. Booths are set up and the company's products are distributed free of charge. Everyone loves freebies.

    Include at your table some information about career opportunities at the company and have a human resources representative and/or a department manager at the booth to answer questions about working at your company. See how it works. You accomplished two tasks at one place by combining your community affairs and recruitment efforts at one event. Consider bringing together the following groups to craft a yearly calendar of events aimed at collaborative opportunities to help recruit indispensable employees:

- Communications.
- Community affairs/relations.
- Human resources.
- Marketing.
- Public affairs.

  It is important for you to be careful about which sponsorships you take out and which group you align yourself with in the community.

4. Take advantage of multicultural marketing and market segmentation opportunities. Think about all of the different types of employees you may want to attract to your organization. From an outsider's standpoint, would you use the same marketing tactics to lure an older customer to purchase your goods and services as you would a 20-year-old? Probably not. Why is it, then, that we don't do a better job at segmenting our market strategies when we are trying to lure different groups to the organization?

   After you've completed your demographic profile and labor forecasting plan and have a good handle on the type of people you have to recruit, why not consider a more targeted approach? Consider how best to get the word out to the different groups you wish to attract. Remember that they may not all best receive their information in one format.

Multicultural marketing

Consider these TV- and radio-related mulitcultural trends:

- Latinos' top preference for radio stations is Spanish-speaking (43.8 percent), followed by Top 40 (14.7 percent), and then adult contemporary (10.2 percent), according to Arbitron National Database.
- According to Deloitte and Touche Impact Resources, Latinos ages 12 and older listen to 12 hours and 18 minutes of radio weekly. This is two hours more (per week) than the general population.
- On average, African American households watch 73 hours and 39 minutes of television weekly. The national average is 48 hours and 25 minutes. These audiences are most attracted to shows presenting African Americans in major supporting or starring roles, according to *American Demographics* (September 1996).

Also consider the statistics of these markets when marketing:

African American market

- Annual buying power: $352 billion.
- Ethnic pride is strongly valued; 90 percent feel proud of their ethnic heritage.

(Source: U.S. Census and Market Segment Research and Consulting, Inc.)

Latino market

- Annual buying power: $248 billion.
- Common bond: Spanish language.
- Most heavily used media is Spanish-language radio and television.

(Source: U.S. Census and Market Segment Research and Consulting, Inc.)

Asian market

- Annual buying power: $200 billion.
- Major languages spoken are Japanese, Filipino, Korean, Chinese, and Vietnamese. 62 percent speak an Asian language at home.

(Source: U.S. Census and Market Segment Research and Consulting, Inc.)

•••

In your recruitment effort, try target marketing that aims at finding a specific audience that shares something together. Marketing yourself as an employer of substance and choice to these groups may prove fruitful in attracting and returning indispensable employees.

Target recruitment efforts can be utilized to:

- Attract certain groups (who you want to be lured) to your organization. This may also create new recruitment opportunities for you as satisfied employees from these groups tell their family and friends about your organization.
- Compete in markets that have been untapped.

Avoid generalizations when marketing

Generalizations can allow human resources professionals and managers to extrapolate broad trends and behavior characteristics for various groups they are trying to recruit (women, Latinos, individuals with disabilities, etc.). However, this information must be viewed as general, and not indicative of every candidate within a particular segment. To prevent overgeneralization of a particular target population, closely examine the degree to which a candidate has either assimilated (adopted) or acculturated (partially adopting without abandoning the native culture) with mainstream values and behaviors.

Company Spotlight:
Unity First Direct, Inc.

The recruitment of people of color in the 21st century requires the personal touch of a credible communications source and broad outreach in targeted markets, both in the United States and across the world. Employers will need to take more action to recruit and retain the most talented candidates in the market, many of whom are African American, Asian, African, Caribbean, Native American, East Indian, and Latino.

Janine Fondon of Unity First Direct, Inc. believes that establishing a 21st-century–style relationship with diverse candidates means that you have to go beyond the "I have an opportunity" phone call. Fondon says, "Employers must develop their own brand image for attracting diverse candidates, and even go beyond what they have already tried in the past. Corporations often have the glitz, glamour, and four-color ads in top publications, but their reputations often lack the well-respected grassroots outreach that signals credibility. Employers must also exhibit a highly publicized commitment and reputation for treating employees of all backgrounds fairly and truly offering an equal opportunity to people at all levels. Above all, there must be commitment to communicate with the diverse market on a regular basis. To recruit and retain quality professionals who seek more than a one-year review, the trust factor and communications gap must be addressed."

Job prospects who qualify for mid- to senior-level professional positions often search the very selective Unity First Job Opportunity Showcase and revisit the Web site on a regular basis because the targeted, Web-based service highlights positions specifically targeted to people of color. "Readers look for jobs on a daily basis and feel comfortable with the credibility of our service and the postings advertised to reach out to communities of color. One job candidate wrote: 'When I got back to my office this morning, naturally, I looked at the job postings you have and one caught my eye in particular,'" Fondon says. Key jobs have been posted for top corporations, educational institutions, and key nonprofits. One of the best-kept secrets to recruiting people of color is the trust factor.

Although employers and recruiters may say they advertise in the top publications, they must also develop strategies for targeting smaller, community-based industry and professional publications, both online and in print. People of color trust their own community-based sources of information. For example, 87 percent of African Americans trust information about companies and product information in Black magazines and 79.7 percent trust local Black-owned newspapers, as reported in a study that was commissioned by the African American Markets Group of Ketchum Public Relations Worldwide. Most often, companies don't run consistent ads or develop complete campaigns targeting community-based, grassroots outlets. As a result, they do not see the result they desire.

With trust being a key factor to successful recruitment and retention, diverse job seekers and potential job seekers prefer opt-in e-mail newsletters, such as Unity First Online's, that they can subscribe to. Readers trust the publications and are willing to accept their advertisements and job leads on related Web sites, job boards, and other Internet-based sources.

Many companies are now reevaluating the power of the ethnic press (radio, newspapers, magazines, Web sites, direct e-mails, and bulletin boards) and developing strategies to reach out to untapped communities. A great example of this is when Viacom purchased Black Entertainment TV, the top-rated network serving the African American community. Viacom is extending its outreach to the African American community.

Diversity-focused Web sites are also proven key attractions for the job seekers of color as well as professionals looking for greater opportunities. People of color participate in great numbers on ethnic outlets, such as direct e-mail services, job boards directed to people of color, and targeted Web sites. The key is finding the sites that help you reach the talent pools you desire, while at the same time building solid relationships for consistent, trustworthy communications and outreach in nontraditional markets.

Companies should not have any doubt about whether to heavily use the Internet to market to all segments of the U.S. population. People from all walks of life and socioeconomic statuses are online users. Mass-market companies are using niche sites to target African Americans and other groups.

Tom Fondon, Chief Information Officer of *UnityFirst.com* says, "Technology is leveling the playing field for the recruitment of professionals of color. More and more, recruiters and employers will have access to candidates of color, if they wish to seek them out."

Companies seeking to deal with these emerging populations will most likely use the Internet or Intranet to distribute information and resources that rank high in helping people of color feel more at ease with gaining access to the organization. In the book *Breaking Through: The Making of Minority Executives in Corporate America*, author David Thomas heard firsthand accounts of the struggles and strides of minorities who spoke of their personal backgrounds and family experiences, prejudice in the workplace, being passed over for job assignments, and the importance of relationships with mentors and others in their support networks, as well as other factors critical to their success in making their way up the corporate ladder. With a wide range of resources, and regular communication on topics and information relevant to the individual's needs, experiences, and career, the Internet or company's Intranet will score top marks in providing information and support contributing to retaining that employee.

Now, and well into this century, Internet outlets will target diverse job populations. They are currently broadcasting a wide range of career opportunities and resources via e-recruiting efforts, targeted job searches, and job-posting services. According to Unity First Direct's Janine Fondon, "Credibility and consistent action will define the players who truly desire diversity at all levels of their organization and a track record of retaining the best talent across all communities and functions."

Chapter 7

Cultivating Community Outreach Efforts and Resources

As we've explored, organizations interested in luring indispensable employees to their doorsteps in a market where passive job seekers rule must employ a long-term and comprehensive approach to accomplish their mission. Simply put, they must craft strategies that look at past, current, and future employees. In this chapter, we will explore some innovative, even radical approaches companies are utilizing to entice individuals into their folds. Let's begin by looking at ways to attract people through community relationships and outreach efforts.

Here are some outlets for organizations to recruit employees by developing external relationships:

- School-to-career initiatives at elementary, middle, and high schools.
- Internships programs.
- Job shadowing programs.
- Job fairs (internal and external).
- College-relations recruitment program.
- Religious settings (churches, mosques, synagogues, temples, etc.).
- Volunteer programs.
- Schools.
- Community partnerships.
- Social enterprise/responsibility.

- Work with community agencies and leaders.
- Specialized search firms.
- Customer and vendor referrals.
- Involvement of candidates' families.

School-to-career initiatives

School-to-career initiatives have become a popular way for businesses to connect with teachers, students, and administrators. In some instances, the business partner becomes "married" to the school and participates in such things as curriculum development and serving as an advisor to teachers and administrators about what should be included in the curriculum to prepare students for the world of work. Internships (summer and year round), college co-op programs where students work part time and go to school as well, and job shadowing programs all help in getting the word out about career opportunities within your organization and industry.

School-to-career initiatives and partnerships can:

- Enhance an organization's image within the community as an employer of substance and choice.
- Improve customer relations.
- Develop students' competencies needed to perform on the job.
- Serve as pipeline for future employees.
- Act as mutually beneficial partnerships that strengthen the community *and* the organization.

Consider a few examples of how business organizations have partnered with schools within their communities in different ways.

School-to-career partnerships: The Massachusetts General Hospital

The Massachusetts General Hospital (MGH), part of The Partners Healthcare System, and the Timilty Middle School formed a partnership in 1988 to enhance science education, promote faculty development, improve academic performance, and better the health status of all students and their families. The school, which has more than 550 students from every neighborhood in the city of Boston, is located in the Fort Hill section of Roxbury.

The school's Family Center was created to increase parental involvement in all aspects of the school and to improve the students' health status, academic performance, and self-esteem by providing support, training, and improved access to a wide range of health and community services.

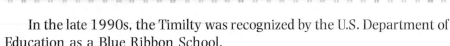

In the late 1990s, the Timilty was recognized by the U.S. Department of Education as a Blue Ribbon School.

Mentoring and job shadowing:
The Brighams & Women's Hospital

The Brighams & Women's Hospital, another affiliate of Partner's Health Care, has also been involved with Project Pro Tech, a program for high school students who are interested in pursuing careers in healthcare. They have provided mentors and job training to high school students beginning in their junior year and continuing through at least their first two years of college.

Career fair:
Peabody Community School

The Peabody Community School Program, an after-school program housed in the Peabody School, located just minutes from Harvard University in Cambridge, Massachusetts, worked with Fields Associates, Inc. to deliver a career fair with a twist. This career fair was based on the premise that in today's job market, employers need to do more about getting a variety of audiences to better understand what they do, the types of jobs they have, and the people they employ. This variety of audiences should include:

- Young people whose career choices are just starting to take shape.
- Teachers, administrators, and guidance counselors who help to steer young minds towards career choices. Because careers have changed (and continue to change) so dramatically and rapidly, these career guides may also need to be reoriented to what people do in occupations and at different companies.
- Parents and guardians of students. These people play a significant and important role in shaping the lives (and ultimately the careers) of young people. Parents might also need kids' help to think about a new career path for themselves. Some adults may be shy about pursuing a new career path, or have always wanted to know what someone in a particular field does for a living but were afraid to ask. At the career fair, they could attend and learn alongside with their children about career opportunities. No one would know if they were there to learn more about the career on their behalf or that of their children.

● ● ●

The idea of a career fair that would attract these three audiences was hatched and proved to be extremely fruitful for all involved—the children, teachers, administrators, guidance counselors, parents and guardians, and employers who participated. What was in it for the area's top employers who attended the fair? A lot. Employers had the opportunity to "do well by doing good." Teachers, parents, and students all learned about the organizations and the career opportunities within them. In some cases, people applied for jobs right at the fair.

Numerous employees from a real eclectic group of industries were in attendance and included representation from:

- Airlines.
- Banking and financial services.
- Biomedical industries.
- Consulting.
- Education.
- Government (city government, fire department, police department, politicians).
- Healthcare.
- High technology.
- Insurance.
- Manufacturing.
- Media and communications.
- Retail.

Internal and external job fairs

Everyone scouring the streets for talent attends their share of job fairs. Here are some ideas whose time may not have yet come for your organization that you may want to consider with regard to job fairs.

Internal job fairs

Host internal job fairs where departments set up booths where employees can stop by and see what type of jobs and careers are available in that area. Quite often staff want to know, but are afraid to ask (or never quite get around to it), what people in such and such a field or department really do. Perhaps if they knew the answers to their questions, they might consider applying for a job there.

A value-added benefit to an internal job fair is that you can increase communication between and among departments as people have an opportunity to find out firsthand what their colleagues in the next department or cubicle really do with their days.

An external job fair with a twist

Partners HealthCare, an organization with close to 40,000 employees, hosted a candidate showcase. Postcards were sent to promising candidates who showed a big interest in wanting to work for the company. Like the recipient of a million-dollar award from a Publishing Clearinghouse–type organization, these candidates received a postcard from Partners letting them know that they had "been selected" to appear in the candidate showcase program. They were asked to give a five-minute presentation at the showcase in front of a variety of hiring managers. In advance of the candidate showcase, hiring managers were provided with the names, resumes, and vital information about the candidates who would be participating in the showcase. The showcase was a smashing success, and human resources and managers lived up to a promise they made to interview candidates immediately after they gave their five-minute presentations.

Community partnerships

In the mid-1980s, hospitals in the Boston area were all experiencing the same problem: a major shortage of certain types of healthcare workers (such as nurses and physical, recreational, and respiratory therapists). Rather than fight and battle against themselves for a limited supply of candidates, they decided to lay down their organizational swords and band together to fight the problem. An organization of 12 Boston hospitals came together under the Conference of Boston Teaching Hospitals. Most of the hospitals were large teaching hospitals affiliated with the Harvard Medical School. They decided on a strategy to help attract talent to the Boston area, which they felt was a major concern. The group focused on marketing the benefits of working in Boston (rather than just one particular hospital) as a healthcare professional. The group was successful in elevating the city's already-stellar reputation as a hub for quality research, teaching, and patient care. Some of the marketing techniques the group employed were:

- The development of a marketing campaign and a slogan.
- The creation of a recruitment brochure featuring all of the hospitals within the organization.
- Attendance at out-of-state job fairs.

Straight from the expert's lips:

"If organizations don't figure out how to tap into talent wherever it comes from and whatever it looks like, then they will be at a competitive disadvantage. Retention must be an integral component of any effective recruitment strategy. Companies should partner with local resources to insure they are addressing the professional, personal and community interests of high-potential employees they wish to retain."

—*Bennie Wiley,*
President and CEO, The Partnership, Inc.

- The establishment of an 800-number to answer calls from people around the country.

Religious settings

In today's high-tech marketplace, many religious institutions have Web sites, and some are willing to post jobs on them. In addition, some organizations have been successful in working together with religious institutions to get the word out about career opportunities within their organization. (For an interesting story on how one organization, Boston Coach, did some pretty innovative outreach efforts to religious institutions, see the Company Spotlight in Chapter 9.)

Corporate enterprise/ responsibility activities

Many of today's employees, whether they were born and bred during the Beatnik, Hippie, or Gen X era, want more out of a company than just a paycheck. Work that has a sense of purpose and does something to make a meaningful difference in the world is what many IEs search for when looking for an organizational home where they can put their feet up and settle. Such employees want to know that their organization is ethically sound and that their job is helping the corporate mission to move forward.

In addition, more consumers are investing their hard-earned money exclusively in socially responsible investments and companies that perform such work. Organizations such as the Business for Social Responsibility (BSR) serve as a professional association for organizations interested in finding out more about how they can practice social responsibility in their work and social enterprise. The notion that businesses can be profitable and socially responsible has become increasingly important.

Work with community agencies and leaders

Politicians, community leaders, and activists, as well as community agency personnel, are all people who can assist you in filling jobs and identifying active and passive candidates. Take time to get to know them. Keep them in touch with your organization by inviting them to appropriate organizational functions or honoring them and their constituents for their fine work in the community.

Specialized search firms

For jobs at certain levels or those that are extremely specialized, search firms (including executive search firms) may still prove to be your best bet. Although their fees may be hefty (30 percent and upwards on average) and in some cases you pay a fee whether a candidate is found after a specified period of time or not, in the end their research capabilities and ability to target quickly the active and passive candidates who are qualified and competent for your job make the price worthwhile.

Here are some particular instances when you should consider using a search firm:

- You need a search firm's skill or expertise.
- The search firm can add value and credibility to what you are doing.
- The "politics" of the situation require outside help.
- In-house resources aren't sufficient.

It is more cost-effective in the long run to hire a consultant than a staff person. In some cases, organizations that have to conduct numerous high-level and specialized searches are hiring an internal search person who is employed by the company to work full-time at beating the bushes for their targeted staff.

Tips for managing outside search firms

1. Know exactly what you want to have done, and approximately how much time it will take.
2. Decide on how much you will pay for the work or project, a payment schedule, and a billing arrangement.
3. Determine how to measure the success of the assignment.
4. Remember to manage the project/consultant. Don't be afraid to ignore advice that isn't right for your organization.
5. Agree up front on expectations and project deadlines.
6. Make sure the consultant has expertise in your industry.
7. Be honest. Don't give consultants the runaround by "picking their brains" and then not using them.

Customer and vendor referrals

Many companies elicit the help of their employees to find staff. But why stop there? More and more companies are expanding their job referral programs to include two groups who know their work intimately: customers and vendors. These savvy employers seem to operate under the philosophy that it doesn't really matter from which source qualified people come as long as they come forward and apply for jobs. Consider these companies' examples of involving customers and/or vendors as referral sources:

- According to a 1997 TMP Worldwide Research report, MT Bank in Buffalo, N.Y. mailed employee applications with monthly bank statements and received 400 responses in three weeks.
- D'Angelo's Sub Shops has a 24-hour 800-number to respond to job inquiries, places ads on carry-out bags, and includes trips to Disney World as part of its employee referral program.

Candidate rejects

What about the candidate who was the bridesmaid, but never the bride? Have you ever thought about what you should do with candidates who were excellent, but for whatever reason didn't get the job? The reason is usually minor, or has to do with politics and having to select an internal person or a referral from some outside top dog.

Why not maintain a database of these people and establish a system to keep them in your loop? To update them regarding your career possibilities, you may want to e-mail, call, or send them a newsletter about career opportunities within your organization from time to time.

Candidates who reject you

Also consider staying in touch with candidates who rejected you. Lockheed has a practice of mailing follow-up letters to candidates who turned down a job offer. Lockheed received a 20-percent return call rate (versus 2 percent, the average return from direct mail).

Family or significant other involvement

Quite often, the decision as to whether a candidate accepts or rejects a job is a family matter. Some candidates (even if they are in love with the job and career possibilities) will turn it down if a person influential in their lives gives the job a thumbs down. That person could be a child, parent, spouse, significant other, or someone else.

Organizations such as the Armed Forces quite often involve the family in the recruitment process. Young recruits bring Mom, Dad, and other parental figures out to meet with the recruiter before they sign on the dotted line.

Executive searches that involve relocation quite often include a trip to the potential employer site with the spouse, family members, or significant other. The company recognizes that if the person's other half isn't satisfied with the move, the employee is probably going to be under pressure and ultimately won't be happy either.

When involving the family or significant other, remember that these days, such people may have a totally different role in helping to sway the job applicant one way or another. For example, a client of mine learned loud and clear the role that the family played with certain ethnic groups it was trying to attract to its organization. In this case, the company held a diversity job fair with the hopes of attracting a lot of Latino applicants. The company got more than it bargained for: Many of the job applicants also came with their extended family members who were not applying for a job—kids, grandparents, spouses, uncles, cousins.

The organization learned a lot from this experience. As the director of employment later told me, "The next time we host this type of job fair, we're going to make sure to include activities for family members."

Organizations that practice social enterprise are often very vocal about what they believe and try to put their money where their social responsibility resides.

Passive job seekers are often drawn to the noble efforts of socially responsible organizations and may not be looking for a job, but like what they hear and see about the good work that these organizations do. When the passive job seeker who is socially responsible is ready to look for a job, then the company that has already established itself as a corporate do-gooder may set itself apart from others.

Volunteer and social responsibility time-off perks

Many corporations today offer employees time off to do volunteer work of their choice and/or company-sponsored volunteer work, where an entire company might become involved in a social or civic activity. Many people are familiar with corporate-wide socially responsible activities, such as Habitat for Humanity efforts, where homes are built for families in need.

Sometimes, for-profit organizations will link their efforts with nonprofit organizations or causes. For example, Timberland and City Year collaborate on efforts that involve the Fortune 500 company working along with young adults who have formed something akin to an urban Peace Corps.

Volunteer activities to attract passive candidates

Remember when you were young and always wanted to work in a hospital, so you became an unpaid "candy striper," where you learned about the hospital, did odd jobs, read to patients, or helped anxious patients as they waited to see the doctor? Not only did you do something meaningful with a sense of purpose, but your volunteer job also exposed you to the world of work and healthcare.

Many people are looking to volunteer time to organizations with noble causes. As an added benefit, they get to know you as an employer. Whether people are in high school, in college, or more mature and looking for something meaningful to do with extra time after their children have flown away from the nest or they retire, these volunteers are potential passive job candidates and can also serve as goodwill ambassadors to get the word out to friends and colleagues about your wonderful organization.

Radical recruitment

Desperate times call for drastic means. Your external recruitment efforts may need to become radical if you are to succeed in finding indispensable employees. Are you out of ideas about new and different ways to get the word out about your positions? Here are some places to post your job openings and/or company logo or slogan that you might not have considered:

Shopping carts

The place on a shopping cart where children sit while you're shopping has become a mini-advertising billboard for companies to advertise their services and wares. Consider this wide-reaching advertising mechanism to keep your company's name on the brains of passive and active candidates.

Restaurants

Recently, I was dining at a restaurant called The Cheesecake Factory. This popular restaurant has pages and pages of luscious culinary items to tease your gastronomic fancies. Inserted between enticing food items are ads for a variety of things. I noticed, however, that there were no ads about coming to work for people or that showed a company as an employer of substance and choice.

Think about it. You've waited for an hour or more to get a table at this restaurant because the food is a gastronomical delight. You are, however, going to comb through the menu as you wait so that when you're seated and your waiter comes to take your drink order you already know what to order for your meal. Think about how much exposure XYZ Company gets if it places an ad in that menu that extols the virtues of working for it. As a passive candidate, I may not just look at the ad, but may even have time to imagine what it is like to work for the company as I wait for my table to be ready. Consider this as a radical recruitment option.

Shopping malls

Americans spend a lot of time shopping for bargains and great deals in malls—Americans of all ages. Think about all the people you could potentially reach, from teenagers hanging out with their friends to senior citizens on their "power walks." Consider establishing a job-shopping store or linking up with mall promotions from radio or TV stations, sport teams, etc. inside malls.

Concerts/sporting events

Concerts offer a great opportunity to set up a booth where people can register online for jobs and/or get information about what it's like to work firsthand at that company from people who are also giving out freebies.

Cisco Systems' Radical Practice: "Oh no, my boss is coming"

Check out Cisco Systems if you ever want to experience a radical recruitment practice. I presented at a conference given by Linkage, Inc. in March 2000 and listened to a speech given by a high-level human resources person at Cisco Systems. He had incredible things to say about some of the strategies Cisco has used to attract top talent and to continue its phenomenal growth spiral. Cisco did its research and found (to my surprise) that most people were applying for jobs during work hours. Naturally, problems arise on the job if you're supposed to be working and instead you're applying for a job. Cisco did something to help people remedy the dilemma of being interrupted by a boss when applying for a job during work hours. This is a truly radical recruitment experience. Cisco's Web site (*www.cisco.com/jobs*) has an "oh no, my boss is coming" icon. When you click this icon, another screen pops up— one more pertinent to the world of work, so that your boss won't suspect a thing.

Because people love freebies so much, they'll be drawn to your booth. Once they're there, you can talk to them about the company.

For some sporting events, such as football games, companies foot the bill for staff to attend. In return, they (the staff) do subtle marketing. For example, they'll hold up signs at every touchdown that read *XYZ Company: A great place to work. Call our toll free number 1-800-ABC-DEFG for more information.*

Check-cashing/money-wiring establishments

Think about establishing relationships with check-cashing establishments and places that wire money. Perhaps there are workers there and/or people waiting in line who might consider your company if they knew more about it.

The Web

Emerging technologies are radically changing the way companies source, screen, and select talent. According to Gerry Crispin, co-author

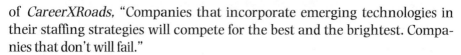

of *CareerXRoads,* "Companies that incorporate emerging technologies in their staffing strategies will compete for the best and the brightest. Companies that don't will fail."

What a boom the Web has been for employers and job seekers alike. For the employer it is a very cost-effective way to showcase the organization and its open positions. Although it might be necessary for visibility's sake to still advertise in the local newspaper, it's less likely that you will need to repeat this expensive practice for the same positions over and over again. The Web has literally opened up the world to your open positions.

One CEO of a 4-year-old high technology manufacturing company posted a firmware engineer position on one of the leading job Web sites. He received resumes from eight international candidates (all needing employer sponsorships to work in the U.S.) and two domestic candidates. His experience 10 years ago with sponsoring a foreigner to work for his company was not a happy memory, so he was not encouraged by the applicant pool. (However, it's fair to say the application procedure for companies sponsoring foreign professionals for hard-to-fill positions has been streamlined, and can now be done in two months on average, according to a Cambridge-based law firm specializing in immigration issues.)

The number of job Web sites is growing daily. My colleague, Deane Coady, remembers the time she received a sales call from Jeff Taylor, founder of *Monster.com.* It was in the mid-1980s, before Internet recruiting was commonplace. Deane remembers being intrigued but skeptical of the benefits of the Web as a job applicant source. All she could envision was overwhelming her recruiters with hundreds of resumes from online job seekers who were not qualified or lived so far away that the relocation expenses would be prohibitive. Screening through volumes of resumes to find the truly qualified was too much to ask of her staff at the time. But times have changed. The technology has improved, and the labor shortage has intensified to such a degree that recruiters are now accustomed to the fact that they must wade through hundreds of online resumes in the hopes of finding a few viable candidates for each open position. Job Web sites that figure out how to decrease this cumbersome, time-consuming task will truly become the job Web sites of choice.

There are now middlemen and middlewomen (that is, Web search consultants) whose sole job is to search for the best Web sites for an employer's open positions. I have found this service to be very worthwhile and cost-effective. For a set fee, and in a matter of days, the search consultant will research and place an employer's open position(s) on free and fee-based job Web sites. For example, a client of mine needs to fill several domestic and international human rights advocacy positions each year. In just a few hours, the company can post its jobs on the following sites and get worldwide exposure:

- *www.idealist.org*
- *www.internationaljobs.org*
- *www.hri.ca*
- *www.opportunitynocs.org*
- *www.nonprofitjobs.org*

What are the benefits, then, of online recruiting for employers? There are many:

- It's user-friendly for applicants. Online recruiting is an easy way for applicants to access comprehensive information about organizations and specific jobs. Many organizations have links to information that prospective candidates might find useful, such as relocation advice/information.
- Employers can list future job openings as a way of becoming more proactive (rather than reactive) about finding talent.
- Online recruiting is usually less expensive, and wider reaching, than print or media advertising.
- Employers can build in candidate evaluation tools into the Web site. A good example is Ernst & Young, which developed a challenging case study that prospective candidates are asked to read and solve. E&Y evaluates the responses. Another example is Cisco Systems, which has a section on its Web site called "Make a Friend at Cisco." Prospective candidates are given the e-mail address of a volunteer Cisco Systems employee. They become e-mail pen pals whereby the candidate can ask questions from an employee and learn the inside scoop on the company. Meanwhile, the employee can be evaluating the prospective candidate.
- Employers can widen their search for candidates from underrepresented groups. Here are some examples:
  - *Listmanager@blackpeople.com*
  - *naaap@listbot.com* (National Association of Asian American Professionals)
  - *www.lpn.org* (Latino Professional Network)
  - *www.hirediversity.com*
  - *www.blackvoices.com*
  - *www.unityfirst.com*

Online recruiting benefits job seekers as well. Here are a few ways how:

- Instant access to hundreds of open positions.
- Quick and easy access to organizations' Web sites with information that is often very useful in preparing for job interviews.
- Easy and quick application for a job.
- Added benefits for the applicant (at some sites). For example, job seekers can request an "online agent" at Hot Jobs (*www.hotjobs.com*). The "agent" sifts through all the openings posted on a daily basis and e-mails appropriate positions to the job seeker.

One note of caution: Statistics still show that the best way to land a new job is networking. A July 2000 issue of *The Wall Street Journal* reported that a recent survey by Forrester Research found that only 4 percent of Internet job seekers landed a job through the Net. Meanwhile, 64 percent landed a job through networking. These numbers may change, and I do believe the Web will grow in importance and effectiveness, as our world increasingly becomes technology-reliant.

Restrooms

Restrooms provide another outlet for employers to advertise and/or market their wares as an employer of substance and choice. Every organization has restrooms, and when people are utilizing them, they are generally a "captive audience." Some organizations put ads up in these most intimate of intimate places. (I must admit that this is an ultra-radical approach, but some companies may want to consider this as a way of getting the word out about career and job opportunities.)

Transportation vehicles

We've progressed from the days of horses and buggies. Think about the various modes of transportation that people utilize or see in today's society. Why not accomplish two things at the same time: transport people and deliver good news about your company? Trucks, buses, subways, mobile vans, cars, trolley cars, and airplanes are highly visible as they complete their mission to get people from point Y to point Z safely. What if they carried a message in their travels that touted the virtues of working for your company and/or gave a Web site address or telephone number to contact if people wanted to learn more about you?

Blimps floating over a beach with your company's Web site address on a hot sunny day, small airplanes trailing a message about your company's Web site, or articles in the in-flight magazines of larger domestic and international airlines are all ways that the sky is the limit when thinking about ways to get the word out about career opportunities in your organization.

Here's another idea: Think about buying some cars to advertise your organization as an employer of substance and choice. The cars, of course, would be painted with a logo of your company, a slogan, and/or some message that would indicate how people would contact you for career opportunities. This is a win/win situation. The drivers of the cars get your message out to the mobile public. In return, they receive free transportation (that you pay for) that can be utilized during their off-driving hours.

Recycled employees

Recycled employees are those who have previously worked for your organization and leave, but at some point are recycled into your workplace. Recycled employees may have left your organization for a plethora of reasons, but because the grass is not always greener elsewhere, they decide to return. Recycled employees include past employees, temporary help workers, and retirees.

In this age of labor shortages, don't burn bridges with staff as they leave. Their employment life can oftentimes be reincarnated with you. They may appear months or even years later, back on your doorstep in the form of a recycled employee looking to volunteer, consult, or work full- or part-time. (See Chapter 11 for more information on recycled employees.)

Retirees

Think about innovative ways to reach out to senior citizens through retirement and assisted-living facilities; social, civic, and religious organizations; and senior citizens' centers. Because the government has relaxed some restrictions on allowing people who collect Social Security to also work, there are individuals who are still ready, willing, and able to work for you.

On-call/per diem staff

Many industries that require around-the-clock staff, such as manufacturers and hospitals, have used on-call and per diem staff for years. This type of staffing may require some getting used to if you are not accustomed to it, but it is a handy way to keep jobs going during times of low staffing, leaves of absence, sick time, and increased work loads. It works like this: Individuals sign up to be put on an on-call list that is used on days when the manager needs an additional pair of hands.

Some organizations have very sophisticated on-call systems. For example, Adrienne Mervin of Orlando, Fla. sometimes works as a substitute teacher. She utilizes a system whereby she calls in (or registers online) for temporary work only when she wants to work. The convenience these systems provide these employees with is hard to beat.

 Company Spotlight:

Timberland

Timberland, a Fortune 500 company, encourages recycled activity from temporary employees and offers liberal community service benefits to provide employees with time off to perform community service. Vidra Harris, director of human resources, explains: "Timberland has a flexible Consumer Service program that hires individuals to staff our consumer call lines. Employees work an average of 15 hours a week, so it's a perfect job for retirees, college students, and parents with children in school. The work is cyclical—heavy call volume beginning around October and leading up to the holiday season, and tapering off around April.

"As the work tapers off, we found ourselves either losing employees who needed to pick up hours elsewhere, or terminating employees in the spring and trying to rehire them in the fall. The retention practice we employed was to leave employees on the active roles when the call volume tapered off if they agreed to return in the fall. Employees on 'hiatus' are invited back for key company and department meetings. It helps them to feel like they are still linked to the company as employees. (More importantly, they get to retain their employee discount!) As a result, our retention rate has significantly improved with this group."

Community service benefits

"Timberland has a policy of providing full-time employees with 40 hours of community service in addition to all of their other time-off benefits. Part-time employees are eligible for pro-rated numbers of service hours. We have found that providing service to the communities we live in accomplishes a number of things:

1. It's a retention tool. Community service benefits the environment and people around us. These are often the

schools, the playgrounds, and the community organizations that our employees and their families use. Employees report that they feel proud of the community service that Timberland provides, and it is one of the benefits that keeps them here.

2. It's a recruitment tool. Service functions as a "candidate magnet" for those who share our values, which helps to reduce potential recruitment costs. People who value community service self-select Timberland as an employer of choice.

3. It's an experimental development tool. Employees get an opportunity to try new skills, work through and with teams, and manage projects. The accounting clerk who aspires to be a supervisor can get hands-on experience leading and managing a project team of 30 people to build a set of docks for a local YMCA campground.

4. It's fun. Employees enjoying participating in service events, and everyone needs a little fun in their worklife."

Chapter 8

Hidden Sources of Employees: Individuals With a Disability

I've heard it said that we are all *temporarily* able-bodied. A Louis Harris and National Organization on Disabilities poll found that 54 million people in America have disabilities. Of that 54 million, only 29 percent are employed, although 56 percent of those in the survey reported that they were seeking jobs.

Employers need to consider what is about to happen in the near future. In 1998, Baby Boomers comprised 53 percent and Matures 21 percent of the nation's workforce, according to the Bureau of Labor Statistics. Additionally, people are not retiring at age 65 anymore. Many people are working well into their 70s these days. What does all this mean? It means this: The number of people with chronic illnesses and disabilities in the workforce is about to increase dramatically.

Don't let the word *disabled* put you off. Many people with disabilities possess incredible skill sets that can be tapped into if only companies would learn how to make appropriate accommodations. Though it's a good start, this mindset cannot be limited to wheelchair ramps. Schedule changes, telecommuting, and flexible schedules are just a few examples of possible accommodations.

Disability knowledge quiz

In 1998 the National Organization on Disabilities and Louis Harris conducted a survey of 1000 American adults with disabilities (age 16+). (The survey allowed for a sampling error of plus or minus four percentage points.)

Answer the following questions to test your disability knowledge. I think you'll be surprised by some of the answers.

1. Joel Reedy's book, *Marketing to Consumers with Disabilities* (Probus Publishing Company, 1993), states that _____ is the age when chronic conditions such as arthritis, hearing impairment, and heart disease become prevalent.
   a. 45
   b. 55
   c. 65+

2a. A 1998 National Organization on Disabilities and Louis Harris & Associates survey revealed that _____ percent of persons with disabilities ages 18 to 64 do not work full- or part-time.
   a. 10
   b. 25
   c. 71

2b. Of these persons with disabilities ages 16 to 64 who do not work, _____ percent say that they would prefer to work.
   a. 13
   b. 72
   c. 50

3. True of false: According to a July 1996 President's Committee on Employment of People with Disabilities, Diversity and Disabilities Fact Sheet, "If you do not currently have a disability, you have about a 2% chance of becoming disabled at some point during your work life."

4. True or false: A July 23, 1998 press release on the National Organization on Disabilities and Louis Harris & Associates, Inc. Landmark Survey indicated that "recent business studies show it requires on average less than $300 to accommodate a worker with a disability."

Disability knowledge quiz answer key

1. a
2a. c
2b. b
3. True
4. True

Disability and employment

According to *Survey Program on Participation and Attitudes* (Executive Summary, 1998), the following are highlights of the 1998 National Organization on Disabilities and Louis Harris & Associates' survey:

- Among adults with disabilities of working ages 18 to 64, 29 percent work full- or part-time, compared to eight out of 10 (79 percent) of those without disabilities, a gap of 50 percentage points.
- The proportion of working-age adults with disabilities who are employed has actually declined since 1986, when one in three (34 percent) was working.
- Among those with disabilities ages 16 to 64 who are not employed, seven out of 10 (72 percent) say that they would prefer to be working.
- 45 percent of adults with a disability say that people generally treat them as equal after they learn they have a disability.
- Two out of three adults with disabilities say that their disability has prevented (41 percent) or made it more difficult (26 percent) for them to get the kind of job they would like to have.
- Among adults with disabilities who work full-time, fewer than half (41 percent) say that their work requires them to use their full talents or abilities.

Tips on recruiting and retaining indispensable employees with a disability

- Audit and carefully scrutinize your organization's current programs and future capabilities to successfully recruit and retain individuals with disabilities. Pay careful attention to:

- Recruitment.
- Retention.
- Mentoring programs.
- Succession planning.
- Promotions, transfers, work assignments.
- Personnel and administrative policies, procedures, and systems.
- Compensation.
- Benefits.
- Training and career development.
- Management development.
- Community outreach.
- Employee orientation and education.
- Utilize disability resources and disability-related organizations to get the word out about job vacancies and the organization's commitment to hire, train, and promote individuals with disabilities.
- To gain insight for tapping into and keeping consumers with disabilities, ask yourself, "Do I include people with disabilities in":
  - My workforce?
  - Sales and marketing teams?
  - The research and development process?
  - Advertising efforts?
  - Annual meetings and ongoing communication initiatives?
- Train staff on proper etiquette for working with and serving customers who are persons with disabilities. For example:
  - Don't pet guide dogs.
  - Don't pat a person in a wheelchair on the head or shoulder.
  - Remember that a wheelchair is part of a person's personal space. Honor that person by not leaning on it.
  - Speak directly to a person. Don't talk to them via a sign - language interpreter.
  - When conversing with a person who is visually impaired, identify who you are as well as others in the room.
- Identify a point person who can help answer questions, provide advice on reasonable accommodations, and give

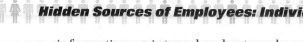

information on internal and external resources to hire and retain people with disabilities.

- Train HR staff and managers on how to recruit and retain persons with disabilities.
- Look at recruitment and retention activities to make sure they include outreach efforts to hire qualified people with disabilities.
- Evaluate recruitment practices.
- Develop comprehensive programs to transition people who are temporarily able-bodied (TAB) and become disabled, including return-to-work programs.
- Make sure your organization and those businesses you use and subcontract to are accessible.
- When drafting communications, consider issues of literacy and craft communications that people of all education and literacy levels can comprehend.
- Make sure advertising and marketing efforts include the presence of individuals with disabilities.
- Market yourself as an employer of substance and choice for individuals with disabilities. This includes job advertisements, applications, in-house and external communications, stories, articles, etc.
- Create a disability or diversity council whose responsibility is to provide insights and direction with regard to the organization's diversity efforts.
- Provide training for employees and managers.
- Ask people what type of accommodation is appropriate; don't assume you know what they need. Provide reasonable accommodation.
- When possible, print things in large print and make sure that the typeface isn't printed in light-colored pastels, which are more difficult to read.
- Train and orient staff and managers. This includes:
  - Working with staff so they better understand why a person with a disability has reasonable accommodation in the workplace.
  - Orienting employees who haven't worked with individuals with disabilities.
  - Teaching staff to examine preconceived notions about what people can't do.

- Training senior and middle managers, HR professionals, and employees on reasonable accommodations and how to work with individuals with disabilities in the workplace.
- Create ways to transition employees who are temporarily able bodies and become persons with disabilities to consider:
  - Social/psychological issues.
  - Reasonable accommodation.
  - Managing them through the transition process.
  - Employee orientation issues.
  - Job restructuring.
  - Getting colleagues to understand the situation.
- Consider telecommuting/home-based employment as an option.
- Help managers and employees to not stereotype when there is a perception and history of disability.

Section 3

The Role of Human Resources and Management

Chapter 9

The Impact of Human Resources on Hiring and Keeping Indispensable Employees

Think for a moment about how much of your organization's overall budget is consumed by the following activities:

- Benefits (health insurance, life insurance, 401K or 403B plans, stock options, childcare, etc.).
- Compensation (wages, bonuses, incentives, etc.).
- Recruitment (hiring and orientation).
- Employee relations (investigations regarding employee concerns, terminations, layoffs, etc.).
- Labor relations (union negotiations, grievances, mediation).
- Employee activities (employee events, fun activities, etc.).
- Training and organizational development (programs to enhance employee skills and competencies).
- Human resources information systems (keeping up with employee vital information, signing up and taking employees off the rolls).

Take a wild guess at how much of your company's budget it can cost. Ten percent? 30? 50? 70? More? My guess is that these activities take a *huge* chunk out of your cash flow. Here's

Straight from the expert's lips:

"Human resources is not just this entity that fills open job requisitions or handles terminations. HR is not just about celebrations and terminations; there's a whole lot in the middle."

—*Mary Aceto, Vice President, Human Resources,*
Boston Coach

a second question: In which department are many of these activities administered? If you said human resources, you're probably right.

If so much of the organization's financial resources flow towards the human resources department, then it stands to reason that smart organizations need to pay very close attention to making sure that the department runs smoothly in order to attract and retain indispensable employees.

Given the monumental and expensive tasks that HR departments must execute, savvy organizations have moved to elevate the function so that it occupies a seat at the senior management table alongside such functions as finance, operations, information technology, sales and marketing, and research and development.

In progressive companies, gone are the days when human resources was personnel—paper-pushing bureaucrats whose departments were filled with nice people that the organization didn't want to get rid of, but didn't know what to do with. Personnel people played the "fall guy" role: Any time a manager had to do something he didn't like, he said, "Personnel made me do it" and was instantly off the hook in his employee's eyes. In the role as company bureaucrat police, personnel also took out the organization's dirty laundry: terminations, layoffs, you name it. If this description sounds too much like your organization, you'll want to start to make some changes to improve the image of this vital function.

The role of management

Managers, not human resources professionals, are ultimately responsible for hiring, firing, promoting, and advancing staff. Human resources should be viewed as its name implies: as a "resource" to management as they carry out these functions.

Straight from the expert's lips:

"In my view, there must be an organization philosophy, modeled at the top levels of the organization, that reflects placing value on people as individuals and team contributors. If it is not there, all the training and consciousness-raising programs by HR mean very little.

"The work for HR, then, is to help senior leadership articulate its philosophy and be visible in practicing it throughout the organization. We must also create pay programs and provide other workplace supports as tools to help the supervisory staff reinforce the right message about staff's contributions and importance. This is not at all original, but I find the basic HR principles are still the best."

—*Laura Avakian, Vice President, Human Resources*
Massachusetts Institute of Technology (M.I.T.)

As such, to hire and attract indispensable employees, management and human resources must form tight alliances in order to win the talent war competition.

There's an old cliché that states, in effect, that people are recruited and attracted to organizations because of their reputation and status, but leave because of management. Managers who think that they can be hands-off and relegate the responsibility of recruiting and retaining staff only to the human resources department need to think again. Sure, HR can beat the proverbial bushes and find good (if not great) candidates, but if management drags its feet and is indecisive about a "hot" job candidate in this job market, the applicant will be snatched up quickly by the competition. In such a case, the manager has no one to blame but himself.

Conversely, if a top-notch candidate is recruited into the organization, but the manager lacks the skills and competencies to manage in a fast-paced environment and doesn't create an atmosphere where the employee feels valued, is treated fairly, and understands his job and how it fits into the mission of the organization, more than likely that indispensable employee is not retained.

Organizations that are successful in recruiting and retaining indispensable employees and conquering the talent war understand the importance of strengthening the human resources department function, as well as fortifying the bond between the human resources department and management. Here are some simple tips that human resources departments and/or managers can utilize to become more effective in recruiting and retaining indispensable employees:

1. Develop a human resources strategy. Successful recruitment and retention requires that your human resources strategy aligns with your organization's mission, values, and goals. Take the time to articulate and commit to paper what your HR strategy is. Also work to better understand what you truly "stand for" as an employer of substance and choice. (Return to Chapter 6 if you need help with this.) To help you in your decision-making process, look at the strategic plan of your organization and how you will accomplish it.

    If you don't have an organizational strategic plan, backtrack and create one so that everyone understands the vision and direction of the company. That includes understanding the demographic profile of your workforce (the attributes, ages, gender, geographic residence, goals, and skill sets of the employees your organization needs to recruit and retain to achieve its objectives).

    Remember that with such a tight labor market, you don't want to find yourself in the situation that some companies have: ready to grow and expand but unable to do so because they can't find the right people to fill the jobs that will let them grow the business.

2. Remember the old saying, "If you fail to plan, you plan to fail." In our new world order, planning is the key to recruiting and retaining the indispensable employees who are going to help your business to prosper. To create a strategic HR plan that supports your organization's strategic plan, mission, vision, and values, you must complete some very important steps. As we discussed previously, to know where you're going, you've got to understand what you've got and what's needed to get to where you're headed. Again, planning is the key. By knowing your employee demographic profile, you'll have a real good sense of the type of people

you're currently attracting. Once you've completed the labor forecasting process, you'll also have a clearer picture of what type of jobs and people you'll need in the future. After all of this is completed, the fun really begins as you craft a long-range strategy that articulates ways you can recruit from external and internal resources to fill future jobs.

3. Craft a long-range recruitment strategy. All too often we want quick fixes when it comes to filling jobs. Many managers panic when an employee gives his or her two-weeks' notice, and demand that HR fills the job immediately. This job market, however, doesn't support this request. Take a longer-range view and think about filling jobs *before* they are empty. This means constantly looking for good talent. Your long-range strategy may include a combination of:

    *   External recruitment.
    *   Internal recruitment (including growing your own employees).
    *   Utilizing recycled employees.
    *   Cultivating relationships with potential future employees (through such efforts as school-to-career initiatives, job shadowing opportunities, and internship programs).

4. Offer exceptional customer service to job candidates. With good candidates in "hot" demand, superb customer service from human resources and management—coupled with a quick turnaround time in processing applications—is essential. In the good ol' days, candidates would attend an interview with the expectation that they were going to be grilled by the hiring manager. They expected to prove themselves worthy of becoming an employee. In today's "no longer a buyer's market," the interview process dictates a more customer-friendly and marketing-orientation touch. Consider improving your customer service orientation if:

    *   Managers are too slow in making hiring decisions.
    *   Human resources staff are drowning in paperwork and/or not adequately staffed, making them unable to process job requests quickly or work with managers fast enough to address employee grievances that may cause them to look elsewhere.
    *   Candidates wait too long to hear about your interest in them.

- Internal and external applicants don't know if you've received their application and/or the status of their candidacy.
- People are kept waiting for interviews.

5. Never forget that it is no longer a buyer's market. You have to market and sell the company *and* the job to prospective candidates. Keep in mind that, even during economic downturns, competition is stiff for indispensable employees, in this country and around the world. Prospects have choices and can afford to shop around for the best and highest bidder. If you are a hiring manager or HR person, before you even start the interview process, think carefully about how you will sell the job and the company to the person interviewing for the job.

   A word of caution: Don't sell candidates a false bill of goods or brag about something that you're not ("We're very flexible in our hours of work." or "Of course you will quickly grow and advance in your career and salary here."), unless you can produce the goods. Otherwise it will come back to haunt you. Honesty is *absolutely* the best policy here. Provide candidates with a realistic view of the job, working environment, and challenges (both positive and negative).

6. Take a critical look at your human resources policies, procedures, structures, programs, and activities. Regularly (at least once a year) conduct an audit, analyze the results, and (based upon your findings) take action to change things or leave them the way they are currently operating. (See the audit exercise that follows to assist you with that effort.) As you are auditing the human resource function, ask these key questions:

   - What are we doing and why? (Look at programs, services, benefits, policies, procedures, and training.)
   - Who do we serve?
   - How are we spending our time? With whom are we spending our time? Is this the best use of our time?
   - How are we organized? Is it an appropriate and efficient structure?
   - Do we have the right skill mix to perform our jobs? Where are we lacking? What should we do to correct things if we are lacking?

> ## Straight from the expert's lips:
>
> "Management is starting to realize that retention is not just a human resources issue. People used to turn to HR not for help when there was turnover, but to say, 'HR, what are you going to do about it?' They are starting to take ownership for retention."
>
> —*Joan Goodwin, Vice President, Human Resources, Evergreen Investments*

- Do we have "seamless" service with people take appropriate ownership of problems and concerns?
- Are we keyed into the voice of our customers?
- Are mechanisms in place to take the pulse of the organization?

7. Involve senior and middle management in crafting strategies to recruit and retain IEs. Without their involvement and support, efforts are bound to be fruitless.

HR department audit exercise

To conduct an audit of your human resources department, answer the following questions. If you answer no to any of them, devise an action item. Include start and end dates for creating and implementing your action process.

Employee relations

1. Do you have a formal grievance system and are employees aware of how to access it?
2. Do employees and managers know with whom to talk in human resources regarding employee relations issues?
3. Do you have formal written policies and procedures?
4. Do managers and employees receive training on your policies and procedures?
5. Are policies and procedures reviewed and updated at least annually?

6. Do you have an HR advisory committee/board or group that can provide information on the pulse of the organization and give advice to HR on upcoming initiatives?

7. Do you offer a regular program of employee activities?

8. Do you have a formal progressive/corrective action policy?

9. Are all formal written warnings and termination notices reviewed in HR or by legal counsel before they are issued to employees?

10. Do you conduct exit interviews, and is feedback given to management regarding why employees leave or stay in the organization?

11. Do you have an updated employee handbook?

12. Do you have an effective employee recognition program?

13. Are managers encouraged to provide ongoing feedback to employees?

14. Do you have programs in place to help employees balance work, family, and personal life?

15. Do you have a childcare or eldercare center and/or offer employees assistance in these areas?

16. Do you have a formal employee assistance program?

Benefits

1. Are benefits effectively communicated to employees?

2. Are benefit enrollment lists audited on a monthly basis?

3. Are benefit programs evaluated annually to determine cost-effectiveness?

4. Do employees receive yearly benefit summary statements outlining their benefits as well as how much the organization contributes towards them?

5. Are employees who terminate employment deleted from benefits lists within one month of termination?

6. Is the COBRA program (continuous health insurance for terminated employees) audited every two years?

7. Are legally required benefits reports submitted in a timely manner?

8. Are mechanisms in place to treat employees who are hurt on the job?

9. Are there programs in place to provide training so employee injuries do not recur?

10. Are managers provided with annual reports regarding em-

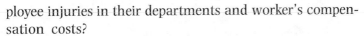

ployee injuries in their departments and worker's compensation costs?

11. Do you have an effective return-to-work program for employees who are ready to return to work following an illness or injury?

12. Are systems in place to review office ergonomics to prevent injuries and/or repetitive strain injury?

13. Do you offer benefits information sessions or brown bag–luncheon programs so employees can find out about their benefits?

14. Are changes in benefits communicated to employees via a variety of mechanisms (written communication, employee forums, etc.)?

15. Do you evaluate the cost-effectiveness of all your benefit programs at least once a year, and is senior management apprised of cost savings in any benefit programs?

16. Do you conduct any benefit fairs, health fairs, or wellness programs throughout the year?

17. Do you conduct any pre-retirement training programs?

19. Do employees know who to contact for benefits-related questions?

Training and development

1. Do you offer career management and/or counseling services to your employees?

2. Is there an evaluation of your training programs (those in place and those needed) at least every two years?

3. Are employees encouraged to continuously learn?

4. Do you measure the quality of your training instructors?

5. Are evaluations conducted and analyzed after every training program?

6. Have you developed a comprehensive training plan that helps address forecasted skills needed by your organization?

7. Are there training programs in the area of customer service, management, and executive development?

8. Do you have a diversity training program?

9. Do you have a formal tuition reimbursement policy, and is it communicated to employees?

10. Do employees know who to talk with if they are interested in attending conferences, seminars, or professional trade

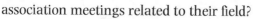

association meetings related to their field?

11. Do you have strong relationships with area colleges, schools, and vocational-technical programs?

12. Do managers routinely talk with their employees about their careers?

13. Does your training function provide information to employees on educational opportunities at colleges, schools, adult basic education programs, English as a Second Language programs, etc.?

Company Spotlight:
Boston Coach

For many years, Boston Coach has been a leader in providing prompt, clean, courteous, safe, and dependable transportation in luxury sedans to employees of Fortune 500 companies. In this tight labor market, the company wants to maintain its reputation for quality and service. Boston Coach is a Fidelity Capital company, owned by Fidelity Investments, that extends beyond its corporate headquarters in Boston with seven sites throughout the United States.

To remain competitive, it has enhanced its capability to recruit and retain a competent workforce. In 1998, Boston Coach hired Mary Aceto as vice president of human resources. Soon after her arrival, an employee handbook was created with job descriptions for all 1,600 Boston Coach employees. Mary called this step "something that needed to happen, so we put our nose to the grindstone and did it."

The next—and biggest—human resources milestone was gaining a seat for human resources at the proverbial senior management table. The human resources team worked hard so that the function was viewed as an essential part of the business. Mary also worked to establish herself as a business partner on the senior management team. She was determined to elevate the role of human resources so it was, as she states, "not just this entity that fills open job requisitions or handles terminations. HR is not just about celebrations and terminations; there's a whole lot in the middle. When you get to the middle, the celebrations and terminations become incidental and a part of what you do everyday—a part of the employee's life span. We don't just focus on the life or death of an employee, but what also happens in the middle."

The company's human resources approach is not to wait for people to come to human resources; HR goes to them. Mary practiced what she preached to the human resources staff. Donning a driver's uniform, she attended the company's Coach College's driver training class. She was oriented alongside new drivers and became certified in a defensive driving course. As part of the training, she took on-the-road training and had to pass the course just as the drivers did.

Boston Coach's human resources staff is constantly seeking to look through the eyes of employees to see what they really do. They visit sites where their employees pick up customers. As Mary explains, "When you have a mobile workforce, you have to go out to them. Talk to employees in their world, not yours, about what's working for them and what they do every day."

Boston Coach makes sure that it keeps in touch with the needs of staff in remote sites. "It's one thing to be in corporate headquarters, but another thing to be in sites such as Philadelphia, Chicago, and New York, to see how things also worked for people there," she stated. She found people were doing some interesting things and decided the entire company could benefit from hearing about each other's recruitment and retention trials, tribulations, and, above all, successes.

Early on, all human resources staff throughout the country were brought together to a retreat where they shared their best practices. Although this may make common sense, a lot of large HR departments look outside for professional support and best practices when what they really need to do is look right under their own noses.

Over the past few years, HR staff company-wide have chipped away at this direction, and they continue sharing HR best practices via a monthly HR conference call. This has particularly helped with recruitment initiatives. What also helps is they can test things in different markets before going company-wide. Here's a good example:

DARP (Donation Appreciation Referral Program) was first launched in Chicago. Mailings were sent out to local temples, churches, and mosques asking if members of congregations were interested in jobs at Boston Coach. If they were hired, a donation was sent to the new employee's religious institution. After this win/win idea was tested in Chicago, other branches tried it with successful results.

Another HR initiative at Boston Coach is employee surveys. The company doesn't just survey employees and put the results away in a drawer, never to be seen again. June 1999 marked Boston Coach's first annual employee survey. The results indicated five key institutional issues. These issues were addressed and then re-surveyed in February 2000 (the mid-point of the year). In June 2000, when employees were surveyed again, there was a 90 percent return rate from Boston Coach's mobile workforce. (This return rate is significant. It's unusual to see so many staff concerned enough to fill out and return surveys!)

Communication was the key to the successful return rate. Everyone from senior management, to shift supervisors, to all employees got on board and realized their common goal: to make Boston Coach a better place to work.

Where most workplace surveys fall short is that once the results are tabulated, only a small group sees them (generally senior or middle management). In some cases employees may get a watered-down version of the results complete with quick fixes. At Boston Coach, HR realizes that these things take time. Once the survey results are completed, the challenge is to communicate them back to respondents, along with action items to correct issues identified.

Boston Coach doesn't stop there. It posts its survey results on a board prominently displayed in each branch of the company quarterly so all staff can see the progress being made at the corporate *and* branch levels. This feedback is helpful for employees and managers alike. The message is given loud and clear: "Your opinion counts. We heard you and are doing something positive about it." The survey is not an event, but rather a living, breathing process.

Mary and her department's efforts have paid off. In spring 2000, Mary Aceto was awarded the HR Leadership Award, an award given to top Fidelity Investments' human resources professionals.

Company Spotlight:
Sepracor, Inc.

Sepracor, Inc.'s human resource's mission has focused on retention efforts. Here's what senior director of human resources, Regina DeTore, had to say about the comprehensive approach:

> "Our overall HR mission has focused on retention efforts: building relationships with employees and managers, without setting unrealistic expectations; providing tools and resources to focus on their professional development and worklife needs, and ensuring value-added benefits and services.

"Over the last few years, our HR team has developed an HR strategy that incorporates the goals stated previously and has developed a quarterly schedule of HR initiatives, such as training sessions and employee programs/workshops to keep connected with the workforce and to enhance productivity.

"Putting a strategic plan in place that is flexible enough to accommodate business needs, yet keeps us focused on the people mission has been a very effective retention practice. This plan provides a baseline for us to continuously evaluate, address, and improve our HR services to our workforce."

Chapter 10

Hiring Indispensable Employees: Tactics, Tips, and Forms

The recruitment process works best when it involves good communication, effective selection, and educating the hiring manager about the process.

The hiring manager needs to "partner" with the human resources professional to help prevent the costly mistake of selecting a poor choice for an open position.

Interview and hiring plan

An interview and hiring plan will force you to think through *exactly* what you are looking for in a potential hire. Refer to the position's job description for important and related information to help you with this process. Here are the questions you need to ask yourself before you begin interviewing candidates:

1. How does this position fit into my overall organizational structure?
2. Have I structured the position appropriately?
3. Should any changes be made to the job description?
4. Why did the last incumbent leave the job? What can we learn from this departure? Is

there a problem with how the job is structured or to whom or where in the organization it reports?

5. Has the job changed since the last time it was open?
6. What career advancement opportunities are available for the individual taking this job?
7. What are the working hours for this job?
8. Will I consider job-sharing, telecommuting, or consultants/contingency workers?
9. How will I recruit for the position?
10. Who will be responsible for screening incoming resumes?
11. Who will be responsible for coordinating the interview logistics?
12. Who will be the point person for candidates?
13. Is telephone interviewing a reasonable first step? Who will conduct these interviews and what questions will be asked?
14. Who will participate on the interviewing team? What roles and questions will we assign to each person?
15. When and where do we want to conduct group interviews with candidates?
16. Who must participate in the actual decision-making process? Who should be involved at the finalist stage?

Recruitment Order Form

A Recruitment Order Form can help you to communicate effectively with the hiring manager. It clarifies the steps involved in the recruitment process and allows the recruiter *and* the hiring manager to determine who will be responsible for each step. The more the hiring manager understands the process, the easier and smoother it will be to fill the position.

This form also aides the recruiter in getting a comprehensive picture of the open position and the hiring manager's likes and dislikes. Once the recruiter and hiring manager have established a good rapport and know each other's styles, many of the questions may not be necessary to ask.

The data on this form clearly show the hiring manager the specific efforts as well as the timelines involved in filling the position. The data are also useful in tracking quality indicators such as length of time to fill positions, number of resumes screened, number of applicants interviewed, and sourcing strategies.

Elements of the Fields Associates, Inc. Recruitment Order Form

- Open position title.
- Hiring Manager.
- Date.
- Reason for vacancy (new position, external position, replacement position, etc.).
- Up-to-date job description.
- Day-to-day responsibilities.
- Selling points of the job.
- Career potential.
- Your management style.
- Department structure/total number of staff and other types of positions in department. (You may want to insert an organizational chart.)
- Office environment.
- Places to find good candidates for this position (organizations, companies, schools, Web sites, print publications, networking opportunities, etc.). Be as specific as possible here with names, contact names, addresses, telephone numbers, and e-mail addresses.
- Travel requirements.
- Relocation allowance (if applicable).
- Qualities of your most recent hire that peaked your interest.
- Flexibility options. (Would you consider a job share arrangement, part-time option, schedule options, telecommuting, or other arrangements?)
- Resume screening process. (Do you plan to have resumes screened, or see them all yourself?)
- Participants in the interview process.
- Salary negotiations. (Will HR, the hiring manager, or both negotiate salary?)
- Reference checking. (How many will there be and who will conduct them?)

Creating a positive interview environment

Creating a positive interview environment is crucial. Establishing rapport early in the interview will lead to a constructive flow and exchange of information from and to the applicant. Issues that must be considered in setting this environment include:

- Physical space/seating arrangements. Select a private space conducive to uninterrupted conversation. Have your telephone calls held and turn off beepers and cell phones.
- Greeting/initial ice breakers. Introduce yourself. Use the candidate's name repeatedly through the conversation. Start with a nonthreatening topic to make the candidate feel at ease and to get him or her talking openly.
- Good listening skills. Listen carefully. Don't dominate the interview; let the candidate talk.
- Body language. Watch your body language.
- Use of silence. When an applicant doesn't answer appropriately or sufficiently, allow some time to pass. Usually the silence will encourage him or her to say more.
- Tone of voice and ability to display interest in candidate. Don't seem condescending or uninterested.
- Using language the candidate will understand. Avoid acronyms, technical lingo, and language understood only in your organization.
- Some special requirements for interviewing individuals with a disability or who require a translator. Don't approach them with pity. Treat them with respect and look at them directly, even if they are accompanied by an assistant or an interpreter.

Crafting interview questions

Remember to be uniform in how you interview all applicants. Use your interview and hiring plan as well as structured interview questions. Ask all candidates the same questions.

Questions to determine the customer service needs of the job

When thinking about the customer service needs of a particular job, and the characteristics that a successful applicant needs to possess, consider the following:

(Note: These are the questions to ask yourself in preparation for interviewing candidates.)

1. What four customer service values are most important to my department?

2. Who are the customers that this position serves? What are their needs?

3. What are the two most common things that make the customers who are served by this position feel that they have received superior service?

4. What are the two most common things that make the customers who are served by this position angry?

5. What are the two things that generally make customers irate with people in this job?

6. What are three routine customer interactions that the individual in this position must perform? What questions should I ask to probe for how employees in this job will handle those interactions?

7. What are my expectations regarding how employees in this position should provide empathy to the customers when they are faced with a difficult situation?

8. How do I expect my employees to function as a team? What characteristics should this new employee possess to fit in with our group?

Questions to determine if a candidate is customer-focused

(These are questions you should ask yourself after an interview with a candidate.)

1. Does the candidate possess the customer service values that are important for the job?

2. Will the candidate work effectively with the customers that this position must serve? Why or why not?

3. Does the candidate have the ability to handle angry customers effectively?

4. Can the candidate provide the appropriate amount of empathy to customers who place them in difficult situations?

5. Does the candidate appear to know how to interrupt or locate me when warranted?

6. Does the candidate know how and when to forward urgent calls or requests?

7. Will the candidate know when to promptly refer complex or difficult questions that are not in the scope of his or her authority?

8. Can the candidate provide clear, accurate information on the department's services and programs?

9. Will the candidate provide timely follow-up on tasks assigned or information that must be given to customers?

10. Can the candidate work effectively with co-workers? Will the candidate fit in with our current team?

11. Can the candidate provide constructive suggestions, ideas, and feedback in a positive manner?

12. Can the candidate work collaboratively with others to effectively resolve issues that impact customer service?

Analyzing resumes

When analyzing resumes, be sure to take particular note of the following:

- **Job progression.** Examine closely how the candidate has progressed in his or her career. Is the progression logical? If not, can it be explained?

- **Typographical errors.** Grammatical errors may signal problems with attention to detail.

- **Too much emphasis on education, extracurricular activities, volunteer activities, hobbies, or professional association memberships.** This could mean that person is inexperienced or places too much emphasis on activities.

- **Functional resumes that do not indicate dates of employment.** Is the candidate trying to mask something regarding dates of employment or skill level?

- **Gaps in employment.** Understand why these gaps exist. How does the applicant explain what happened during those times? Keep an open mind; there may be legitimate reasons for a hiatus.

- **Job hopping (short periods of time in a job/many jobs in a short period).** Find out why candidate changed jobs so frequently. Does applicant easily get bored in a job or is there a legitimate reason?

- **Language qualifiers.** Carefully review the language presented in a resume. Probe when you see language such as "knowledge of," "in conjunction with," "assisted in," "worked with," "had exposure to," or "coordinated/helped to coordinate." What message is the applicant conveying? Did he or she actually do the work, or just help?

- **Order of information.** Often, the least important or impressive information is placed at the end.

- **Education.** Remember what the minimum educational or experience requirements are for the job, and don't be over-impressed by a person whose educational background exceeds job requirements. For example, does an administrative assistant really need a Ph.D.? Also, watch for signs of weak educational attainment, especially if the person lists a lot of seminars and conferences, but no degrees attained.

Analyzing interview data

- Be uniform in your assessment. Base decisions on the candidate's ability to perform the essential functions of the job with reasonable accommodation (if appropriate).
- Document your decisions. Keep a separate record as to why a candidate was rejected or accepted. Do not make notes on the resume/application.
- Closely examine the candidate's motivation for taking the job. Don't force a job fit even if you're desperate to fill the job.
- Be wary of individuals who "bad mouth" an organization or previous boss. They might do the same to you someday.
- Limit the number of people who will make the final hiring decisions. If it is a team decision, determine up front which team members will participate in the final hiring decision.

Even if you are grossly understaffed, think again about candidates who:

- Arrive late for an interview.
- Want to know immediately about salary and benefits.
- Spend an inordinate amount of time asking questions about when and how they might be promoted and/or time-off issues (such as vacation and holiday schedules).
- Haven't done much research about the organization.
- "Bad mouth" previous or current employers.
- Are willing to quit a job without providing adequate notice. As a rule of thumb, this is typically two weeks for hourly paid (nonexempt positions) and four weeks for professional and managerial positions
- Accept a salary offer, but try to raise the amount by saying that their employer is willing to make a counteroffer.
- Are wary about having you call references.

- Are willing to take a substantial cut in salary or job responsibilities. The exception is a case where the candidate is making a career change.
- Divulge confidential information.
- Have a hard time explaining their strengths and weaknesses/areas for improvement.

Valid reasons for rejecting applicants

Employers are not obliged to hire individuals who are not qualified to perform the essential functions of the job with reasonable accommodation (if appropriate). The law, however, *does* require that employment decisions be based on valid and job-related criteria that are applied consistently to all candidates for a position. Some valid reasons not to select job applicants are that the candidate:

- Does not meet the minimum qualifications (requirements) of the job as posted.
- Cannot perform the essential functions of the job with reasonable accommodation (if appropriate).
- Has less related, or more unrelated, experience than the individual selected.
- Has a lower skill level than the person chosen.
- Has less related education/training than the individual chosen.

Reference checks

Reference checks, preferably done orally (as opposed to a person only producing a written statement), from at least two former supervisors are very important to obtain. One deterrent to obtaining references is the unfortunate trend of companies having a policy of not giving out information about current or former employees except perhaps dates of employment. Because this information is inadequate, one technique that some organizations employ is to ask candidates to submit their most recent performance evaluation.

Create a form for checking applicants' references. This way, you'll be sure to get all the information you want/need. Each form should indicate the applicant's name; the reference's name, title, and phone number; the name of the person checking the reference; the date the reference check was conducted; and the length of the conversation. Also include the answers to the following questions on each form:

Verification

1. How long have you known the candidate and in what capacity?
2. Would you please verify that the applicant has worked for your company from _____ to _____ as a _____ at a base salary of _____?
3. Would you please describe what his or her job responsibilities are/were?
4. What would you say were this person's most important accomplishments while he or she worked for you?
   - Follow-up question: The applicant said that one of his or her most important accomplishments was _____. Does this sound right?

Performance

1. Could you please comment on the applicant's attendance and punctuality and how it compares with your other employees?
2. How does he or she respond to work pressures and deadlines?
   - Follow-up question: The applicant said she handles pressure in this way. Does this sound right to you?
3. Are there any types of people with whom he or she has problems?
   - Follow-up question: The applicant said he had trouble with this person. Does this sound right?
4. Could you please tell me what you consider to be his or her strengths and weaknesses (or areas to improve)?
   - Follow-up question: The applicant said a weakness was _____. Does this sound right?
5. Did you do the applicant's last performance evaluation? If so, please comment on what areas you praised him/her for and what areas you indicated as needing improvement.
6. (This question is applicable if the applicant was a supervisor.) How many people does/did he or she supervise and how effective is/was he or she in working with staff?
   - Follow-up question: The applicant said his or her greatest strength as a supervisor was _____. Does that sound right?

7. This question is a little awkward, but I'm obliged to ask it: Was this candidate ever involved in any kind of misconduct, found in violation of work rules, subject to any disciplinary actions, or terminated?

Development

1. What kind of professional growth have you seen in this person from when he or she first started working with you?
2. In your opinion, what is his or her growth potential?
3. What piece of advice would you give this candidate that would help him/her to be a top performer?
4. Why did he or she leave?
5. What did you do to try and keep applicant?

Skills assessment

Would you please rate this candidate on a scale from 1 to 10 (with 10 being the highest) on the following skills:

1. Communication skills.
2. Customer skills.
3. Team-building skills.
4. Problem-solving skills.
5. Interpersonal skills.
6. Ability to take constructive feedback.
7. Ability to give constructive feedback.
8. Flexibility/dealing with change.
9. Ability to deal with multiple priorities.
10. Supervisory skills (if applicable).
11. Other skills according to the position (i.e. equipment, computer).

How would you rate this applicant overall as a candidate for this position? Do you have any additional comments that might be helpful to us regarding this candidate's work performance and ability to perform our job?

Capturing time-to-fill data

You should track the time it takes to fill each position so that you can see any patterns that develop. Create a form to track this information that includes:

- The position.
- The recruiter.
- The hiring manager.
- The department.
- The date the staff member gave notice.
- The date the requisition was signed.
- The date the position was posted.
- The date the offer was made.
- The date the new staff member will start work.
- The total number of days it took to fill the job.
- The approximate number of resumes that were screened.
- How the staff member was found (agency or search firm, school or colleges, newspaper ad, referral, career or job fair, Internet site, internal transfer [from which department], etc.).

Be sure you leave room for any additional comments.

Evaluating recruitment effectiveness

After you've hired someone, find out how the hiring process went from *his* perspective. Create a form whereby you present statements and the employee decides whether he "strongly agrees" or "strongly disagrees" with each on a scale from 1 (strongly agree) to 5 (strongly disagree). Be sure to let the employee know how pleased you are that he's joined your organization and thank him for taking the time to complete the form. Here are some statements whose responses will help you improve the quality of your hiring process.

1. I was contacted soon after I submitted my resume/application.
2. I was treated with respect and care by HR staff members.
3. The interview process went by smoothly and relatively quickly.
4. I was kept informed of my status throughout the interview and selection process.
5. I easily got answers to my questions about the new position (benefits, salary, work location, job duties, etc.)

Also ask what impressed him the most during the interview process and give him the opportunity to suggest improvements.

"Having been an HR generalist for more than 20 years, I've found there are no secrets to successful recruitment. It's common sense. If companies take a commonsense approach to recruitment and treat applicants with the utmost respect and dignity, they have an immediate competitive advantage. Here's where the golden rule applies. I treat applicants the way I want to be treated. What do I want from companies interviewing me? I want to feel warm and welcome when I enter their doors. Those that acknowledge my value and show their sincere appreciation for my taking the time to talk with them are big winners.

"If pay is relatively competitive (it doesn't have to be highest), I'd go with the company that takes the time to say it cares about who it hires. It's more than okay to have a structured interview process that includes seeing several people. A structured interview process geared to finding out whether the candidate is a good fit is the only way to truly enhance a company's chances of finding the right people. Devote the afternoon or the day, but don't make me come back multiple times. Let me meet the president or have coffee with the COO to demonstrate how important you feel about hiring the right person. Tell me what you value.

"Ask behavior-based, probing questions to find out how I've handled situations in the past. These certainly include asking open ended questions such as "How would you handle...?"; "Tell me about a time..."; and "Please share some examples...." Make sure I know what to expect up front, and coordinate the interviews so different people don't ask me the same questions. Treat me like your best customer. And go the extra mile if you really want somebody. We not only have to hire people; we hire the whole person. So take the time if needed to invite them to dinner and include spouses or even children.

"Ask their family what they want from their husband or wife's new company. Include other employees in the process to be ambassadors for the company. After the offer is made and I accept, make sure the good experience continues. Make my first month the best I've ever had. Let me never look back at having made the decision to come to work for my very special company. Set high expectations. Let me learn and grow.

"Give me a manager who truly has the ability to stretch my potential, who recognizes my contributions, and who isn't afraid to deliver bad news or give me constructive feedback. Enhance the experience with great communications and good work-life balance and I'm hooked."

—*Diane Hammer, HR Generalist ,*

Fidelity Investments

 Company Spotlight:

Butler Home Products, Inc. (formerly Easy Day Manufacturing)

Geri Weinstein, director of human resources for Butler Home Products, Inc., has developed an HR strategic plan for her company. This savvy HR pro also knows that a variety of creative recruitment resources must be mixed together to recruit indispensable employees. Here are some of the variety of approaches this manufacturing company utilizes:

- Referral bonuses.
- Sign-on bonuses.
- Advertising on *Monster.com.*
- Framingham Cablevision (no cost to place ad).
- Outplacement firms.
- Contacts companies that are downsizing.
- Job fairs (in-house and local fairs).
- Advertising in regional newspapers.
- Internship programs with local high schools and colleges.

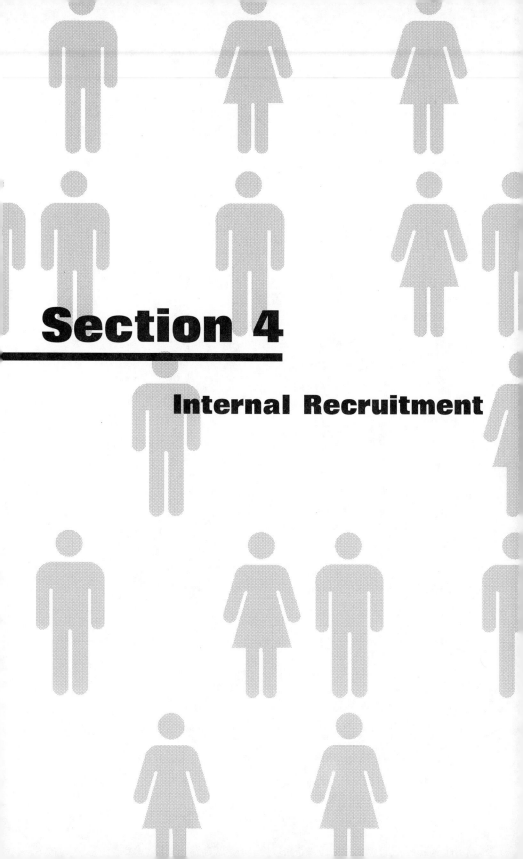

Section 4

Internal Recruitment

Chapter 11

Your Managers and Employees as Goodwill Ambassadors

As we learned in Chapter 3, internal recruitment efforts assist the organization to recruit staff from within as well as utilize employees as a source to recruit outside talent. Central to this notion is turning employees into goodwill ambassadors to get the word out about the employer as an employer of substance and choice. With only 1-percent workforce growth in coming years, the employees you currently have are basically what you'll have to work with in the future.

Internal recruitment efforts also involve cultivating the talents, skills, and competencies of staff already on board so that they can become a possible recruitment source to fill vacant positions. "Growing your own employees" through mentorships, educational opportunities, succession planning, and redeployment of workers will increasingly become a major recruitment source.

As we discussed in Chapters 1 and 2, the labor shortage should last for many more years. The Bureau of Labor Statistics (BLS) projects low unemployment through 2006. Why do you think there will only be 1-percent workforce growth per year? This is due in large part to the Baby Boomers who did not have children in large numbers between 1964 and 1990.

Birthrates and the labor shortage

In 1964, birthrates in the United States started to plummet. The Baby Booming, flower children just stopped having babies in the record numbers that their parents had. Millions, not thousands, of fewer children weren't born each year starting in 1964.

Remember how Baby Boomers structured their lives. Baby Boomers did get married (although later in life than their parents), but in large part they didn't start to produce or adopt children until later in life. In the 1980s, birthrates plummeted to an all-time low as the "me" generation discoed, boogied, and went on a generation-long buying spree. Reflect for a moment on the 1980s. Do you recall what happened in certain parts of the country as Baby Boomers came of age and married, but weren't really sure about having kids?

The decade-long spending and condo conversion spree, however, came to an abrupt halt in the late 1980s as the stock market crashed (in October 1987). This jolt also woke up Baby Boomers to a sobering reality: The biological clock hadn't stopped ticking, and if they really wanted to settle down and have kids (as their parents and generations previously had done throughout history) they'd better start working.

By the 1990s, birthrates were prosperous again as the Boomers had children in record numbers. Baby Boomers didn't come close to producing the high numbers of children that their parents had hatched, though.

We are now living with the aftermath of millions of fewer children born between 1964 and 1990. That is why we only have 1-percent workforce growth per year between now and 2006. The kids just weren't born, and population growth has not kept pace with job growth.

So what does all this mean? Generation X has now come of age and met the Baby Boomers and Matures in the workplace. In many cases, because of technology, they are more advanced than their older colleagues in the workplace—people who are their parents' and grandparents' ages. All these dynamics lead us to a point where we're going to have to focus on our internal staff more closely in order to keep indispensable employees within our organizations in the future.

Here are some other reasons why there is a need to focus on our internal employees as a source to fill jobs:

- Seasoned/older workers are the fastest-growing segment in the workforce.

- The definition of "most experienced" has changed so that in some cases young people are more experienced than their older counterparts.

With fewer new workers to select from, the signs strongly point to one message: The workers of today are pretty much what you'll have to work with in the coming years. They can also be the best way for you to recruit talent into the organization. All of this sounds like common sense, but unfortunately many organizations are just starting to key into this reality and are realizing that the answers to solving their labor shortage (and finding and keeping indispensable employees) may be right under their noses.

Career counselors consistently tell job seekers that networking is the best way to find a job. Sixty-four percent of people find jobs by networking and only 4 percent via the Internet. Smart organizations have come to realize that the key to solving their labor shortage is their own employees: A 1997 survey by the Society of Human Resources Management found that employee referrals were seen as the number-one recruitment source.

As we learned in Chapter 5, turnover costs can put a gargantuan strain on an organization's budget. Outdated recruitment and retention practices are costly.

Internal recruitment efforts

Because the number-one way that people find jobs is by networking with people who are employed, why is it that companies don't better utilize their staff to get the word out about job and career opportunities? Why don't many work harder to get employees to be their goodwill ambassadors and tell others about their jobs? Why don't they make this their number-one approach to solve their labor shortage instead of focusing on the traditional approach of searching for people who are actively looking for jobs? (Remember that with low unemployment rates, most people aren't looking for jobs because they're already employed.)

As we've discussed, internal recruitment efforts must focus on two issues:

1. How to make employees goodwill ambassadors and headhunters who can help you market your organization as an employer of substance and choice.
2. Crafting ways to better utilize in-house talent to fill jobs through lateral and promotional opportunities as well as mentor and succession planning programs.

To accomplish this, managers must learn how to be career coaches.

Turn your employees and managers into headhunters

Many organizations are taking steps to turn their employees and managers into headhunters. These companies believe strongly that recruitment is everyone's job—not just the people in the human resources department.

Here are some interesting practices that you may want to consider as you turn your employees and managers into headhunters:

- Look at and zero in on exactly who your ideal candidate is (for example, he or she has five to eight years of experience, holds an Ivy League degree, etc.).
- Have a picture in your mind of what one ideal candidate will work like, but be open to change as you find out what's available in the marketplace.
- Network, network, network.
- Attend professional association meetings.

Cold calls

You need to target your market. To find out who is working in what position, make some cold calls. Ask if your contacts know anyone who might fit into your organization. Get their referrals.

Keep an internal database of your contacts and consider buying other databases that will provide useful contacts.

Wining and dining clients

Give human resource staff and managers who constantly must recruit talent a credit card to entertain internal and external prospects. Establish a dollar amount per month that they *must* spend and report on what activities transpired (taking active and passive job seekers out for meals, a concert, high-profile community event, etc.).

Community outreach

To get the most out of your community outreach efforts, develop your annual calendar of events to include:

- Marketing efforts.
- Community-based initiatives, such as job fairs.

- Fund-raisers.
- College recruitment.
- Internet activities.

Hire today, gone tomorrow

Qualified individuals who walk in the door will eventually walk out. Forget lifetime employment. The new goal is lifetime *affiliation*. Walking out the door doesn't have to mark the end of your relationship. It can mean the beginning of a new stage in that relationship.

Utilize alumni

Florida-based HR consultant Adrienne Mervin tells us to forget such terms as "ex-employees" and "former colleagues." The new term of choice is "alumni." Turn them into advocates, clients, business partners, and so forth. Walking out the door is just one more step along a career path. Keep great people working *with* you, even after they've stopped working *for* you.

Stay connected with good people after they leave. Be sure to get their new phone number, address, and e-mail. Offer to send them your annual report and company newsletter. Explain to them, "You never know when there will be an opportunity for us to use your services, for you to use ours, or for you to come back and join us." Send invitations to attend cocktail receptions or to participate in panel discussions. Produce a biannual newsletter that chronicles developments at the firm as well as the professional achievements and personal milestones of other alumni.

Why pay so much attention to people who used to work for you?

Alumni send a strong message to people who are thinking about working for you and to people who are already there. The message is, "We are going to make you more marketable." People who are still working for you see that you are not kicking ex-employees on the way out the door, and they know that you'll do the same for them. People who once worked at your company and who still work for your company are the most credible spokespeople you have. Even if they never return, they remain part of the fabric of the firm and may be a source of employee and/or customer referrals. Build a network of people who share a common heritage and a loyalty. Create a family-oriented environment so that when people leave, it is like moving away from home.

What to do when a valued employee quits

First, act fast. This means within five minutes. Cancel the next activity on your schedule. Any delay (even saying, "I'll talk to you after the staff meeting") is unacceptable.

Second, listen hard, and then fight hard. Is the employee looking for a better job, more money, or a fundamental career change? You can make a good argument that it's in his or her best interest to stay 90 percent of the time. The employee needs to know that quitting was a mistake and that you will personally work to rectify that mistake.

Third, call in the big guns if necessary. If it requires the company president to get the job done, then the president has nothing more important to do than sit down with the employee.

Boomerangs and green grassers

Boomerangs and green grassers are the most loyal employees. This category includes current employees who have returned to your company after spending some time away. They come back with a rich set of experience from different companies. They have inspected the grass on the other side of the fence, and found it not so green. What is your boomerang rate?

There are only so many good people out there. If you cross off the ones who have already worked for you, you've limited the number even further. Time is freed up when boomerangs are brought back because they already understand the value your company places on sharing information and the emphasis on client service rather than the ego of the designer. They also understand more mundane things, such as paychecks, policies about continuing education, and time slips. Furthermore, boomerangs bring a wealth of new ideas to the table and keep the culture from getting stale. They promote cross-pollination, introducing the organization to new building materials, new contractors, and new processes.

 Company Spotlight:

Fitzgerald, Stevens and Ford

Stephen Ford, president of Fitzgerald, Stevens and Ford, describes a process his company has developed to help employers keep in touch with their alumni employees:

"We have been working with a number of organizations to reduce turnover and increase employee loyalty and commitment. In our discussions on turnover and recruiting, we have identified a recruiting strategy that many organizations aren't using. We call it *Alumni Minding*.

"There are many soft costs in turnover, usually substantially more than most organizations realize. One of the largest soft costs is having a new employee become able to execute successfully within your organization. This requires knowledge of the organization's culture, values, personnel, products or services, customers, etc. It takes time and money, but is critical for someone to be able to deliver maximum results.

"There is one pool of candidates who doesn't have this learning curve: your previous employees. It used to be that once an employee left your organization, he or she often wasn't welcomed back, especially within a couple of years. Now that person may be your best recruit. Organizations should develop a strategy to leave the door open with those leaving and then to keep in touch with them. This is not unlike what colleges and universities do to keep visible and maintain credibility with their alumni. These tactics may include sending past employees the in-house newsletter or e-mail updates on organization successes. As long as they are not working for a competitor, you might invite them to technical or product updates. Previous peers or bosses can place occasional calls to check in. Anything you can do to keep your name, and credibility, with those alumni, can make it easy for them to return.

"Because not many people like conducting a job search, and new jobs often don't work out as well as hoped, it seems easiest for past employees to contact their old boss and talk about returning. It is the path of least resistance, particularly if they believe that they would be welcomed back. One organization has been able to recruit 25 percent of the employees who left within two years. And the per-hire cost is very modest!"

Chapter 12

Growing Your Own Employees: Utilizing Internal Staff to Fill Positions

As we've discussed throughout this book, the job market doesn't always lend itself to a readily available pool of qualified talent. Many organizations are filled with people who really would like to remain with the company but find themselves having to move on in order to move up. Complaints from employees who had to seek greener pastures elsewhere sound similar to this one: "I started in the organization as a clerical staff. Then I went to college and even got my MBA. Still, I couldn't move up but so far in my organization. It's like I was in a time warp in their eyes: They always seemed to see me as that 18-year-old clerical person."

The "growing your own employees" process is one that more organizations are beginning to embark upon. Why lose talented people to a competitor or spend months, if not years, trying to acclimate a new employee to the organization's complex corporate culture, then not benefit from their expertise? Here are some of the type of activities organizations are utilizing to grow their own employees:

Growing your own programs
- Management programs for new managers.
- Internships.
- Job rotation/shadowing.
- Internal career fairs.

179

- "Take your kids to work" program.
- School-to-work career initiatives.
- Parents, kids, and teachers career fairs.

Skill enhancement programs

- ESL (English as a Second Language).
- Management and executive development.
- Diversity and globalization.
- Communication (oral, written, and interpersonal).
- Computer skills.
- Accent reduction programs.
- GED (General Education Development) testing.
- The 3R's (Reading, Writing, Arithmetic).
- Customer service.
- Computer skills.

Consider

Here are some considerations when growing your own employees and filling jobs internally:

- Create a consistent way to publicize internal transfer opportunities. Be clear about qualifications for the job and the process for applying for internal transfers and promotions. Many employee relations issues arise if internal staff feel they were not given an opportunity to apply for a job and that an outside person was brought in over them to fill it.
- Be clear about which jobs get posted. In some organizations, jobs at a certain level are not posted. Let staff know what your policy is regarding job postings. Consider whether certain types of jobs are exempt from posting, and also be sure to explain any criteria around how long a job must be posted before it can be offered to a candidate (for example, all jobs must be posted for three days before an offer can be made).
- Be clear about internal hiring preference practices. Do you have a policy that favors hiring internal candidates over external ones? If you do, make sure you clearly delineate the circumstances that might cause you to select an internal candidate over an external one. For example, some companies have internal preference policies that state something

to the effect that, if all things are equal with regard to qualifications and skill sets, preference for hiring will go to the internal candidate. Such a statement does *not* imply that only internal candidates will be hired for an open job. You may need to do some explaining to internal candidates about the subtleties of your statement.

• Publicize the internal job application process. Be clear about when and with whom internal candidates will interview when a job is open. For example, some companies will have a recruiter (usually a member of the human resources department) interview all internal candidates as part of an initial screening process. After this step, only those candidates who are deemed "qualified" interview with the hiring manager. In other organizations, all internal applicants, regardless of whether or not they are qualified for the job, are guaranteed an interview with human resources *and* the hiring manager.

• Don't lose valuable talent to the competitor because you don't want a colleague or rival department to "get his hands on your employee." It's really frightening, but I can't tell you how many times I've seen top talent leave one organization and go to a competitor just because a manager would rather see the employee go elsewhere than fly from her nest and into the tree of a fellow colleague. Sounds petty? It is, but it truly does happen. Take time in your organization to craft ways to share talent pools. Allow managers to get comfortable with this notion of in-placement.

• Let staff know about career opportunities available to them within your department and the organization. To help with this effort, some organizations are creating career ladders and/or internal career fairs where staff learn what other departments do and about career opportunities within the organization.

• Treat internal candidates with the same royal treatment that you do outside applicants. I once was appalled when I heard a recruiter talk about not having time to contact internal candidates who had applied for jobs. What was even more amazing was that so many employees in the organization were complaining about never being able to be seen in HR for jobs. The recruiter may have had extra time on his schedule by filling the open job with a willing internal recruit. Make sure that your hiring systems and processes include internal candidates in the mix. Treat them the same way you treat candidates from the outside.

A common scenario

Roberto, a 10-year employee, is quite angry. He just found out that Susan, a two-year employee, was just promoted. He tells you that he is tired of orienting and training new employees to their jobs, only to see them leapfrog over him when a promotion comes up. He also tells you he thinks it's because he's Latino.

What steps should the organization and/or individual take to address the issues raised in the case? As a manager, you should do several things:

- Acknowledge the employee's feelings.
- Not jump to conclusions about whether this is or is not a racial issue. Check out the facts first.
- Make sure he understands the application process for internal positions (lateral and promotions). He may be passed over because he is not applying for jobs and is waiting for someone to tell him of the promotional opportunity.
- If he is being passed over due to performance issues, address them. Use this "Feedback Model":
  - **Step 1:** Ask the employee what he believes he does well.
  - **Step 2:** Reinforce what the employee says by adding other areas where he does well.
  - **Step 3:** Ask the employee where he believes he needs improvement.
  - **Step 4:** Add your own observations about areas that could use improvement.

It's up to you to be clear with your employees about why they aren't being selected for internal positions and, more importantly, what they can do to be viable candidates when positions open.

Manager as career counselor

Managers can provide invaluable career counseling and development opportunities by using the performance appraisal process as a time to meet with employees to:

- Review their job descriptions.
- Discuss future career plans, education, and/or skills needed to achieve those objectives, along with any suggestions for mentorships, networking, or job rotation/job shadowing opportunities.
- Develop goals for the upcoming year, including career development goals.

For more on the performance appraisal process, see Chapter 14.

Encourage continuous learning

Offer training and tuition reimbursement and put out the message that learning is a must for success. Many companies offer seminars in:

- Change management.
- How to be an effective mentor/coach.
- Industry-specific core competency skills.
- Team-building skills.
- Conflict resolution.
- Interviewing skills.
- Performance management.
- Communication skills.
- Leadership skills.
- Negotiating and mediation skills.
- Strategic planning and goal-setting.
- Project management.

Reinforce that staff should take advantage of company-sponsored training programs, tuition reimbursement/assistance programs, and attendance at conferences and meetings.

Mentorships and succession planning

Managers can assist employees with their careers through career counseling sessions or by referring them to a company career development program or counselor (if resources are available). In addition, managers can provide career development opportunities through mentorships and succession planning. Succession planning involves formulating a plan that identifies an individual (or individuals) who will succeed a person in a given position.

Coaching

Managers provide coaching to staff regarding negative performance and behavioral issues. (Coaching employees on issues related to their career development as well as positive performance issues also exists.)

Basic components of a coaching session

Because discussions about unacceptable performance can incite resentment, be sure these few criteria are met.

1. The coach should present his concerns regarding the employee's performance in a cordial manner.
2. The coach must make sure that an employee understands the problem and why it is occurring in his or her performance.
3. Both parties (employee and coach) must realize what the actual performance problem is. Differences should be mutually discussed. Outlooks on the specific problem could very well vary.
4. The coach must make an effort to help the employee improve upon shortcomings and encourage them for the future.

Possible reasons for shortcomings in employee performance include:

1. Uncertain goals.
2. Lack of motivation.
3. Lack of proper training or knowledge.
4. Co-workers failed to complete assigned duties.
5. Improper prioritizing.
6. Bad judgment of time.
7. Not enough staff, budget, or support services.

Coaching do's

When coaching indispensable employees, keep these things in mind:

1. Provide timely feedback to employees.
2. Give feedback as often as possible so employees can learn.
3. While giving feedback and coaching, provide specific examples and documentation of issues.
4. Remember that the object of coaching is to redirect negative behavior to improve performance.

5. Focus on one issue at a time in order to avoid confusion or misdirection.

Mentoring

Mentors are people who serve as seasoned counselors or advisors to employees. Having already forged a path in their own careers, they serve as a personal guide to an up-and-coming employee. Mentorships may occur through formal programs or on an informal basis. Today, many organizations are encouraging events or activities at all levels of the organization, because there is always someone who knows more than you. Mentors can be peer to peer, or subordinate to superior. Young people can be mentors to older people and vice-versa. Jack Welch (CEO of General Electric) utilizes young computer whizzes in his organization to boost the computer knowledge of seasoned people in management.

6 focal points

When mentoring indispensable employees, mentors should:
1. Pay attention to the concerns of mentees.
2. Give feedback to the concerns raised by mentees.
3. Encourage mentees to check out options.
4. Get mentees to confront negative behaviors and intentions.
5. Help mentees to focus, change, or broaden perspective.
6. Provide needed information about an organization, job, industry, career life decision, etc.

Succession planning

Succession planning is a defined program that an organization systemizes to ensure leadership continuity for all key positions by developing activities that will build personnel talent from within. By having a succession planning process, organizations identify individuals who could replace key people in the organization.

The reasons for having a succession plan are many. One is that you can identify talented employees and therefore establish a "pool" of employees to refill positions. Thus you are promoting employee development while at the same time redefining corporate planning. Successful companies always have a plan for the future, and succession planning is a strategy to do just that.

Typical succession planning programs first target essential positions at the senior levels of the organization (president, CFO, vice presidents, directors, and managers). However, succession planning activities can take place for virtually every position in an organization.

Good plans set forth the objective for establishing the succession plans, a list of targeted positions from which the plans will be developed (and a list of individuals who will be mentored for such positions), and comprehensive individual succession development plans. These particular plans outline specific development, educational, and skill enhancement activities that the mentored employee will need in order to assume the position when it is vacated (and when this learning process will begin and end).

A succession plan can do several things:

- Establish a plan for existing resources and staff.
- Justify new resources.
- Make it easier to contend with corporate changes.
- Present alternatives in a new environment.
- Provide direction for corporate long-range planning.
- Prepare individuals for achievements.
- Define goals and missions.
- Provide development programs to ensure growth and continuity.
- Help assess corporate functions and results.

Starting a succession plan

Here are the steps to get you started:

1. Develop a mission statement that answers the why, how, and who of the plan.
2. Write a policy design (implications of plan, assumptions, limits to be imposed, areas of plan to be stressed).
3. Incorporate plan procedures (guidelines for plan to be carried out; procedures for actual plan).
4. Define target positions.
5. Define additional succession positions.
6. Develop and prioritize program activities so plan participants succeed.

A different kind of career planning

Although many employers offer career planning activities to help staff chart their career direction, some organizations go one step beyond and

Straight from the expert's lips:

"At Harvard, where salaries and benefits are competitive and the university environment is a plus, we nevertheless see rising termination rates in this booming economy. A recent survey of employees pointed to two key areas of dissatisfaction: management competency and communications. As a result, we will be focusing our efforts on both as we work to retain valuable employees.

"We recently implemented a new initiative directed at our entry-level service employees. The Harvard Bridge to Learning and Literacy provides employees with paid release time for English as a Second Language, basic literacy, GED, and computer literacy classes. We hope these employees will develop the skills they need to move into higher-paying positions either at Harvard or elsewhere.

"Finally, in order to improve our recruitment of minority employees, we have partnered with local professional organizations (the Latino Professional Network, the National Association of a Asian American Professionals, and the National Association of Black Accountants) in order to broaden our pool of talent and to strengthen the perception that Harvard has a welcoming and nurturing environment for talent from all backgrounds. We have definitely begun to see fruit from our efforts in terms of increased applicants and actual hires."

—Polly Price
Associate Vice President for Administration, Harvard University

encourage employees to actively look for jobs elsewhere. Experts tell us that many people will have six careers and 15 jobs in a lifetime. Think about developing management training programs for non-managers. Through such programs staff will acquire the skills needed to manage people so that when positions become available, they might be able to fill them.

Pacific Enterprises has a career development program in which employees are actively encouraged to look for jobs elsewhere. G. Joyce Rowland, vice president of human resources at Pacific Enterprises, said in *Fortune* (August 3, 1998), "We want our employees to be prepared to interview well for jobs in our organization...but we also want them to see what's out there so that they come back more satisfied with where they are now." The company offers workshops in resume-writing and job-interviewing.

Company Spotlight:
Harvard University

Harvard University is more than 360 years old. The faculty and staff number 14,000. There are more than 5,000 exempt-level employees. Harvard contains a decentralized administrative structure. Harvard pursues "employer of choice" along a few fronts. It engages administrators, managers, and employees in collective discussion of diversity. It's no wonder Harvard continuously benchmarks results.

Ways Harvard pursues "employer of choice" status

- Defining what it means for Harvard.
- Conducting "Great Places to Work" employee survey in central administration.
- Defining management competencies that support performance.
- Aligning training/development with the acquisition of core competencies.

Efforts to build awareness of commitment to diversity

One way to build awareness of commitment to diversity is to build an infrastructure both centrally and across faculties. Harvard recruits and retains employees for the long-term by fostering productive relationships. In addition, managers and employees at all levels are kept informed and involved.

Building the infrastructure

One way that Harvard is building its infrastructure is by creating key positions to build the staffing function across the University. HIRES, a Web-based job posting and applicant tracking system, was developed to establish common forums for sharing recruitment and training information. A

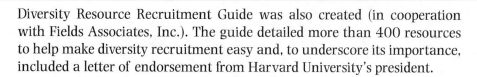

Diversity Resource Recruitment Guide was also created (in cooperation with Fields Associates, Inc.). The guide detailed more than 400 resources to help make diversity recruitment easy and, to underscore its importance, included a letter of endorsement from Harvard University's president.

Recruit for the long-term

Harvard outreaches to community groups, municipal agencies, and does job training programs. It builds relationships with multicultural professional organizations and supports the volunteerism of their employees. An Annual Harvard Career Forum is also held.

Ways Harvard educates and involves managers and employees

- Interactive workforce management conferences.
- Supervisor orientation and training.
- A foundation for leadership management development program.
- Biomedical careers programs.
- Education initiative for entry-level workers.
- Local diversity initiatives and media efforts.

Results to date

The results have been astounding. The number of open positions has decreased 20% over the last year. There has been a 25% increase in people of color hired in the central administration. The turnover rate has decreased 25% within the IT staff in one year.

Continued challenges

Although great strides have been made, there is always room for improvement. One continued challenge is the accountability and consistency in a decentralized environment. Another challenge is retaining the best employees by partnering with local managers and HR staffs.

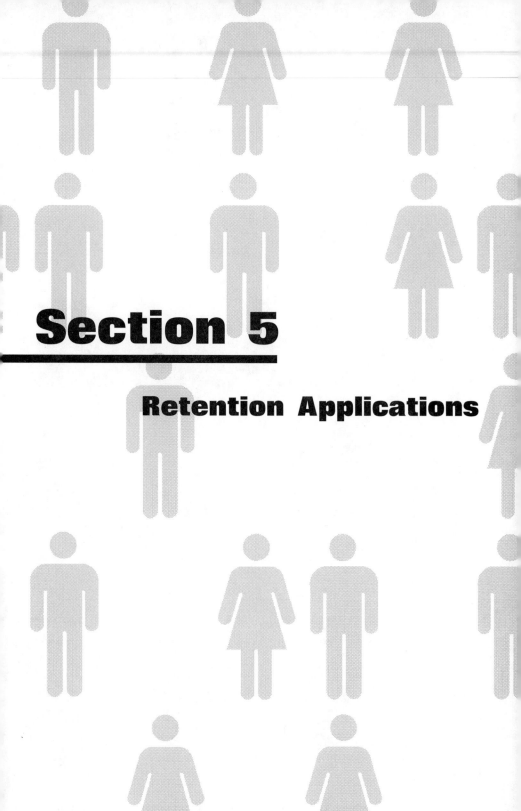

Section 5

Retention Applications

The Best Form of
Recruitment Is Retention

To say that competition for a limited number of competent and talented employees is fierce would be an understatement. Companies everywhere are feeling the pressure from having the financial resources to grow, but not the people. Look around at the number of businesses that have had to curtail their hours of operation because they can't staff properly.

The ability to provide quality customer service is also eroded when organizations don't have enough people—and/or the ones who *are* there to service the customers are overworked due to the staffing shortage and become, well, less hospitable to the customer. Who among us hasn't been to a retail establishment (store, restaurant, movie theater, etc.) and had a frustrating experience because there was no one around to ask a question of or take care of your purchase in a timely manner?

Think about this: What would happen if there was an employer that treated its staff *so* well that they not only wanted to stay there and couldn't be lured away by the competition, but the staff adored their work so much that they became goodwill ambassadors for their company and were constantly telling their friends and relatives about their wonderful employer? Their associates, most of whom were working for lousy companies that didn't seem to value them, were genuinely intrigued by their friends' glowing reports about their positive work environment and ready to jump ship in a hot second when a job for which they were qualified became available at this great company. *Dream on,* you say? Not necessarily. This fantasy could become a reality for companies that start to seriously embrace one of my favorite philosophies: The best form of recruitment is retention!

If you hung out and eavesdropped by the water cooler listening for employees' biggest gripes with the organization, what do you think they would be? You should know the answers. Finding out about and fixing problems is essential to lure-proofing your employees from competitors.

Organizations are taking multiple measures to hold onto their employees. In January 1998, *Inc.* magazine reported that one organization, the RHS Help Desk in New York, cut its turnover from 300 percent to 25 percent by improving its employee orientation program, establishing a career ladder, and communicating at least weekly with its field staff.

As a short-term retention measure, UPS promised its employees a $1,300 bonus if they stayed with the company until the end of the year (that is, until the end of the holiday rush), according to a November, 1999 *NBC Nightly News* broadcast.

Of course, sometimes turnover is positive. The key lies in recognizing when an organization needs turnover—and managing it effectively. (Remember our discussion of good and bad turnover in Chapter 5?)

Understanding the changing employer/employee relationship

Not all managers have realized that it is no longer an employer's (buyer's) market. Given the critical labor shortages that most organizations face now (and those they'll face in the future), managers must work harder to recruit and retain a competent staff. It is important that managers understand what it takes to manage today's workforce more effectively, given the changing employer/employee relationship. Start by bringing them up to speed by raising the following questions with them:

- Is the labor shortage here to stay?
- How has (and will) the workforce changed?
- How can managers recruit and retain a competent and diverse workforce?
- How do you manage staff before, during, and after organizational initiatives that alter the way work is conducted?
- What are some ways to manage across generations?

The relationship between recruitment and retention

Retention initiatives are often thought of as separate from recruitment. They are, however, inextricably tied together. An organization may have the most elaborate and sophisticated recruitment program imaginable, but once individuals are hired, if the environment is inhospitable, given the choices that employees have in this labor market, companies will soon find themselves looking for another replacement. They'll also see the huge impact that turnover has on the bottom line.

We all know that bad news truly does travel fast. Unfortunately, in this labor market, employee war stories about bad treatment by employers abound. But what about the other side? How many stories do you hear from people whose work experience is *nothing* but positive because their employer treats them like royalty? Are you hard-pressed to think about someone you know who fits into that category? I'd bet that you are. There is a lot of room for improvement with regard to retaining employees. Unfortunately, employee tales of terror thrive while those where employees enjoy workplace bliss are few and far between.

Why is there a need to seriously think through strategies for attracting and keeping staff and linking recruitment and retention? Let's review some of the trends we've discussed:

- There is a shortage of competent knowledge workers and a limited talent pool that is projected to continue well into the future.
- High turnover rates exist due to employee dissatisfaction and/or moves to get higher pay or better job opportunities.
- Population growth can't keep pace with job growth.
- Fierce competition exists for top talent across and between industries.
- It's becoming increasingly difficult to fill vacant positions. This erodes a company's ability to expand and offer top-quality customer service as staff are overworked, are undertrained, don't feel valued, and therefore aren't loyal.
- Workers learned from the downsizing of the late 1980s to mid-1990s that cradle-to-grave employment and company loyalty are things of the past. Job hopping is very much en vogue.

On the surface, the news about employee retention appears rather bleak. A number of studies point to the fact that although employees may not be actively looking to leave their organization, the thought has certainly crossed their minds. There are a lot of less-than-happy souls out there—and these people become the prime targets for labor-hungry employers savvy enough to seek out and penetrate the passive candidate market. For its *Recruiting, Retention and other Employment Practices: 2000 Report,* Pricewaterhouse Coopers surveyed investment management employees. The results follow:

Survey says...

Question: "Thinking about your own company and other mutual fund companies you are familiar with, what percentage of employees believe they could do better financially at another company?

a. 37%   b. 53% c. 67% d. 84% e. 100%

Answer: **e**

All of the people surveyed said they could make bigger bucks elsewhere. Amazingly, the same report also indicated that *everyone* believed that if they left, not only would they be difficult to replace, but it would cost more for the company to replace them that the company spent to hire them in the first place. To add insult to injury, the following observations were reported:

- Sixty percent of respondents were actively looking for a new position.
- Seventy-five percent of respondents said they're unaware of their career path in their current company.
- Eighty percent of respondents said they would leave their current job to follow a good mentor.
- Ninety percent of respondents felt proficient in their job, but weren't sure that it's the best showcase for their talents.

What motivates indispensable employees to hang in there?

In a July 20, 2000 presentation to Fidelity Investments, Pricewaterhouse Coopers outlined seven factors people consider when deciding to commit

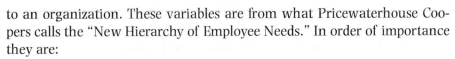

to an organization. These variables are from what Pricewaterhouse Coopers calls the "New Hierarchy of Employee Needs." In order of importance they are:

- **Learning Opportunity.** The opportunities created by the organization to improve intellectual capital.
- **Competitive Compensation.** Reassurance that compensation is competitive with the external marketplace and that there is a direct linkage of performance to incentives.
- **Career Opportunity.** Visibility of career progression within the organization and a recognition that the developmental activities provided promote internal career interests but are also transferable.
- **Quality of Management Mentoring.** The recognition that "someone" has accepted on a proactive basis the responsibility for development of skills and there is an organized approach for doing so.
- **Firm Reputation.** Reputation of the firm within its industry for innovation and progressive human capital practices.
- **Employee Benefits.** The appropriate array by employee life cycle of employee benefits (such as demonstrated sensitivity to diversity, quality of work life, and retirement post-age 45).
- **Environmental Clarity.** Employees understand how they contribute to organizational accomplishment, with clear guidelines around performance expectations, career growth, and organizational support.

Retention research

Studies, books, and research identify certain things regarding what the best companies do to recruit (and, more importantly, retain) IEs. Here are a few of them:

Inspirational, visionary, characteristic leadership

These leaders walk the walk, and their talk turns to action. Their vision is made clear to the masses, and the troops like what they see and want to be a part of the winning team when it reaches the summit. Leaders such as Herb Kelleher of Southwest Airlines, Jack Welch of General Electric, and even Colin Powell come to mind. Not only do these people spread the organization's vision through their thoughts, words, and deeds, but they also have managers underneath them who are visible, accessible, and able to also chant the organization's mantra. Indispensable employees can help them to breathe life into the vision and resurrect it into reality.

Workers in these organizations know the direction that the company is headed. They know how their jobs and contributions to the company are helping to propel the organization—and are also cognizant of how the company can help them to achieve their personal and professional life goals.

A challenging and supportive work environment

This environment should mutate regularly to keep up with the times and:

- Allow individuals to balance work and personal life activities.
- Have a well-defined culture. People understand how their performance is measured and what gets rewarded and punished.
- Foster learning opportunities to improve workers' intellectual capital and sustainable marketability in a world where continuously learning in order to keep a job is a given.
- Have benefits that are in line with where individuals are in their life cycle.

Growth and advancement opportunities

Companies that recruit and retain know that all indispensable employees seek growth and advancement opportunities, whether they are looking to climb the corporate ladder or just stay put on one of its rungs. Internal promotion is absolutely encouraged, as is taking advantage of developmental opportunities (internships, job shadowing, rotating jobs to learn more skills, etc.). People also know and understand how to achieve career progression within the organization and the industry. Mentoring, succession planning and training, development, and career planning programs help people move ahead.

Communication

Smart people know that in the absence of information, people make up their own. Rumor mills run overtime, and the grapevine blossoms. Companies that do a stellar job with communication make sure that employees hear information through straight talk and are provided with a variety of opportunities to respond in a way that is uncensored and unplugged.

Staff opinions are valued and encouraged, and staff are called upon regularly to "tell it like it is" through such vehicles as employee attitude surveys, focus groups, suggestion box programs, town meetings with the

CEO, and (in the unlikely event they leave) exit interviews. Communication flows up, down, and sideways in these organizations. Executives speak with and listen to managers, and supervisors in turn communicate up and down to employees at all levels.

Creative and competitive compensation and rewards

If your salaries are not even in the ballpark of your competition (or the marketplace, for that matter), don't even think about truly trying to compete in the talent war games for indispensable employees. Pay has got to be within the range of your competition or you'll have a hard time even making it to first base. That's the bad news. Fortunately, there is a lot of good news regarding salary and perks in the talent war games.

With all things equal on the salary front (that is, you're paying people at least at the minimum of what the market dictates), a more level playing field is open to those who can produce the goods of the other themes we've discussed in this chapter (benefits, mentoring, etc.). Simply put, study after study has shown us that compensation is *not* the number-one thing that indispensable employees are looking for in an employer with which they can settle down.

IEs are looking for much more of what we've traditionally called the "soft stuff": a company with a reputation for innovation, excellence, and making a memorable difference in the world; stellar practices toward their most important resources (their human capital); and a place guided by visionary, inspirational leadership, where employees know that their work is valued, appreciated, and appropriately rewarded.

People who are satisfied and love what they do—and those around them (including the customers they serve)—have no need to look elsewhere. Why would they ever want to leave Nirvana when they know from their friends and relatives that it doesn't generally exist in other places? Once again, it is underscored that the best form of recruitment is retention.

It pays to be nice

"Employers barely paused when the worker swooned from overwork or fell into a rendering tank. They just got another working body to replace him."

—Upton Sinclair, *The Jungle* (1906)

According to the *Wall Street Journal* (July 22, 1998), Sears Roebuck, one of the nation's top retailers, regularly conducts research on employee productivity and customer satisfaction. The company's conclusion is that happy employees produce satisfied customers.

Sears has found that employees' attitudes about their workload, treatment by bosses, and other such matters have measurable effect on customer satisfaction. Happy employees will not only stick with the company, but they'll provide better service to the customer.

Tools to evaluate retention efforts

Use the following tools to evaluate your retention efforts:

- Exit interviews.
- Turnover statistics.
- Listening to the voice of the customer via:
  - Surveys/questionnaires.
  - Focus groups.
  - Attending staff meetings.
  - Employee open forums.
  - Suggestion boxes.

Retention tips

Here are some other retention tips:

- Increase managers' awareness of why retention efforts are important in a tight labor market, and provide them with tools and training to improve their management styles.
- Offer management and employees skills-development programs.
- Improve HR service delivery to internal and external customers.
- Provide career management programs and information on career paths and promotional opportunities.
- Link employees' jobs to the strategic direction of the company.
- Keep benefits and perks in line with employees' needs.
- Survey employees regularly. Don't guess what they want. Ask.
- Promote social enterprise (responsibility and profitability).
- Develop a business plan and training to address diversity issues. (See Chapters 15 and 16 for more information.)
- Create a strategic HR recruitment and retention plan. Before you can solve a labor shortage problem, you need to

have a strategic plan. You need answers to the following questions:

- What are your company's mission, values, and goals?
- How are the mission, values, and goals linked to your human resources function?
- What do these mission and value statements say about the kind of staff you want to hire?
- What do your goals demand in the way of qualifications and skills of your current and new staff?

Once these questions have been answered, you will have a clear understanding of the mission, values, and goals for the company and how these are linked to human resources and the kind of staff you want to recruit and retain in your company. Analyzing these questions can help you to develop a retention strategy that will typically include training for supervisors.

An interesting retention practice

In the medical field, physicians do a lot of information-sharing about case studies, the latest in research, and tips on how to perform better through a process called grand rounds. They also keep in tune with the pulse of their customers (patients) by regularly conducting rounds where they visit patients directly in their space (their hospital room). They go to the patient's room and get a real feel for how the patient under their care is doing and whether or not any interventions are needed.

More and more companies are adapting this process of conducting grand rounds to improve their management's ability to keep its pulse on the temperature of its organization, what employees are doing, and, most importantly, what employees need to perform better in their jobs.

As reported in the May 29, 2000 issue of *Fortune*, several organizations are utilizing this approach: At Home Depot, part of the job of senior executives and board members is to regularly visit stores; top management at Southwest Airlines must spend one day in the field each quarter.

Concern about the employee entering and exiting processes

The manner in which staff are treated through the interview process, in the first few days of their immersion into the organization, and as they exit the organization are perhaps the most important "moments" in the life of an employee. Employees remember if people welcomed them with warm, helping hands and guided them through each of their job responsibilities and the organizational idiosyncrasies, or if people simply pointed them in a vague direction to figure out, through baptism by fire, what they were supposed to do.

Employees at Tufts Health Plan are ushered into the organization with a greeting from the company's president *and* the company's CEO, who discuss the organization and its values at new-employee orientation programs. I'd bet Tufts Health Plan's employees remember their first day fondly. Likewise, if at the end of their tenure, employees are given the cold shoulder by their boss or are unceremoniously told to leave immediately after years of loyalty because of a layoff or merger, employees remember.

What lessons can employers who are trying to recruit and retain indispensable employees learn from this? A lot. The most important lesson, though, is to work to improve your entrance and exit processes. The way you bring employees in and dismiss them should be done with thought, care, and compassion. Here are some things you may want to consider in order to improve your chances of recruiting and keeping indispensable employees.

An effective orientation process

A successful orientation program not only helps new staff members form a lasting attachment to your organization, but it also helps them become acclimated to your corporate environment, as well as become productive within their positions. Unsuccessful orientation programs can result in low productivity and costly employee turnover.

Monitoring whether or not your orientation process is on track is important to your organization's bottom line. For instance, are new employees satisfied with the process? Does the process include a mentoring program or a buddy system? Do new supervisors, managers, and executives have their own specialized orientation programs?

Your company's ability to ensure that new staff are as productive as possible and that they develop a lasting attachment to your company begins with the orientation. What is your company's orientation process? Is it effective? Are staff really learning what they need to learn?

Orientation tips

- Orientation programs should include an introduction to the organization, the industry, and the individual's department or job.

> ## Straight from the expert's lips:
>
> "State Street is focusing on the retention of all employees, with particular emphasis on new hires into our training programs. We are taking a three-pronged approach here: revising the design and content of the programs to ensure alignment with the demands of the jobs and the learning needs of the participants; developing skills trainers and first-line managers to enhance their ability to work with a multicultural group of new hires; and providing a range of support mechanisms to new hires both in the classroom and on the floor to increase the likelihood that they succeed in the class and in the work unit.
>
> "In terms of recruiting, State Street is working closely with its employee affinity groups to develop recruitment strategies and community outreach programs designed to effectively reach members of diverse communities."
>
> —*Susan G. Aaronson,*
> *Vice President of Diversity, State Street*

- Conduct an evaluation with employees and their managers three to six months after the orientation program to determine its effectiveness.
- Identify skills particular to a job and communicate them to new staff.
- Consider the orientation needs of certain groups (people of color, women in senior level and managerial positions, individuals with disabilities, and so on).
- Develop orientation programs specific to new supervisors, managers, and executives.

Managing transitions

To develop a culture after a merger, acquisition, or major organizational change, consider refining your transition process. Despite all the best efforts of a company, some staff will leave. It is essential to understand why they are leaving and where they are going. Management needs to know why staff are leaving, so exit interviews are important in helping to craft a solution to the labor shortage problem.

Company Spotlight:
The Gillette Company

Deborah Perry, manager of diversity resources at The Gillette Company, had this to say about some of Gillette's retention efforts:

"People come to an organization first for the opportunity, but [they] will always factor in their personal and professional development. They need to have a good sense of the company's internal culture in order to determine whether they could *belong*.

"People need to be valued and included in any environment. It's all about ongoing communication and education of employees. At The Gillette Company we continue to implement programs and resources to help build a culture that's inclusive and supportive of all people."

Company Spotlight:
Giga Information Group

According to Sandra Casey Buford, vice president of human resources, Giga strives to create a work environment in which all employees are valued and can realize success in their careers. Because of its effort in this regard, Giga continues to excel in its ability to attract and retain top talent in the industry. Giga differentiates itself as an employer in the IT Research industry with three distinct, cutting-edge retention strategies:

- Continually benchmarking against best-in-class companies and seeking to go beyond the standard and traditional.
- Fostering and rewarding a spirit of innovation and out-of-the-box thinking.
- Involving employees in defining their work environment.

"We work continuously to improve our work environment, giving as much attention to the less obvious, non-job related aspects of an employee's life as we do to the larger items. We also work hard to build a sense of community in the company by acknowledging the various life events that occur in our employee's lives. We realize that when it comes to retention, more is involved than compensation. It is a total package, a far-reaching philosophy that ensures that each employee's work contribution is valued, that each employee is recognized and valued as an individual. The following are some features of our retention strategy:

Benefits

"In addition to providing a top-notch benefit package that includes health, dental, disability, life, 401K, EAP, etc., Giga offers benefits that help employees achieve a healthy balance between work and personal life, including paid parental leave (for mothers and fathers) and domestic partnership coverage.

Culture

"Although our employees are scattered across the country and the globe, we foster an atmosphere of community through personal connections to acknowledge and accommodate employees as individuals.

"Elements of the Giga Community Connections Program include:

- Life event recognition (whereby the CEO and executives recognize personal life events such as births, deaths, sickness, and other milestones).
- "Knowledge Saloons" (fun after-work events designed and run by employees).
- Annual social events such as baseball games, holiday parties, etc.
- New-hire orientation programs.
- Welcome baskets during the first week of employment.
- Personal welcome e-mails from the CEO and other executives.
- An infrastructure that supports a quick-start for all new employees.
- Flexible work arrangements (including telecommuting and home offices).
- Periodic surveys and incentives for timely feedback.

Continuous learning

"As a company, we have to remain firmly on the leading edge of technology. But we also encourage our employees to continue their learning beyond their immediate field of expertise. This includes:

- A language readiness program that includes on-site offerings, as well as opportunities for coursework through accredited programs.

- Cultural awareness seminars and workshops.
- A broad range of continuous learning opportunities, both on- and off-site.
- Support for online degree programs.

Rewards and recognition

"The reward system at Giga is performance-based. Our employees are assured that financial rewards follow personal and team achievement. Examples of rewards include:

- Personal and corporate bonus programs.
- An employee referral program, designed with direct input from employees and featuring cash payouts.
- Stock options and a stock purchase program.
- Awards for top salespeople.
- Promotion from within. (More than 80 employees were promoted to positions with increased responsibility and pay last year.)
- Divisional awards and recognition programs.
- All-company awards programs."

Chapter 14

Improving Management and Executive Development as a Way to Enhance Retention Efforts

A s you now know, the best form of recruitment is retention. Recruitment efforts are made easy when the people in your organization tell their friends, families, and significant others about your organization. How, then, do you beef up your employee referral efforts? Create an environment that beckons your IEs to realize they've got a terrific deal and to want to stay put.

Although this approach makes common sense, many organizations have been slow to put as many resources into retention efforts as they have recruitment efforts. I talk to many consultants and experts who lament that organizations appear to wrestle with providing adequate resources to train and develop executives and managers to improve their ability to retain indispensable employees. Conversely, these same organizations don't seem to blink at allocating tremendous amounts to recruitment efforts. In fact, they'll gladly spend 30 percent or more of annual compensation to pay a search firm to recruit a new employee. Think about it. Thirty percent of a $50,000 managerial job is $15,000. For an executive job that may start at about $100,000, 30 percent is $30,000.

Although high search fees may be completely in store for certain positions to better recruit and retain IEs, organizations

Straight from the expert's lips:

"For a retention strategy to be effective, it must be delivered by supervisors and managers. They can be trained by good organization development staff in methods of coaching, praising, counseling, rewarding. But most importantly, employees must be treated with respect and have their contributions valued by their bosses."

—*Laura Avakian, Vice President for Human Resources, Massachusetts Institute of Technology (M.I.T.)*

need to shift the heavy focus on recruitment efforts to retention strategies that produce managers and executives who know that:

1. It is no longer a buyer's market when it comes to finding and keeping IEs, and
2. The old approach to management ("my way or the highway") is dead.

The name of the game in this job market is nurturing and working with your indispensable employees so that they *want* to stay and be a part of your company.

Improving your managers' and executives' skills through a variety of executive development activities is one major way to enhance retention efforts. Even seasoned managers will admit that they've never really witnessed such monumental management challenges as they have in today's workplace.

Let's begin by looking at performance management as a retention tool. Do you know anyone who has experienced the following scenario? (Perhaps it's happened to you in your own career.)

You nervously sit in your boss's office waiting for her to come in for your annual performance appraisal. By all accounts, you feel you've done a terrific job this past year, and your boss has never told you anything to the contrary. The two of you exchange pleasantries about the weather and how your family is doing. You're only half-listening, because all you want to do is hear the wonderful accolades she has to give you about your performance. More importantly you want to hear how big of a salary increase you can expect in your next check. Truth be known, you've already thought about how the extra cash will be spent.

Then the moment you've been obsessing over comes. Your boss starts talking about a few wonderful things you've accomplished, and then lets out a long "but...." This is followed by a litany of things that she feels you need to do to "improve your performance." What she says is a total surprise: She's not happy with the quality of your work, which translates into no merit increase, and she's putting you on a performance improvement plan. If things get better in three months, she'll reevaluate your performance. You leave your boss's office in a state of complete devastation.

What's wrong with this picture? Plenty. Any manager who wants to cultivate indispensable employees should realize the importance of providing *ongoing* feedback to staff. Here are some ways to manage the performance appraisal process so you can better keep indispensable employees.

Performance management

Supervising employees' performance is an essential part of management. Performance management supports an organization's business objectives by linking individual as well as team performance to them. To be effective, it must be an ongoing process. People should be told about the good, bad, and ugly aspects of their performance throughout the year— not just in their annual performance appraisal.

Employees should be aware of what is expected from them, how effectively or ineffectively they are performing against those expectations, and how they can maintain the standard or improve upon their performance.

Think of performance management as cyclical. It's a step-by-step process, one with different components occurring sometimes simultaneously. The four major components to performance management are:

- Establishing goals and objectives.
- Preparing the performance appraisal.
- Providing ongoing feedback.
- Conducting the performance appraisal meeting.

Establishing goals and objectives

Establish performance goals yearly with your indispensable employees. Review work regularly and modify them to meet changing workplace and personal needs. When developing goals, assess:

- What kind of goals are they?
- What is their order of priority?
- What standards of performance are needed?
- What are potential obstacles?
- What are the rewards for reaching the goal?

Approaches for goal-setting

You can utilize one of two ways to set individual goals with your indispensable employees:

- Manager *to* employee: Manager determines goals to be met and then gives them to employee for comments, alterations, negotiation, and finally, acceptance.

  or

- Manager *and* employee: Both manager and employee develop goals separately. A meeting is held to discuss results, negotiate, and come to agreement.

Either approach is acceptable and effective, as long as you're consistent among employees within a particular job category.

Preparing the performance management appraisal

Here are the basic steps in preparing the review:

1. Begin the process early.
2. Inform the employee of the process.
3. Gather the information.
4. Schedule the meeting.
5. Review the information/write the review.

Begin the process early.

Begin the performance management review process at least one month before it is due to human resources. Approach the process with a positive attitude.

Inform the employee of the process.

Inform the employee of the performance management review process. Give the indispensable employee a self-evaluation form two to three weeks before you need it back from him. Tell the employee the date it should be returned.

Gather information.

Establish and maintain a folder (hard copy and/or online) for each employee that includes compliments, comments, concerns, and complaints from customers, other managers, peers, and you.

Have each employee submit a monthly report of accomplishments, obstacles to doing work, and upcoming activities. (You can simplify this process by developing a monthly report form.) The monthly reports will be invaluable as you prepare to write the reviews of each employee.

Schedule the meeting.

Schedule a mutually agreeable time with the employee to discuss the performance appraisal in a private, confidential location. If a face-to-face meeting isn't possible, send the appraisal in advance and have a confidential phone meeting. E-mailing a performance appraisal with no face-to-face or voice communication is not appropriate, especially if the employee has major areas that need improvement.

Review the information/write the review.

Just before writing the evaluation, review your information as well as that submitted by the employee. After you write the performance appraisal, review it for potentially controversial issues. Also obtain any appropriate signatures.

Above all, do the performance appraisal on time. Think of the message you are sending to your indispensable employee if you are late with your review: Other things are more important than you. Think about how you would feel if your boss gave you a late review.

Providing ongoing feedback

All too often employees and managers alike fear that one day of the year when the employee receives his or her annual performance appraisal from the boss. These performance review meetings should be painless. Effective managers constantly give performance breakdown to their indispensable employees—and all employees for that matter. Because the positive feedback and information regarding areas of improvement is ongoing, there should be no surprises in that annual performance review. Here are some tips to make for "hassle-free" performance appraisal meetings:

- Meet with employees in person at a private place to discuss performance. Conducting a performance appraisal via e-mail is not appropriate. Let the employee know about his or her performance regularly so there are no surprises on the formal evaluation.

Straight from the expert's lips:

"It is important to regularly acknowledge good performance. Recognition takes other forms beyond increased compensation. We all like to know that our efforts (and results) are appreciated. Sometimes it is just a matter of saying, 'I appreciate and value what you are doing!'"

— Henry Ryan, Corporate Director, Employment and Training, Partners HealthCare Systems, Inc.

- Establish goals and objectives for the next year at the time of the formal evaluation. Make links between attainment of goals and impact on the bottom line and the organization's strategic direction.
- Conduct ongoing evaluations and provide feedback on performance and career goals. Consider working with the employee to develop an individual development plan.
- Make sure written performance evaluation presents a "balanced" view of the performance. Don't sugarcoat evaluations. For example, if problems with performance arose during the year but have since improved, indicate that on the written performance appraisal document.
- Use performance appraisal meetings to review career development plans and the job description. Point out where additional skills and training are needed and how they might be obtained (such as a return to school, on-the-job training, or developmental opportunities).
- Make sure evaluations are objective and performance-based, not subjective and personality-based.

Conducting the performance appraisal meeting

The meeting has four main parts: a beginning, a review of the written performance evaluation, a discussion of the future, and an end. Here's what you should be doing at each stage:

Starting the meeting

- Meet in a private place and avoid any distractions (telephone calls, cell phones, beepers).
- Put the employee and yourself at ease. Remember how you feel when you have your meeting with your boss.
- Repeat the purpose and objectives of the meeting.
- Make sure that employee understands the process.
- Indicate that this will be a two-way conversation.
- Avoid surprises.
- Be sure to address any concerns the employee has.

Evaluating the employee's performance

- Review goals and objectives from the last evaluation and assess whether or not they were met.
- Review the employee's own evaluation of his or her performance and then give your evaluation.
- Look at accomplishments and then review areas for improvement.
- If discipline is involved, review that process.
- Discuss whether changes are needed in the employee's job description.
- Resolve disagreements.
- Develop individual development plan, career goals, and competencies (skills) needed now and in the future. (See the "Manager as career counselor" section that follows.)
- Ask for reactions (positive and/or negative) to your evaluation.
- Give the employee the opportunity to raise any other questions he or she has.

Giving effective feedback

- Start with the positive aspects of the employee's performance.
- Be specific. Discuss particular tasks, behavior, and issues.
- Address one issue at a time (such as punctuality, accuracy, or productivity) before addressing another.
- Describe the impact (positive and negative) felt by others, the organization, the team, and the employee himself by his behavior.
- When feedback is negative, be sensitive and supportive. Offer alternatives to improve performance.

Dealing with unsatisfactory performance

- Create a nonthreatening environment where shortcomings can be discussed.
- Be aware that the employee may not realize that he or she is not meeting expectations.
- Take disciplinary action soon after the event in accordance with company policy. Don't wait for the appraisal meeting.
- Figure out the reason for problems. Are they a function of management practices or of individual motivation?

The realities of an unsatisfactory performance

Mediocre or below-standard performance impacts upon morale negatively. Here are some suggestions for improving this situation:

- Coaching.
- Mentoring.
- Providing guidance, direction, and training (if necessary).
- Offering assistance in any way it will be accepted.
- Communicating needs and listening to desires.

Planning the future

- Present goals you have determined for the employee. Keep in mind that performance is affected by expectations for good and bad performance.
- Exchange goals that each of you has developed.
- Negotiate/reach an agreement on goals.
- Discuss expectations for each goal.
- Determine next actions.

Ending the meeting

- Summarize the meeting, focusing on agreements you and the employee have reached.
- Convey your confidence in the employee to meet the goals set.
- Give the employee a chance to bring up topics he or she wants to discuss or reconcile.
- Schedule another meeting if necessary.
- Put agreed-upon objectives (and their action plans) into written form.
- Express feelings about the meeting and allow the employee to do the same.

Manager as career counselor

Managers can provide invaluable career counseling and development opportunities by using the performance appraisal process as a time to meet with employees and review their job descriptions. Discuss future career plans. Also discuss education and/or job skills needed to achieve those objectives, along with any suggestions for mentorships, networking, or job rotations/job shadowing opportunities. Develop goals for the upcoming year, including career development goals.

As part of your role as a career coach, help your employees to better plan their careers by developing an individual development plan (IDP). An IDP is a written career management plan that identifies short- and long-term career goals, as well as the training and education needed to accomplish them. Often, managers use the annual performance meeting as a time to review and update IDP with employees.

What an IDP can do for you

An IDP can help indispensable employees to:

- Develop short- and long-term career goals that are realistic, attainable, and compatible with their life's work/purpose.
- Identify what knowledge, skills, and abilities are needed to meet personal career goals, life's work/purpose, and organizational needs.
- Design a plan of action (including a timetable) to acquire the training and skills needed to achieve desired career goals and life's work/purpose.
- Better communicate their life's work/purpose and career desires to mentors, superiors, and others who may be instrumental in helping them to achieve their goals.

Prior to completing an IDP, encourage employees to think about:

- Their skills and abilities.
- Jobs and skills needed by organizations both now and in the future.
- How their career plans match the jobs and skills that will be needed in the future.
- Their current and future job and how their life's work/purpose fits into the scheme.

Straight from the expert's lips:

"Before making the final decision for a new manager or team leader in sales, have the team discuss the professional skill set and personal qualities required, then have them meet the prospective manager as you note the synergy and fit. This enhances the success in finding the right manager and ensures retention and performance success!"

—*Sidrah Jackson,*
Vice President, Fleet Boston Financial

IDPs should be evaluated every three to six months to determine what needs to change and what progress is being made.

Keep abreast of changes in the world, United States, and workplace. Encourage indispensable employees to mutate regularly so they can adapt to these changes in their career and the environment that surrounds them.

Rewards that fit
your indispensable employees

As you will discover in the next two chapters, today's workforce is extremely diverse, and managers must manage three (and in some cases four) generations in the workplace: Baby Boomers, Gen Xers, Matures, and Gen Yers. More organizations must begin to look at "synergy and fit" in new ways as they work in the international arenas and incorporate more people from different racial, ethnic, and international backgrounds into their folds.

In this age of diversity, one size certainly doesn't fit all employees when it comes to the rewards and perks that are given to thank employees for their contribution.

Wise organizations know that in this day and age when it comes to recruiting and attracting employees, they must examine more closely their awards structure and fit it to the needs of their indispensable employees.

Here are some tips on how you might go about matching rewards to indispensable employees:

1. Don't guess about what indispensable employees want in regards to rewards and perks. Ask them. As you are surveying staff about attitudes towards work and conducting focus groups or exit interviews, take some time to ask them about the type of rewards they'd like to receive for outstanding performance or contributing significantly to the organization's bottom line or helping a team perform more productively.

   HQ Global Workplaces has surveyed new employees. Among the questions asked of employees are their favorite magazines, restaurants, foods, authors, and hobbies. Imagine an employee's surprise when he receives, in praise of an accomplishment, his favorite author's new book or a gift certificate to his favorite restaurant.

2. Make sure that rewards and perks align with indispensable employees' value systems. For example, some employees don't celebrate holidays such as Christmas or Thanksgiving. A Christmas party or Thanksgiving turkey, then, wouldn't be an appropriate reward.

   Other employees come from cultures where their work ethic dictates that compensation and status in the organization is based upon how well you perform as a team player (as opposed to individual contribution). In fact, in these parts of the world, a person who outshines his fellow working buddies may be viewed as less than a team player, something that is certainly taboo. In cases where employees are reluctant to showcase their individual contributions, they might not accept a reward as the Employee of the Month happily.

Management and executive development programs to improve retention

Continuous learning is the name of the game today, whether managers are just starting their management careers or are more seasoned. Most must routinely brush up on effective management techniques to handle a workforce that is probably older and grayer, more international in focus, knows its value, and isn't afraid to walk out the door if treated unfairly or feels unwanted and unchallenged by management.

What type of training programs and approaches can help managers and executives bone up on their competencies and expand their knowledge base so they can better recruit and retain indispensable employees? Following is a brief overview of management and executive programs you may want to offer, as well as an explanation of each's benefits. These training opportunities help management build their skills and abilities to better retain indispensable employees.

- **Delegation:** Management will learn techniques that ensure their success as well as that of their staff.
- **Disciplinary action and handling difficult employees:** Management will learn proven approaches for handling disciplinary action and difficult employees.
- **Effective communication skills:** Management will learn how to communicate up, down, and across the organization.
- **Effective interviewing skills:** Management will update skills to select the right candidates the first time around.
- **Human resources and the law:** Management will cut through the legalese and human resources jargon. This practical knowledge will help to avoid costly mistakes.
- **Human resources management for non-human resource professionals:** Management will be provided with the essential human resources–related tools and knowledge so they manage more effectively and are more attuned to potential legal liability issues.
- **Individual career enhancement:** Management will convey the "upside" of change and how it can positively affect an employee's career.
- **Management roles and responsibilities:** Management teams will be elevated in order to clarify, understand, and successfully conduct their managerial functions.
- **Managing across generations:** Management will be taught the skills necessary to manage this newly emerging workforce diversity issue.
- **Managing diversity and diversity awareness:** Management will learn to manage and value diversity in the evolving workplace.

- **Meeting management:** Management will learn to make all meetings more productive and effective.
- **Motivational leadership:** Management will become leaders who energize and empower others to excel and achieve.
- **Performance management:** Management will be given tools to link individual, team, and organizational objectives.
- **Project management:** Management will learn to manage projects successfully from start to finish.
- **Rewards and motivation during constant change:** Management will understand how to maintain high staff morale and reward and motivate them in these ever-changing times.
- **Strategic planning and goal-setting:** Management will set measurable goals and craft a shared vision and strategic direction.
- **Team building:** Management will learn how to develop and motivate teams.
- **Time management:** Management will use time management effectively to avoid undue stress, achieve a greater balance between work and personal life, improve productivity, and attain goals.
- **Train-the-trainer programs/effective presentation skills:** Management will teach others how to deliver powerful and memorable presentations.

Management and executive training programs for continuous learning

No two organizations are alike. Make sure your organization offers practical, custom-tailored seminars (both on- and off-site) that maximize learning and allow participants, regardless of their level within the organization, to use the knowledge gained immediately.

In-house training programs are often a cost-effective way to educate managers and ensure that everyone obtains the same knowledge base at the same time. Multifaceted approaches, ranging from innovative seminars for all levels of staff to executive and managerial coaching, should be utilized.

On-site seminars

Whether you use internal trainers or hire outside consultants (or a combination of internal and external personnel), make sure they evaluate your organization's unique circumstances and priorities before implementing a program. Conducting a pilot program or dry run prior to implementing the training is advisable. This process allows you to work out the kinks before "going live," and it helps you to better tailor the program to the unique needs of your organization. It is extremely important to prepare the right delivery for your audience and adapt the training style, program duration, and communication mediums to your organizational culture.

Real-life learning labs

The key to successful learning is that what is taught in the "classroom" relates directly to the workplace. This is especially true for the adult learner. Through a "learning lab approach" participants learn, go back to work, and then return for advanced sessions to expand their knowledge base and reflect upon their real-life experiences.

Make sure there is follow-up and support for your training programs. Avoid holding short training programs where participants are enthusiastic immediately following the training, but because of a lack of follow-up, they lose the enthusiasm and never get around to fully implementing what is learned in class. Provide follow-up training several months after your classes and/or evaluation mechanisms to examine and measure what changes have been achieved for managers as a result of the training.

Executive coaching

Personalized and confidential work with high-powered CEOs, presidents, board members, senior managers, and project teams can assist managers in refocusing their strategic plans and directions and with setting measurable goals. This process can also help them with change management and connecting human resources with business strategies so that what is aimed for is attained.

Through the coaching process, executives and managers enjoy total confidentiality as they expand their knowledge and skills.

Company Spotlight:
Fitzgerald, Stevens and Ford

Stephen C. Ford, president of Fitzgerald, Stevens and Ford (FS&F), outlines the company's innovative Executive Assessment Program:

"The first step in professional development for an executive is to understand his or her own personal leadership and behavioral style, its impact on others, and how this affects his or her success as a leader and manager. Executives who understand their own style are better leaders because they understand others' styles, build better teams, and are less stressed. Executives or managers who have high potential and need to be prepared to move to another level, as well as those who need to improve their performance at their current level, should begin their development process with assessment.

"The Executive Assessment process begins with a discussion of the goals of the process. This is based upon the reasons why the organization, or the individual, believes that the assessment process will be beneficial. The consultant meets with the executive and with his or her manager. Depending upon these objectives, one or more instruments is selected. The assessments include a 360° feedback instrument and a behavioral style assessment; other instruments may be added to address all of the goals.

"The assessment process can also be used very effectively with members of a team to achieve maximum effectiveness.

"Executive Assessment and Development is a very effective tool in retention of key staff. The executive becomes focused on gaining or enhancing the competencies needed to be most effective as a manager and leader. Executives and managers are more loyal to an organization that is investing in them and providing career opportunities. They are, thus, less likely to jump to another organization.

"The assessment process also helps improve the effectiveness of management training and executive coaching by identifying key areas for development and establishing benchmarks for measuring progress.

Step 1

"Determine the goals of the organization for the executive; what are the needs, issues, and interests that lead to the assessment process?

Step 2

"The executive(s) begins with a 45-minute to one-hour overview meeting with the consultant, who will explain the assessment and feedback process, distribute the instruments, and review the directions. The goals of this meeting are: 1) to have the participant understand the assessment process and its objectives; 2) to have the participant understand how to complete the instruments and be comfortable with how the resulting information

will be utilized; 3) to address any questions the executive(s) may have about the process and/or its objectives; and 4) to select the other individuals (subordinates and peers) who will complete the group.

Step 3

"The executive and his or her manager, peers, and subordinates will complete the 360° feedback instrument and the executive will complete any additional instruments selected. The consultant interprets the information developed, integrates it with the personal information and experience learned in Step 1, and then prepares for the feedback session, a process that takes several hours.

Step 4

"The consultant will provide the 360° feedback, integrating supplemental insights gained from the additional instruments. This meeting will last approximately two to three hours. Due to the comprehensive nature of the feedback, the feedback session will be audiotaped for the executive.

Step 5

"To ensure that the information is understood and the executive has a clear plan on how to utilize the information, the consultant will conduct two follow-up meetings (each up to two hours in length). These second and third meetings address any additional questions from the feedback session and then build upon the information to develop a specific Action Plan. The Action Plan is the blueprint for the executive, and a commitment by him or her, to develop the skills, competencies, and knowledge needed to be a successful leader and manager in their future or current roles. This completes the value opportunity presented by the assessment process.

Step 6 (optional)

"After the feedback session and action plan development, FS&F can assist a team or groups of executives in: 1) the development of more 'downstream' team-based plans for increasing and/or maintaining the group's ongoing effectiveness and/or 2) the provision of follow-up coaching for one or more of the participants."

Company Spotlight:
Ezenia! Inc.

Any company whose business involves the Internet and/or information technology has to live by one rule: Change is constant. Ezenia! Inc. is a company that is constantly looking for ways to differentiate itself in the marketplace, both with its product line and in the eyes of its employees. Barbara Colangeli, director of human resources, works closely with her CEO and boss, Khoa Nguyen, to ensure that employees at Ezenia! are a top priority. In the competitive world of the Internet, Ezenia! knows that top technology people can be snatched away in an instant. To keep indispensable employees from straying, Barbara and her staff are constantly crafting surprise events and developing benefits, perks, and events that are fun, memorable, and that differentiate them from the competition.

Quarterly, staff are brought together to hear about the company's progress. Not only do they receive information about the organization's financial health, but they hear directly from CEO Khoa Nguyen and his senior management team about the direction of the company. Employee recognition awards are frequently doled out, and there is usually some type of a theme to these meetings. For example, in May 2000, Ezenia! rented a luxury cruise liner, *The Odyssey,* and bussed the entire organization into a sunny location in downtown Boston, where the ship set sail for an almost-three-hour tour of the lovely Boston Harbor. The theme of the cruise for a day was "We're turning around." The quarterly meeting aboard the ship provided staff some time to unwind and included information shared by the CEO and management about the organization's new strategic direction. Each staff member received a compass, a reminder that he or she was needed to help the organization chart and keep its course.

Barbara and her HR team plan impromptu events at their corporate headquarters for staff. They also regularly host employee "Surprise Days." During a hot summer day, for example, you might see an ice cream truck, complete with jingling music and chimes, pull up to Ezenia!. The voice over Ezenia!'s loudspeaker lets people know that if they are so inclined, they can get a free ice-cream treat from the truck outside.

Barbara Colangeli sums up her organization's approach to retention: "The bottom line is that people have to be excited and feel rewarded for their work contributions. They have to feel very good about the company. Given today's work hours, there has to be a fair amount of flexibility. When you're fair and flexible with people, they'll give you back double."

Chapter 15

Staff Diversity and Globalization Issues

t's hard to pick up a magazine or newspaper, or turn on the television or radio, and not see a story about diversity. Organizations throughout the United States are attempting to become more diverse.

In order to survive and thrive in the new world order, most organizations must operate in a diverse and international arena. With the advent of the Internet, the world shrunk. Business is easily and quickly transacted around the world. The organization that understands and meets customers' needs gets their business.

An organization interested in entering or further penetrating ethnic or multicultural markets (international or domestic) will be unable to do so if its employee population does not understand the unique customer service needs of these groups. Consequently, an organization with the best, most innovative product or service may not be able to capture a market if its staff are not diverse and able to handle worldwide or domestic customers with traditions, beliefs, attitudes, wants, and needs that may be different from their own.

Valuing diversity is not just the right thing to do; it's what a business *must* do in order to survive, thrive, and succeed. The shortage of technically proficient workers will soon leave organizations throughout America with millions of unfilled positions.

Consequently, experts predict that competition will be fierce to attract and retain those with exceptional skills. In the past, some organizations have done a good job of recruiting a diverse workforce, but in many cases, their efforts have proven fruitless because of their inability to retain qualified talent. As one African American woman who was recruited by a major Fortune 500 company put it:

> "They wined me, dined me, and promised me the world when I was recruited. I wish I had known then what I know now: The company really wasn't serious about its diversity efforts. Within a year, I knew that as an African American woman, and as a woman, I would never be given the opportunity to advance into a senior management position, so I left and went to a company that hired me as a vice president and has a diverse and inclusive environment."

●●●

How will your organization:

- Attract highly skilled employees during workforce shortages?
- Satisfy dual-career families and others seeking to balance work, family, and a personal life?
- Compete in a diverse global economy?
- Create a productive organizational culture that retains and motivates employees coming from a myriad of ethnic backgrounds, nationalities, age groups, and lifestyle choices?
- Market to ethnic, gay, and lesbian consumers who do not necessarily respond to typical mass-marketing strategies?

The answer is that your organization will need to foster an inclusive workplace that values both differences and similarities, one that understands the unique needs and preferences of a vast array of both national and international consumers and employees. Before we start to think about accomplishing this daunting feat, let's backtrack for a moment to define diversity.

Diversity is about recognizing differences and honoring them—as well as recognizing similarities among people. Traditionally, organizations have focused their diversity efforts on issues related to race and gender. Today, many companies are taking a broader view and have developed diversity programs and strategies that cover these differences:

- Sexual orientation.
- Religion.
- Personality.
- Socioeconomic status.

- Education and learning ability.
- Balancing work, family, and a personal life.
- Ethnicity.
- Age.
- National origin.
- Physical challenges.
- Length of service and expertise.
- Work style.
- Health.
- Background.
- Job function.
- Gender.
- Race.

Diversity is evolving

When Tiger Woods won his first Masters golf tournament, he didn't describe himself as being Black exclusively (as some people thought he should). He wanted to honor all of the races that are part of his heritage, including his mother's roots from Thailand. He called himself "Cablinasian" (Caucasian, Black, Indian, and Asian). For the first time, due in large part to pressure from parents and people with multiracial backgrounds, the 2000 Census allowed people to identify themselves as being from more than one racial group. If a person is of African, Native American, and Irish decent, for example, she now has a choice as to how she identifies herself.

There is also diversity within groups. Many groups have their own story. Within white American groups, for example, are Irish, Italians, and Germans. Asian includes Chinese, Japanese, and Filipinos, to name just a few subgroups. Haitians, Africans, and Jamaicans may fall under the Black category, but they are not African American because they weren't born in North America. In the Native American group are Cherokee, Lakota Sioux, and Navajos. Between and among each group there is diversity.

Labor shortages

In the late 1980s, the Hudson Institute, in its landmark research in the book *Workforce 2000*, accurately predicted what the workforce of the future would look like. The new millennium has come and gone, and the folks at the Hudson Institute were right: By the year 2000, 85 percent of the new entrants into the workforce *were* women, immigrants, and people

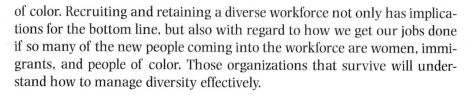

of color. Recruiting and retaining a diverse workforce not only has implications for the bottom line, but also with regard to how we get our jobs done if so many of the new people coming into the workforce are women, immigrants, and people of color. Those organizations that survive will understand how to manage diversity effectively.

The concern about diversity

There are many reasons why organizations have embraced—and continue to embrace—diversity, aside from the fact that it's the right thing to do. Here are some compelling reasons why organizations are seeking to recruit and retain a diverse workforce:

1. The impact of diversity on the bottom line.
2. Shifting workforce and population demographics.
3. Labor shortages.
4. Expanding domestic and international markets (which yield an increase in diverse and global consumers).

Diversity and the bottom line

How can an organization's profitability be enhanced by a true understanding and appreciation of diversity? Enhancing diversity and knowledge of different cultures and lifestyles can help organizations to:

- Compete in international markets and underutilized domestic markets, such as gay and lesbian populations, people of color, and women, due to fine-tuned customer service, as well as multicultural and targeted marketing and sales.
- Enlarge their customer base and marketing opportunities.
- Attract top talent by creating a reputation for valuing diversity, flexibility, and being inclusive of different people.
- Increase productivity by creating good morale and workforce harmony.
- Prevent high turnover rates, low productivity, and difficulty in retaining indispensable employees.
- Maintain lower levels of absenteeism and increased loyalty to the organization.
- Decrease the number of lawsuits, grievances, and discrimination claims.
- Tap into the creative side of a diverse group of people for suggestions, ideas, products, and services.

Here's what some of the nation's top business magazines have to say about the impact of diversity on the bottom line:

In an article in *Harvard Business Review* (September–October 1996), David A. Thomas and Robin J. Ely wrote:

> "...diversity goes beyond increasing the number of different identity-group affiliations on the payroll to recognizing that such an effort is merely the first step in managing a diverse workforce for the organization's utmost benefit. Diversity should be understood as the *varied perspectives and approaches to work* that members of different identity groups bring."

Hemisphere, Inc. reported in *Forbes* magazine that in 1994 General Motors "sought to improve the environment at the [Fort Worth Service Parts Operations] Warehouse by implementing a management system that values diversity." To accomplish this goal, a new female manager who allowed women and people of color to have more authority was appointed. She also developed new standards of performance-based rewards and enhanced communications between professionals and hourly employees. In one year, the plant boosted productivity by 21 percent, making it one of the leaders in the company. Even more impressive, the plant achieved $4.4 million in savings that year.

The next generation of diversity issues

This generation is described as "the first generation to accept mixed races, nontraditional families, and gender-bending sex roles as mainstream" (*American Demographics,* October 1995, pg. 22). One third of young Americans are Black, Latino, Asian, or Native American. Eighty percent of these have friends outside of their race. Take the hip-hop culture, for instance. Hip hop is a $1-billion dollar industry. Guess who purchases 60 percent of rap music? White American teens.

Here area some "next generation" diversity issues that you may face as you try to recruit and retain diverse indispensable employees, including women, people of color, Gen Xers, and Matures:

- Shifting workforce demographics.
- Globalization issues.
- Hiring global workers.
- Managing across generations.
- Socioeconomics (gender and racial pay-scale inequities).
- Managing individuals with disabilities.

Shifting workforce demographics

Organizations that are looking at statistics, such as those published by the U.S. Census Bureau and the Bureau of Labor Statistics, are seeing that the workforce composition is changing. In addition, labor shortages will force organizations to consider a variety of diverse candidates to fill positions due to a shortage of qualified workers. Consider these statistics:

- As predicted by the Hudson Institute (in its landmark research found in the book *Workforce 2000*), in the late 1980s 85 percent of new workforce entrants were women, immigrants, and people of color.
- Close to 50 percent of the workforce is women.
- A shortage of qualified workers with adequate technical skills has resulted in millions of jobs going unfilled. Furthermore, population growth is expected not to keep up with the increase of new jobs created by organizations.
- Most future jobs will require more than a high school education. Illiteracy is rapidly becoming a concern.
- The immigrant population is now at its highest level since World War II.
- Not only are the demographics in the workforce changing, but in the general population as well. White Americans represent the smallest-growing racial population in the United States. Factors contributing to this include a decline in births among whites and a decline in the number of white immigrants, particularly those of European descent.

As population demographics have shifted, in some areas the minorities have turned into the majority. People of color are or will be the majority in California, Florida, and Texas. Those states account for 45 percent of the U.S. population growth. Of this number, Latinos and Asians have had the most rapid growth. Another minority-turned-majority is women.

White males and diversity

White males make up approximately 39.2 percent of the population. In the Forbes 400, out of those who earned at least $265 million, 82.5 percent were white males. White males make up approximately 77% of Congress, 92% of state governors, and 70% of tenured faculty. They also account for 100 percent of U.S. presidents.

Diversity backlash

As noted earlier, minorities are becoming the majority in some parts of the country. But does that mean that top jobs are being taken over by women and other minorities? In some instances, yes, this is the case. But in many cases, though, the numbers don't support this theory. Unfortunately, as organizations try to enhance the ranks of minorities and women, they sometimes have to deal with a backlash and "reverse discrimination." Decide how you'll deal with such backlash if it occurs in your organization. Texas Instruments offers a good example: It developed a comprehensive diversity program and has conducted workshops in its Attleboro, Mass. plant for white males (the group that, for the most part, typically held those top jobs) so they have a platform to discuss their opinions on diversity.

Minorities and women

Asians, Blacks, Latinos, women, and individuals with disabilities want advancement, but statistics are slow to change. According to the March 2000 edition of *HR Magazine,* Blacks and Latinos account for less than 2 percent of executive positions in the United States. In 1983, 25 percent of employed blacks were clustered in low-paying service and unskilled jobs. In 1999, that number dropped only slightly, to 22 percent. In 1979, black males earned 75 cents to every dollar earned by a white male. In 1999, the ratio was identical.

The October 1999 Congressional Record showed that women earn 76 cents for every dollar earned by a man. *HR News* magazine reported in August 1999 that 89 percent of human resources professionals still see a glass ceiling for women. Seventy-nine percent of them still see a glass ceiling for minorities.

Continued challenges

The following are workforce challenges that your indispensable women continue to face in the new millennium:

- A corporate culture that favors males.
- Stereotypes/preconceptions about women.
- A lack of women on boards of directors.
- Exclusion from informal networks.
- Management's perception that family responsibilities will interfere with work.

Your indispensable minorities also continue to face challenges in this new millennium. These include:

- Race- and ethnicity-based stereotypes.
- Exclusion from informal networks.
- Lack of mentoring opportunities.
- Lack of role models.
- Perception that corporate cultures favor non-minorities.

Globalization issues

Diversity issues differ in other parts of the world. Getting managers accustomed to doing business around the world and dealing with global employees sometimes produces a problem. Consider offering culture classes in which managers are taught to value the differences and similarities between American culture and other cultures—and to value those differences. Another problem is acclimating global workers into the U.S. workforce. As more cultures invade the workforce, employers will need to handle more issues related to English as a Second Language, including policies regarding speaking English only. Take a look at the following scenario, one that isn't nearly as uncommon as you might think:

Mary Ellen, one of your outstanding employees, has come to you very upset that five of her co-workers are constantly speaking in Spanish. Mary Ellen tells you that "those people are in America now." She thinks that what they do outside of the office is their business, but while at work, they should speak English only. After all, she explains, it is disrespectful of people who don't speak the language because it isolates them. Besides, they could be saying something bad about her or some other American.

This is obviously a sensitive situation. Here are some steps to take to handle it:

- Acknowledge the employee's feelings and talk with her about why she feels people should not be allowed to speak their native language at work.
- Get more information so you have a good picture of what is happening, and when.
- Encourage the employee to speak directly to her co-worker(s) rather than you being the intermediary. Coach the employee on how to handle the discussion. For example, ask the employee how she might begin a discussion about this issue. Also, talk with her about the fact that she may want to learn some Spanish words so she can communicate with them better and know what they are saying. They

have learned English so they can communicate, so perhaps she'll consider learning some of their language as a gesture of goodwill.

- Ask her how she would feel if she was working in a non-English-speaking country and wasn't allowed to speak English with her English-speaking co-workers.
- Get a commitment from the employee regarding when she will speak with the other employee(s).
- Schedule a follow-up meeting to see how it went and to offer further coaching if necessary.
- Consider having a staff meeting to discuss this issue if it continues and/or becomes more widespread. If you do have a staff meeting consider these steps:
  - Let the group know at the outset that you can't prevent them from speaking their language with friends and co-workers on their own time, but that they might want to include English speakers in the conversation by having someone translate what's being said. Also let them know that you want their thoughts about this issue.
  - Ask the group to brainstorm about the positives and negatives of employees speaking their native language at work. List their answers on a flip chart so everyone can easily see them.
  - Ask the group to brainstorm about solutions to the issue.
  - Follow the rules of brainstorming (no critiquing of ideas when they are expressed; everyone participates; when all the ideas are up on the flip chart, then it's okay for people to ask for clarification and/or to state their opinions of any of the ideas).

Hiring global workers

In a speech given by India's Minister of Information Technology on May 26, 2000 at Harvard University, he noted that India currently produces about 50 percent of the information technology and engineers of the world.

Many organizations are recruiting well-trained foreign workers into their organizations and/or are exporting work to foreign countries. American managers will not be successful in keeping their indispensable foreign workers if they are not aware of how to manage a multicultural, multiracial, and diverse workforce. For example, if an Indian worker is a Hindu and the manager decides to reward the person by taking him out for a juicy hamburger, he would be missing the reward and motivation boat with that employee. Why? Because cows are sacred in the Hindu religion. As your workplace starts to contain more workers from around the world, sensitize managers to issues that are related to culture:

- Work ethics.
- Rewards and motivators.
- Compensation and benefit expectations. (In some cultures people receive additional compensation when they get married or have a child.)
- Performance measurements. (In some cultures, team, performance, rather than individual, is stressed, and rewards are based on team performance.)

Managing across generations

Special concerns are raised when Baby Boomers and Matures meet Gen Xers. What happens when young people begin to supervise people who are their parents' or grandparents' ages—and vice versa? Think about the dynamics (and sometimes fireworks) that are created by such situations. Age diversity will surely continue to be one of the biggest management challenges in the years ahead. (See Chapter 16 for more information on how to handle diversity related to managing across generations.)

Socioeconomics

What would we find if we took a comparison of celebrity salaries, teacher/daycare worker salaries, and millionaire employees? It doesn't take a rocket scientist to figure this one out. Work on closing the gaps between pay scale inequalities based on races and gender.

Managing individuals with disabilities

According to the March 20, 2000 issue of *Business Week*, the percentage of adult Americans with disabilities who are working age and unemployed is 75 percent. Believe it or not, chronic illnesses (such as heart disease and strokes) can begin to set in around age 45. With the vast majority of your workers in the 35-years-old-plus category, issues surrounding disability are rapidly becoming a major concern.

When chronic illness sets in, how can you help employees? Some employee benefits could include assisted living, burial benefits, back-to-work programs, and grief counseling. Reasonable accommodations and adapting the workplace for those with disabilities could help, too. (See Chapter 8 for more information working with indispensable employees who are individuals with a disabilities.)

Diversity as a business imperative

Here are some tips to help your managers embrace diversity issues:

- Develop a business plan and brief them.
- Show them how diversity impacts the bottom line.
- Educate boards of directors, shareholders, and managers.
- Start planning now.
- Provide ongoing training on managing a diverse and global workforce.

Setting yourself apart

Is there anything to differentiate your organization to diverse indispensable employees who may be underrepresented in your organization? Consider these items:

- Promotional opportunities.
- Like (similar) people from whom employees can learn and grow.
- Learning opportunities.
- Diversity programs and mentoring.
- Affinity groups.

Develop a recruitment and retention action plan

Develop a strategic direction to attract a more diverse workforce, particularly at senior levels within your organization. Utilize a comprehensive approach. Include your strategy and tactics related to:

- Multicultural marketing.
- Marketing segmentation.
- Community outreach.
- Brand image as an employer of substance and choice.
- Internal recruitment activities.

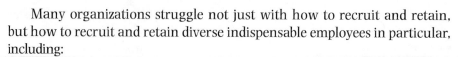

Many organizations struggle not just with how to recruit and retain, but how to recruit and retain diverse indispensable employees in particular, including:

- Women.
- People of color.
- Older workers.
- Generation Xers.
- Individuals with disabilities.

Depending upon what part of the country or world that your organization is located in, the challenge could be even more difficult. I read a very compelling article entitled "The Diversity Myth—True Multiethnic Counties Are Concentrated in Just a Few Areas" in the June 1998 edition of *American Demographics*. The article shed some light on demographic population shifts and how difficult it might be for some employers to recruit a diverse workforce. The reason is that diversity is found in pockets in the United States. Many people come to, relocate to, or stay in areas where there is a critical mass of people like them. Census 2000 data seem to corroborate many of these points from the article:

- The nation has only a few "melting pots" with a significant presence of two or more minority groups.
- Latinos and Asians usually enter the United States through, and remain in, major gateway cities (Los Angeles, New York, San Francisco, etc.). Forty-three percent of all U.S. Asians live in these three areas.
- Blacks are more scattered than Asians and Latinos. They are concentrated in northern urban centers but are moving to the South (particularly to Atlanta).
- Whites are moving where jobs and good weather are (the Southeast, Texas, and Rocky Mountain states near California).
- Job growth for Whites centers around technology and information-based industries.

Think about the implications of the information that you just read. If your organization is interested in becoming more diverse and attracting diverse indispensable employees, it may have to work even harder at it, especially if it is not located in areas of the country where the pockets of diversity exist. Unfortunately, for most of us, diversity recruitment is (and will continue to be) a challenge. The recruitment challenge, however, is far more simple than the retention one.

TR²

TR², which stands for Targeted Recruitment and Retention, is an approach my firm invented that helps organizations to not only target certain groups for employment, but also to retain them, which is a major problem for many organizations.

Recruitment is only the beginning of a good placement. TR² recognizes that in order for there to be a smooth transition for candidates from diverse backgrounds into your organization, you must help new hires with acclimating to the workplace and thereby maximizing their performance. In addition, the organization may have to adjust and change in order to accommodate people it has previously not employed or has only hired in small numbers.

Organizations that actively recruit talented individuals who are a good fit for their organization need to work on how to retain them. This can be a challenging proposition. However, through external retention services and special support, at least through the first year of employment, the candidate's chances of successfully gaining tenure in the organization can be improved.

TR² services to provide

Consider providing these TR² services when you are trying to retain diverse staff:

- A meeting with those involved in the hiring process to develop job specifications.
- A "Diversity Recruitment/Interviewing Briefing" for those directly involved in interviewing candidates. Private coaching can also be made available.
- Upon final selection of the candidate, managers in the new hire's work unit should attend a briefing that will focus on diversity retention issues.
- An executive coaching session for the new hire and/or manager on a monthly basis or for the first four months to debrief on any issues that arise, preferably with a multiracial group of executive coaches.
- Follow-up coaching sessions are provided at the sixth, ninth and twelfth month of employment for the new hire.
- Resources/support services to help new hires navigate their way through the community with information about schools, social activities, and even where to get a haircut.

Innovative diversity and globalization services

As part of your retention of indispensable diverse employees, consider programs that include:

- Affinity group development (diversity councils).
- Annual reports and brochures.
- Audits/needs assessments/focus groups.
- Business plans.
- Networking/ relationship-building.
- Customized training for managers and/or employees.
- Diversity recruitment and retention.
- Handling diverse customers.
- Management and executive development programs.
- Recruiting and retaining underrepresented minorities and women.
- Services to enhance community and global outreach efforts.
- Videos.

Expanding domestic and international markets

The workforce in and the population of the United States are not the only things that are changing. In order to survive and thrive, more and more organizations are finding out that they must compete in a global marketplace, as well as learn how to service the unique customer needs of diverse customers in the United States and around the world. Consider these bloopers that companies have made (from the *Boston Sunday Globe*, November 22, 1998):

- Pepsi's "come alive with the Pepsi generation" slogan translated to "Pepsi will bring back your dead ancestors" in Taiwan.
- In China, Kentucky Fried Chicken's "finger-lickin' good" translated to "eat your fingers off."
- GM introduced the Chevy Nova in South America, not realizing that "nova" means "it won't go." GM renamed the car "Caribe" for Spanish-language countries.

The new global consumer

Unfortunately, many companies have learned the hard way that in order to penetrate multicultural and worldwide markets, they have to produce products and provide services needed by these groups, and they must teach their employees how to serve global customers and to be "culturally sensitive" to their needs. What works in America may not work outside of the United States. Marketing products effectively to people from different racial, ethnic, or age groups may require different approaches.

You may have heard people speak about the new global economy and the world marketplace. What does this mean? Basically, it means that technology has made the world a lot smaller. You can order something from Brazil and have it delivered overnight. The world becomes your shopping mall—and potentially your customer as well. And competition has certainly improved.

Japan, for example, was once known as the epitome of cheap products. Now Japan is a world leader known for producing many top-quality products. Additionally, there are many emerging countries producing items that may not be the latest state-of-the-art, but the products can be produced more cost-effectively by lower-paid workers, and in some cases, without regulatory or union concerns. To survive, many companies must compete in the world markets and learn how to service and meet the varied needs of their international customers.

In addition to international markets, organizations are also endeavoring to be more competitive by expanding into domestic, ethnic, and other multicultural markets that are proving to be profitable. Such markets include people of color, women, older people, Generation Xers, gays and lesbians, and individuals with disabilities.

Show me the money

People of color are a large consumer base. According to George Hererra of the U.S. Hispanic Chamber of Commerce, the combined buying power of Latinos and African Americans is $800 billion. Women are heavy decision-makers when it comes to the purchase of automobiles and healthcare. There is no wonder, then, that there is an enormous demand for services and people who "look like me." Consumers want to be represented and to see a representative who looks like them when doing business. Therefore, it has been a challenge to organizations to build more diverse teams and do more multicultural marketing.

Tips for recruiting indispensable diverse employees

1. Advertise job openings in ethnic/affinity and community newspapers and publications. Focus on those read by:
   - People of color.
   - Individuals with disabilities.
   - Generation Xers, Baby Boomers, and Matures.
   - Women.
   - White males.
   - Veterans.

2. Attend conferences and job fairs held by groups that represent professionals of color, such as the National Black MBA Association.

3. Create your organization's own diversity job fair and have booths with representatives from your affinity groups, diversity committees, and recruitment and retention committees.

4. Utilize a diverse range of recruitment sources, including local agencies, state and federal agencies, and search firms that specialize in recruiting specific populations.

5. Structure formal programs to turn your own satisfied managers and employees into headhunters and goodwill ambassadors who will get the word out about your organization and its career opportunities.

6. Recruit from colleges with a high ratio of women and people of color.

7. To increase your workforce visibility in the community, encourage employees to do volunteer work on behalf of your company (on company time) in various communities.

8. Send press releases to community newspapers and invite the media to attend diversity-related events.

9. Create an employee referral bonus program. Consider non-employee referral bonus programs.

10. Create a people-of-color network made of employees who talk with candidates as well as community groups and educational institutions about your organization, what it is like to work there, and how their careers have advanced within the organization.

11. Participate in career day activities at local schools.

12. Establish internships for people of color and women.

13. Collaborate with area schools to develop career programs/internships for students.

14. Consult the Small Business Administration and other sources for minority vendors.

15. Think of ways to get your customers involved in sending you candidates. Consider including direct-mail pieces with invoices or other correspondence to customers. Set up community task forces to help you. Tap into key community leaders and agencies and send your listings there.

16. Tap into community events. Serve as a sponsor at such events. Create a yearly calendar of events of programs and initiatives you want to support. Build relationships with a number of community organizations for win/win outcomes. These include minority newspapers, Spanish-formatted radio stations (as well as other languages), Black Entertainment Television, and so forth.

17. Examine how different underrepresented minorities get their information and pursue ways to better market yourself as an employer of substance and choice to them.

18. Join forces with organizations that service the social, civic, religious, and educational needs of the groups whose representation you are seeking to improve.

19. Aside from large media and advertising outlets, consider smaller ones that are in tune with the audience you are seeking to attract.

Diversity profile exercise

Take a moment to answer the following questions. (Give approximate numbers if you don't know exact answers.) This exercise should help you to better understand the diversity (or lack thereof) within your area(s) of responsibility and can serve as an instrument to help you think through what should you do to improve diversity within your area(s) of responsibility.

1. What is the number of employees in your department?

2. How many employees are Matures (54+ years old)? How many are Baby Boomers (35 to 53 years old)? How many are Gen Xers (18 to 34 years old)?

3. How many employees are male? How many are female?

4. How many employees are Black? How many are Asian? How many are Latino? How many are Middle Eastern? How many are Native American? How many are White?

5. How many employees are married? How many are married with dependents? How many are single? How many are single with dependents? How many are domestic partnered? How many are domestic partnered with dependents?

6. How many employees are exempt (salaried)? How many are nonexempt (hourly)?

7. How many employees are openly heterosexual? How many are openly gay or lesbian? How many are openly bisexual? How many are openly transgender?

8. What, if any, issues have arisen in your department in regards to the following:
   • Age.
   • Gender.
   • Sexual Orientation.
   • Race.
   • Religion.
   • Socioeconomic status.
   • Job function.
   • Disability.
   • Other.

9. On a scale of 1 (lowest) to 10 (highest), please rate how well you think your staff currently gets along with regard to:
   • Age.
   • Race.
   • Gender.
   • Sexual orientation.

10. What are the diversity strengths within your department?

11. What keeps you awake at night with regard to diversity in your department?

12. Where are your "wheels stuck in the snow" with regard to diversity in your department?

Interview questions
diverse candidates may ask

• How many people like me do you have in the organization?
• How many of them are in middle and senior management positions? In professional and technical positions? On the board?

- What are my chances for progressing/advancing my career in this organization?
- Do you have a formal mentoring program and/or career development programs for women? Minorities? Aspiring managers? Middle and senior managers?
- What does the organization do with regard to community outreach efforts?
- Do you have any employee groups that focus on the needs of people like me?
- Are managers taught how to communicate and manage diverse employees?
- What initiatives, events, and programs has your organization participated in regarding diversity?
- Do you offer a diversity program (e.g., awareness and management)?
- Because there are few people of color in this city, where do people like me live? Go to church? Socialize? Get their hair done? Send their kids to school?

Diversity and participatory management

Participatory management is a leadership style that is becoming more prevalent in successful and innovative organizations. It involves senior and middle managers working with staff to:

- Empower people.
- Share leadership and decision-making.
- Align with a broad vision and strategy of diversity.
- Build relationships, strategic alliances, and networks.
- Participate on multidisciplinary or cross-functional teams.
- Focus on the customer.
- Collaborate.

Organizations that are not sensitive to diversity may experience negative effects that can be long-lasting. For example, a Texaco incident involving a taped conversation of racial remarks made by high-ranking officials showed a level of insensitivity at the company. That incident cost the company millions of dollars ($175 million in settlement claims to employees) and produced negative reactions internationally by customers, vendors, and employees.

In another case, the U.S. State Department paid $3.8 million for a suit by African American Foreign Service officers for alleged discrimination and denial of promotion and other advancement opportunities.

Characteristics of successful diverse organizations

Here are some characteristics of organizations that have been successful on the diversity front:

- Senior management "buy-in" and commitment is in place.
- The diversity effort is part of an organizational strategic plan.
- Accountability, compensation, and incentives are tied to diversity outcomes.
- Efforts are widely communicated to internal and external constituents.
- Learning, evaluation, and continuous improvement are part of the diversity effort.
- The organization assists staff to balance work, family, and personal life.
- Ongoing communication and employee involvement is encouraged.
- Career development and management opportunities are provided. Diverse staff are at all levels.
- Recruitment and retention committees are in place.
- Specialized recruiters are in place.
- Targeted, global, and diverse marketing exists.
- People of color and women-owned vendor/supplier programs are in operation.
- Diversity annual report is prepared.
- Translation/interpreter services are made available.
- In the wake of competing organizational priorities, ways are found to sustain the diversity momentum.

The following practices are used by organizations to assure a diverse, sensitive environment. Incorporating these practices helps to build an organization's positive image in the world community and creates a motivated and productive workforce that is ready to face the many challenges of a rapidly changing world:

- **Benchmarking and case studies.** Benchmarking can be a valuable mechanism to better understand what successful companies have done in the area of diversity.
- **Training for management, executives, employees, board members, and key stakeholders.** Training is an essential component to making diversity a business imperative within your organization.
- **Testing and measurement of diversity programs.** Evaluating the effectiveness of diversity initiatives is a key element to achieving success.

Some of the current workforce trends (highlighted in *Business Week*) that may affect organizations include the following critical issues:

- The falling number of workers.
- The rising average age of workers.
- More working women.
- People of color as a growing percentage of the work force.
- Increasing immigration.
- The world as a global labor market.
- A decreasing percentage of white males entering the labor force.
- More access to the workplace for individuals with disabilities.
- More visible and outspoken gay men and lesbians.
- An increasing skills gap between employer needs and employee ability.
- More demanding work/life balance for employees.
- More demanding and less loyal employees.

Diversity efforts

Here are some specific ideas regarding diversity that you might consider implementing within your organization.

A diversity business plan

A diversity business plan, with a well-defined mission, measurable goals, and a realistic timetable, will enable organizations to roll out diversity initiatives in an efficient and effective manner. This plan must include who is responsible for achieving the goals, what financial and human resources are available, how efforts will be evaluated, who will be responsible for carrying out the plan, a timetable for implementation, and a definition of the board and management's involvement.

Senior management involvement

As with any other business initiative, diversity becomes part of the organizational culture when senior management is actively involved. This involvement can be anything from written and verbal communications from senior managers to being personally involved on a diversity council or part of a training team.

Compensation, rewards, and incentives

Some organizations have found that when diversity initiatives are part of the performance appraisal process, they are taken more seriously. Diversity goals can be tied to compensation through merit increases, bonuses, and other incentives. These incentives are then seen as part of the overall business strategy.

Training programs for all levels

Appropriate training is required for all levels of the organization—from the board to new employees at all levels. The board and senior managers need regular briefings and updates on the diversity efforts. Diversity training needs be integrated into all programs. In addition to the awareness and sensitivity training programs specific to diversity issues, other training programs need to address diversity (for example, training programs involving sexual harassment, worldwide marketing, and customer service).

A calendar of events

Diversity is inclusive; it is about all of us. A calendar of fun events, lectures, activities, and holidays of significance to all cultures will show employees that *everyone* is included. For example, by highlighting *all* holidays and festivals no one feels left out. Celebrate Black History Month (February), the Chinese New Year, Fourth of July, Gay & Lesbian Pride Month (June), Native American Celebrations, National Disability Employment Awareness Month (October), holidays specific to an organization's employee population, and so forth.

Diversity councils/employee involvement

Employee involvement and buy-in is key to a successful diversity initiative. Employee involvement could be useful in developing a diversity business plan. Employees from all levels of the organization should be involved in the development and evaluation of all efforts undertaken. The type of activities that a diversity council could work on include study groups about a particular issue/problem, internal glass ceiling studies, employee attitude surveys/needs assessments, networking directories, and diversity events and training.

Formal mentorships

Many mentor relationships happen naturally in the workplace when people "recognize" themselves when they were just starting out in a new employee. With a diverse employee population, long-term employees may not "recognize" themselves. For this reason, mentorships need to be formally structured.

Diversity coordinator

Although any successful diversity effort will depend upon everyone's involvement, there needs to be a position or person identified who can serve as a resource and help to make sure the efforts are carried out.

Recruitment and retention committees

In order to have a more diverse employee population, organizations need to concentrate on the recruitment and retention of a diverse workforce. Evaluating turnover, identifying candidate pools and developing relationships with schools, communities, and institutions that are historically for women and people of color are just a few of the activities that a committee or specialized recruiter could spend time on.

Targeted global marketing campaigns

In order to have a more diverse customer base, organizations need to understand who their customers are. Individual cultures have different ways of communicating and satisfying their needs. Organizations that spend time researching new markets through a diversity lens will avoid costly mistakes and increase customer satisfaction.

Vendor/supplier programs operated by women or people of color

Vendors and suppliers owned and operated by women or people of color should be utilized. Organizations may need to initiate special outreach programs to find and support these companies.

Diversity annual report

An annual report on the impact and effectiveness of diversity efforts and initiatives will enable organizations to measure how far they have come, where they need to go, and where to make adjustments and revisions to the plans and goals.

Translation/interpreter services

Good communication is vital. Many organizations have employees and customers who do not speak English well (or at all). If this is the case, establish a translation and interpreter services program. All organizations need to be aware of how to communicate with people who are deaf or hearing-impaired. Employees should either have access to a TDD or should be made aware of the "relay service" now offered by telephone companies.

Ongoing program evaluation

Diversity programs need to be evaluated periodically and have goals reviewed and updated. Some tools that can be used to evaluate diversity programs and initiatives include focus groups, needs assessments, audits, surveys, interviews, and an analysis of employee turnover.

Comprehensive communications

The communication about the diversity initiative can and should take many forms. Speeches by and open forums with the CEO are very effective and well-received by employees. Other communication methods include diversity videotapes, diversity mission statements, internal trade shows, diversity newsletters, brochures, management handbooks, and a dialogue/training on the changing employee/employer contract.

Flexible work arrangements

As an organization's workforce becomes more diverse, flexible work arrangements may be required. At first, this may take some creative thinking on everyone's part, but the long-term effect is a more productive workforce. Organizations with a more diverse workforce are now offering flextime, cafeteria-style benefits, earned time, job sharing, telecommuting, and flexible scheduling.

Balancing work, family, and personal life

With an increase in the number of households where both parents work, the large number of single parent homes, and the increasing number of grandparents who become parents again, the balancing of an employee's work, family, and personal life is an issue that organizations need to face.

Some examples of what employers are doing about this include childcare and eldercare centers and referral services, parenting classes and lectures, breastfeeding rooms, paternity policies, and sick child centers.

Career development and management

Many organizations have an overall employee population that is diverse, but where the senior management levels of the organization remain either all or mostly white and male. With many people of color and women in entry-level positions, career development and management programs will enable an organization to become more diverse at all levels. The following are programs that many organizations have found useful:

- Mentor/buddy relationships
- Formal succession planing.
- Career ladders.
- Developmental assignments (lateral, rotational, short-term).
- On-the-job training.
- Tuition reimbursement.
- English as a Second Language programs.
- Remedial education.
- Retirement planning.
- Career counseling.
- Job-hunting courses.
- Information sessions on area colleges and adult education/vocational programs.

Resource guide

You may want to develop a resource guide for your organization that includes listings for Internet and print media; consulting firms, multicultural marketing firms, and reference tools; demographic data of cities with the largest minority populations and the largest newspapers; colleges, universities, and broadcast media; professional organizations; community organizations; and career centers, training programs, and search firms.

Harvard University created such a diversity resource guide in conjunction with Fields Associates, Inc. that has proven to be very beneficial.

Diversity and retention tips

Here are some tips for retaining a diverse workforce:

- Create affinity groups, diversity committees, diversity recruiting committees, and advancement committees for women and people of color.
- Set up a "buddy" system for new workers whereby employees have someone who will take them to lunch, introduce them to others, etc.
- Hold multicultural festivals and celebrate Black History Month, Asian Heritage Month (offer special related activities such as Japanese Origami and Korean costumes), and so on.
- Communicate to managers and employees there is not one style/way of accomplishing a task. Remind them of this often.
- Mediate disputes promptly.
- Take complaints seriously and show your commitment to resolving the issues with timely actions.
- Establish mentoring programs.
- Provide career counseling opportunities.
- Provide access to cross-training and special projects.
- Help employees balance work, family, and personal obligations.
- Ensure that all management/department activities are appropriate for everyone and that everyone is invited.
- Discourage ethnic and sexist jokes in the workplace by adopting a zero-tolerance policy towards them.
- Take a firm stand against sexual harassment and any form of discrimination. Follow through with consistent disciplinary actions.
- Establish grievance procedures.

Company Spotlight:
Fleet Financial

Here's what Michelle Adams Bolden, director of diversity of Fleet Financial, has to say about her organization's diversity programs:

"Human resources professionals need to be fully conversant in issues of diversity. We take seriously our ability to recruit a diverse workforce.

How we're viewed is in terms of our technology. We've spent a lot of time building our technology so we can attract Gen Xers, and we've developed some approaches that target and appeal to that group. For example, we have a college recruitment effort where we go on campus to recruit. We've set up computers at our events so people can apply for jobs or check us out on the spot. Anyone who applies online at our recruitment events gets a free gift, such as a Fleet T-shirt. Other initiatives that we undertake include:

- Building partnerships with the Black MBAA, Hispanic, Inroads Groups, Urban Bankers, and NABA (National Association of Black Accountants). We put major money to build partnerships over two or three years, and this helps market Fleet and tap and cultivate a diverse set of employees that we can bring into our organization over time.
- Visiting historically Black colleges—not just sending junior recruiters, but managers and executives that the students can see role models. These successful executives are proof to these young people that people who look like them do exist in large banks such as Fleet.
- Supporting the United Negro College Fund to build relationships with kids from out of town so they understand that Boston can be a great place to work, despite its checkered racial past.

"It is relatively easy to get people into a company, but the challenge is retaining them. We work hard at re-recruiting people. We want to keep top talent. Our re-recruitment efforts include a career development program, a mentoring program, and formal succession planning.

"In our succession planning efforts, top people are identified, and we make sure women and people of color are identified. Our diversity office runs reports on who the highest-rated people are so that when jobs become available there's a pool of ready candidates. We also introduce them to a human resources colleague so they have one-on-one contact with the HR and recruiters know who the talent is when positions become available.

"Get to know the people in your organization. That's your first opportunity to recruit talent. Recruitment is everyone's job. People come into organizations because they know people they trust and respect. They leave because they get to know people that they can't trust with regard to mentoring them and providing them with an opportunity for growth. So, they go elsewhere.

"Sit down with people and show them opportunities that exist and how they might help out."

Company Spotlight:
DiversityInc.com

Allegiant Media, publisher of *DiversityInc.com*, is a unique company providing a unique service to the business community. Through a combination of original reporting, exclusive interviews, and unparalleled industry knowledge, *DiversityInc.com* gives businesses and the people who run them awareness, understanding, and well-crafted content on the role of diversity on the corporate bottom line—information that is unavailable elsewhere.

"A common trait among most people is a suspicion or fear of the unknown," says company president Luke Visconti. "What brings people together is knowledge and understanding; working together generates respect. Companies that work hard at being inclusive can bring together the best possible people. That enables the companies to gain the varied perspectives of people with different decision-making and problem-solving skills. That is the basis of diversity being a competitive edge."

That's certainly true at *DiversityInc.com*, based in New Brunswick, N.J. The company's workforce is more than one-third multiethnic and more than half female. The close-knit company's emphasis on learning from each other and respecting differences has paid off. Traffic on *DiversityInc.com* grew more than 300 percent in 2000 and continues to grow at least 10 percent each month. *DiversityInc.com* recently added a career center/resume bank, published "The Business Case for Diversity," a definitive document that proves that diversity is an essential bottom-line issue, and received national attention for its hard-hitting journalism.

Chapter 16

Managing Across Generations

I often hear managers complain about how they feel about their new multipurpose management role. They state that they teach people what their parents didn't teach them (manners, courtesy to customers, etc.). As if that's not enough, they are also psychologists, financial counselors, doctors, drug abuse counselors, and so on. Most importantly, they have to manage a workforce comprised of three (and in some cases four) distinct generations of people.

J. Walker Smith and Ann Cluman, in their powerful book *Rocking the Ages: The Yankelovich Report of Generational Marketing,* give us a sense of what the demographics of today's workforce are:

- Matures (born between 1920 and 1945): 21%
- Baby Boomers (born between 1946 and 1964): 53%
- Generation Xers (born between 1965 and 1981): 26%

In a workshop I ran recently, after discussing that a large number (74 percent) of the workforce is 35 and older, one participant explained, "I find that figure so hard to believe. There seem to be so many Generation Xers around." Another attendee commented: "There seem to be more of them because they are so vocal and aren't afraid to voice their opinions."

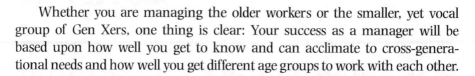

Whether you are managing the older workers or the smaller, yet vocal group of Gen Xers, one thing is clear: Your success as a manager will be based upon how well you get to know and can acclimate to cross-generational needs and how well you get different age groups to work with each other.

Shifts in generational composition

As stated earlier, population growth is not expected to keep up with job growth. Also, remember that from 1965 to 1990, millions of fewer children were born. Consequently, America's workforce is likely to grow very slowly; in fact, most of today's workers have already been born. According to the Bureau of Labor Statistics, the workforce will continue to grow annually at the meager rate of 1 percent through 2006.

According to Claire Raines' book *Beyond Generation X*, in 1964 and before, more than four million new babies were born each year. In 1965, birthrates plummeted and didn't reach the four million mark again until 1990. As a result of this, we have fewer people entering the labor force.

The average age of the American worker is expected to increase until the year 2020, with the normal Social Security age already scheduled to increase to 67 (according to *Workforce 2020*). Many Baby Boomers will continue to work past normal retirement age, mainly because they lack the financial means to retire sooner. Also, the large number of Boomers expected to retire may very well saturate the Social Security and Medicare benefits system.

Gradually replacing the Baby Boomers will be the much smaller cohort of Baby Busters (pre-Generation Xers, born between 1965 and 1981). Due to their relatively small size, the Busters will not be able to finance Social Security benefits through their payroll taxes. As the chart on page 255 from the American Association of Retired People (AARP) illustrates, significantly fewer people are working versus those who are retired.

Organizations that want to meet the challenge head on must recognize that although the future labor pool will consist of several generations, the aging Baby Boomers will dominate in numbers. Additionally, employers must address the impact that America's aging population will have on the workforce. Think about the following:

- Workforce planning will become uncertain as retirement dates become unpredictable. Forecasting vacancies will be difficult, at best.
- Training issues will arise: What are the training needs of older workers? What methodology works best? What resistance can be expected?

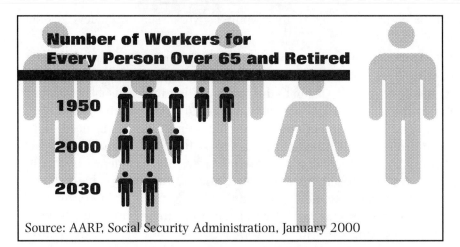

Number of Workers for Every Person Over 65 and Retired

1950	👤👤👤👤👤
2000	👤👤👤
2030	👤👤

Source: AARP, Social Security Administration, January 2000

- Older workers need different health insurance benefits. In fact, as *Workforce 2020* suggests, America may need to consider the overhaul of the insurance system itself. Coverage may need to be expanded to include arthritis, hearing loss, and long-term care, as well as eldercare programs for those employees with elderly living parents. As Medicare benefits decrease, older workers may be tempted to remain employed for the sake of retaining employer-provided healthcare coverage.
- Retirement packages may need to include health insurance and nursing home coverage.

Meet people where they are

To manage indispensable employees effectively, it is important to meet them where they are. This involves understanding where people are in their life cycle and what types of programs, benefits, work arrangements, and so forth might be appealing to them. Gordon F. Shea, in his book, *Managing Older Workers*, talks about the age of people and what their reality might be. If you know your employees' demographic profile you can begin to better tailor benefits to their needs. For example, age 21 is the legal adult age. Early retirement from pension plans typically begins at age 55.

Organizations are finding creative, even radical ways to meet their IEs where they are. For example, some companies with large numbers of young, unmarried employees who do not have children have found that they must tailor their benefits to this important group. Although they continue to offer such things as family health insurance, they understand that such a benefit has little or no relevance to their younger workers, so they devise something that will.

Timberland, an organization that has made the *Fortune* 100 Best Companies to Work For list on several occasions, is a great example. Timberland has done much to listen to the voices of their indispensable employees (who, by the way, are surveyed often in order to keep up with what employees want, not what Timberland, as the employer, thinks people need). After hearing from staff, Timberland concocted a benefit that would play well among many staff, including people who were young, unmarried, and didn't utilize their family health insurance plan. You may not believe this one. Timberland developed a pet health insurance plan. Some of their young indispensable employees may not have sick kids to contend with, but a sick dog can also be taxing—not just on your emotions, but also on the pocketbook if he gets sick and has to go to the vet. That's pretty radical, but Timberland's approach puts it on the *Fortune* 100 Best Companies list.

Generational differences

Generation X grew up with so many TV stations that they needed a remote control to manage them. Baby Boomers grew up with only three TV stations. Matures had no TV; they had radios and their imaginations for entertainment. As we all know, Generation X is advanced in technology. They have grown up with computers, e-mail, fax, call waiting, and caller ID. What a stark contrast with the Matures and Baby Boomers and their pens and pencils, mimeograph machines, and party lines. These differences—and the general composition of the workforce—often cause some friction in the workplace.

Part of managing across generations is to understand the differences and similarities between the generations and to try to build bridges to lessen the gaps.

Think of the bandwidth of your typical Mature worker: He or she has experienced the Depression, World War II, post-war prosperity, and suburban sprawl, and music from Bing Crosby to rap music. Contrast that to a Generation Xer, who also has some serious bandwidth expansion in his background—parents getting laid off from jobs, the advent of the personal computer, and unprecedented economic times—but of a different variety than the Mature.

A key to understanding how to manage indispensable employees from different generations is to take the time to understand the society in which

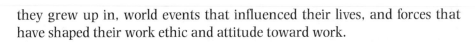

they grew up in, world events that influenced their lives, and forces that have shaped their work ethic and attitude toward work.

Matures

Matures were born between 1920 and 1945. They were raised during the Depression, one of the most catastrophic times the United States has ever seen. Their lives were impacted by the era of Mussolini and Hitler. Franklin Roosevelt's New Deal introduced Social Security and other financial recovery programs. The Japanese took the United States by surprise with Pearl Harbor. The Atomic Bomb changed their lives. Matures had to rebound and restructure during and after World War II. A sense of "the good of the country" (duty and obligation), self-sacrifice, and saving for a rainy day were common themes.

Baby Boomers

Baby Boomers were born between 1946 and 1964. In their era, the post-war economy thrived but the Cold War began. New highways spurred the growth of suburbs. Rock and roll was born and Berry Gordy founded Motown. African Americans demanded that America live up to "all men are created equal." Women's lib, Civil Rights, and antidisestablishmentarianism picked up speed. The Space Race began. Lyndon B. Johnson declared war on poverty. Color televisions became commonplace. Things were groovy; people made love, not war. Spend now, challenge authority, and demand freedom were themes of the Baby Boomers' lives. (Not saving for a rainy day contributed to the concern over decreasing Social Security and health insurance.)

Generation Xers

Generation Xers were born between 1965 and 1981. During their youth they saw the fall of President Nixon, the pain of Vietnam, the death of Elvis, and gasoline shortages. People confronted the possibility that things may never get better. Patriotism and a booming economy spurred the 1980s attitude that America is number one again. The Soviet Union and Communism collapsed. Gen Xers are the first to do worse than their parents. The uncertainty in the workplace that Gen Xers saw (as their parents were laid off) likely contributed to the lack of loyalty given to one company.

•••

As you can tell from these brief overviews, these three generations of workers come from different times, had different childhoods, and have different values. Understanding these backgrounds will help you manage across generations more effectively.

Generational differences and similarities exercise

As an exercise with your staff to get them to open up to each other about their generational differences and similarities, have everyone jot down a few words they'd use to describe Mature, Baby Boomer, and Generation X workers. Also ask them what issues, if any, the department faces regarding people from different generations. As your staff make their lists, you should do the same. You should also think about how you can better manage the performance of each generation of workers.

Grandkids supervising grandparents

Not too long ago, I taught a seminar at the Harvard Business School and a 60-year-old participant revealed that his boss was just 33. These types of situations are becoming more commonplace. Think about how we've redefined in recent years the notion of who is more experienced in the workforce.

For most of the last 50-plus years, experience in the workforce was largely defined by two variables: age and tenure. The older you were (age) coupled with your length of time in the job (tenure) equaled experience. That definition has changed radically.

Matures and Baby Boomers were spoon-fed a cradle-to-grave employment and grew up with the notion that once you went to college, graduated, and got your degree, you had proven yourself and could pretty much rest on your laurels. Except for those occupations that required you to become recertified or take courses to keep your license current, many people did not have to go back to school in order to keep their jobs and/or advance in their careers. You could become a supervisor, move to a managerial position, and eventually become a vice president or president without having to step foot on a college campus.

Today, however, the picture has changed dramatically. After the 1980s drove cradle-to-grave employment into the burial plot, new technology sprouted up, and with it came a whole new definition of what constitutes experience.

Experience now relates less to your age and tenure and is more about your current knowledge: what you know, and what you're doing to keep your brain (and skills) fresh. Lifelong learning rules, and you have to constantly learn new things in and outside of the workplace just to keep your job, let alone get promoted.

As so many managers have learned, when it comes to recruiting and retaining indispensable employees, age has almost become irrelevant. If you're 20 years old and have the technological know-how, then you're the most experienced.

Young people are increasingly found supervising people their parents' and/or grandparents' age. Mature workers, on the other hand, may be challenged when they supervise people who seem to possess a different work ethic from those in their generation and are willing to say "I'm outta here," if the work isn't satisfying.

Over the years, *Fortune* has done a good job of articulating the complex challenge that managers face as they struggle to manage people in the workforce from different generations. Check out some headlines from its June 13, 1994; March 16, 1998; and February 1, 1999 editions, respectively:

- "You will be employed by us as long as you add value to the organization, and you are continuously responsible for finding ways to add value. In return, you have the right to demand interesting and important work, the freedom and resources to perform it well, pay that reflects your contribution, and the experience and training needed to be employable here or elsewhere."
- "Companies used to pay for experience. Now they want potential-on the cheap. Just ask veteran marketing executive Mike Bellick, 46. He lost his job to a 28-year-old."
- "I want a fat salary, a signing bonus, and a cappuccino machine—oh, and I'm bringing my bird to work. I'm the *New* Organization Man. You need me." —Roberto Ziche

Loyalty

Quite often we hear employers lament that loyalty is dead. What happened to those employees who were at one time committed to the organization? Although it is my belief that loyalty is not down for the count, there are certainly many challenges that organizations face in getting people to see more than the WIFM (What's in It For Me) in their jobs. Quite often, people point to Gen Xers as the poster children for lack of loyalty to an organization. It is important to note that although some Generation Xers are not prone to be loyal to any organization, there are still many people who will believe in and stand by an organization as long as the organization practices the same way of thinking.

To put the loyalty factor into perspective (especially as it relates to Gen Xers, who we want to keep as indispensable employees), it's important to reflect on what has driven them to where they are. To better understand where some indispensable employees may be coming from, we must reflect on what's happened in the workplace since the downsizing, rightsizing, reengineering era of the late 1980s through the mid-1990s. This was a very traumatic time for many American workers and their families. So the next time you think that a Gen Xer is disloyal, consider what his experience may have been throughout those years and how it has colored his perceptions regarding loyalty in the workforce. Think about what the following scenario reveals:

Sally is a 25-year-old Gen Xer in your organization. Ten years ago, she experienced a change in her family situation that will forever impact her perception about what it means to be loyal to an organization. Her mother had been a stay-at-home mom and attended all of her sports events and extracurricular activities. Her dad was a company man, and for as much time as he spent at the office (some days it approximated a 24/7 schedule), he should have had the company's logo tattooed on his heart.

One day the bottom fell out of Sally's world. Her dad came home with a strong vodka odor on his breath and told the family that his company of 25 years had just literally given him a pink slip. He got four weeks' severance pay, a pat on the back, and some kind words from his boss ("This could not have happened to a nicer guy"). Home life was never the same again.

Mom was lucky and found a full-time job. She had not been in the workplace for years and, even with her college diploma, in a labor market where just about everyone was downsizing, she was lucky to land a secretarial job that barely paid minimum wage, but it helped to pay the bills. Sally's dad did not fair quite as well. His drinking increased as he pounded the job-hunting pavement in vain for more than a year. He wasn't alone though; several neighbors and scores of family members were also going through a similar ordeal as family breadwinners lost their jobs.

Because Sally's mom had to work full-time and had a boss that wasn't very family-friendly, she seldom made it to Sally's functions. In fact, there was little money for extracurricular activities anymore, so Sally took a part-time job at the local burger place, a few blocks from her house. When Sally wasn't working, she became a latchkey kid and learned how to entertain herself and make do on her own. Finally, Sally's dad did find a job, albeit at a very reduced salary.

Now Sally is 25 years old. She's a survivor who worked her way through a top business school and has more than a promising future ahead of her as an Information Technology Specialist. She has learned, however, some important lessons from the hard school of life that she went through:

1. Be loyal to a company, but also to yourself. Job security is only a retro memory of days gone by.
2. Make sure you make time to balance work and life. Look at what Sally's dad missed out on as she was growing up. Was it really worth it?
3. Also look for balance unless you want your kids to grow up as latchkey children.

•••

This scenario makes you think a little deeper about why so many people, especially Generation Xers, might just approach the notion of loyalty from a different perspective from previous generations of workers.

The influx of Gen X employees into the workforce has forced companies today to:

- Recognize that people do, in fact, have lives outside of work.
- Understand that Xers aren't lacking dedication, but rather have focused their priorities to achieve a fuller life balance.
- Find new ways to recruit, motivate, and retain indispensable employees.

Life stage management

When managing across generations, consider where different staff are in their life stages. Consider how to accommodate them and their needs with regard to:

- Benefits.
- Work/life balance.
- Flexibility.
- Training/education.
- Career management.
- Recruitment and retention (portable or cradle-to-grave ethic?).

Tips for cross-generational management

- Construct benefits and rewards that cross age lines. Ask employees what they want.

- Consider life stages and how to accommodate the needs of pre-retirees (Matures), those paying their children's college tuition (Baby Boomers), and first-time home or car buyers (Gen Xers).

- Consider where people are with regard to work ethic/attitude toward work and leisure time.

- Find ways to get Baby Boomers and Matures to brush up on their skills. Recognize that many of them remember when you could rest on your laurels once you got a degree. Some are not necessarily interested in spending their spare time studying or going back to school.

- Provide career advancement advice (Individual Development Plans, in-house training/in-service opportunities, tuition reimbursement, external training opportunities, etc.).

- Offer job rotation and job shadowing programs.

- Provide mentoring programs that include reciprocal (ways for people to find and be a mentor), radical (accelerated programs to enhance skills), reverse (young people mentoring older people), peer-to-peer, and mentoring for diverse employees.

- Hold "can't we all just get along" activities that help staff understand cross-generational differences and similarities. Retro days/activities (where employees dress as people did in the 1960s, 1970s, and 1980s) are popular in many organizations.

- Make sure that generic management skills are updated and mutated regularly. Provide management training for Gen Xers who will be managing co-workers who are their parents' or grandparents' ages.

- Get managers and employees to rethink age myths (for example, Gen Xers are not loyal and slackers; older people can't learn new tricks, are too slow, and can't keep up with technology). Emphasize the similarities of people at different ages.

- Make sure staff understand the organization's vision and mission, and how they fit into them.

- Provide ongoing feedback on individual and team performances.
- Offer socially responsible activities. Help your organization make a memorable difference in the world.
- Practice labor forecasting so that you know what jobs are needed and whether internal staff could fill them.
- Be more flexible and inclusive with regard to your management style. If appropriate, consider allowing telecommuting, flexible work schedules, and job sharing.
- Realize the implications of the changing employer-employee relationship. Make sure managers clearly understand that it's no longer a buyer's (employer's) market.
- Recognize that employees are at different life stages and that one size doesn't fit all when it comes to benefits, compensation, career mobility, work schedules, etc.
- Link recruitment and retention efforts.
- Help staff continuously sharpen technological, interpersonal, and written communication skills.
- Recognize that employees are portable and that their skills can be used "here or elsewhere."
- Teach staff how to operate in a global arena.

Managing different work and lifestyles

In today's fast-paced work environment, there are as many work and lifestyle arrangements as there are ages of people in the workforce. Employers that want to be successful in retaining and attracting indispensable employees are open to exploring a variety of work arrangements with staff: telecommuting, job sharing, flexible scheduling, compressed work weeks, and so forth.

They also work to meet staff where they are in regards to their careers. Here are some types of indispensable employees in the workforce who span the generations:

- **Lifers.** These are employees who have chosen a career with one employer, but have mutated regularly by changing positions within the company or learning new skills so that their current job remains challenging and keeps them gainfully employed.

Straight from the expert's lips:

"To recruit mature workers effectively, work with non-profit organizations that specialize in referring experienced workers, such as Operation A.B.L.E. (Ability Based on Long Experience), Green Thumb, the Urban League, etc. Preferably have a mature worker conduct the pre-employment interview; younger recruiters can get intimidated.

"Retention of mature workers is accomplished by including them on all assignments, and considering them fairly for promotions."

—Ruth Ann "Rickie" Moriarty,
Former Executive Director of Operation A.B.L.E. of Greater Boston

- **Job-hoppers.** Short-term stints in jobs are what satisfies these indispensable employees. They have no preconceived notion about organizations owing them cradle-to-grave employment. They are the captains of their career ships and have worked hard to create Me, Inc., their own company that can survive any corporation.
- **Reincarnated workers.** These are people who have in some way found their work life reincarnated (people who owned their own business and then went back to work for corporations; mothers who took a hiatus from the world of work to take care of little ones; etc.).
- **Second-career workers.** Sometimes people change their lives and take on a second career. Say, for example, you were in the Army for 22 years and at age 42 you're retired but not ready to spend your days fishing and watching TV.
- **Un-retired workers.** Sometimes people retire, thinking it's just what they want, only to find that they have more time on their hands than they wanted. They now want a new job, but not one to pay the bills. They have enough money; this job has to be special and appeal to their soul.

Take time to think about ways you might incorporate these types of indispensable employees into your workplace.

Chapter 17

Plate Spinning: Balancing Work and Life

We live in a complex, unprecedented time in our worklife, homelife, and society in general. This makes balancing our lives even more complicated. According to a May 1999 issue of *The Wall Street Journal*, one third out of 400,000 employees surveyed find it difficult to balance work and home. A lot is written about balancing work and life, and in my travels, I hear a lot of people complaining about never seeming to be able to achieve balance. I believe they are feeling this way because people mostly *don't* balance the two. Think about the scales of justice in your life: How often are they totally even? Isn't one usually tipped more than the other?

In our ever-changing society and workplace, however, it is important that people do try to bring some type of harmony into their lives by managing chaos and ambiguity. In order to accomplish this, think of this process as plate spinning. Here's how it works.

Perhaps you recall the original *Ed Sullivan Show* (if this was before your time, maybe you remember seeing reruns on "Nick at Nite"). Ed Sullivan had an act on his show that worked like this: There were a series of about five poles on the stage. A gentleman would come out with plates and begin to spin them on these poles. He'd start with the first pole, move to the second one, and so on. By the time he got to place the final plate on the pole, guess what was happening to the plate on the first pole? You guessed it: It started to wobble. The man quickly went back to that first pole and any others that were showing signs of not doing what he intended for them to do, namely spin, and made sure he gave them the appropriate attention, until all five plates were spinning in perfect unions (albeit for a nanosecond).

The plate spinning act is probably more in line with how work and life issues play out in most of our lives. We get one plate spinning (work) and leave it alone for a second when we go home to pick up our children or be with our significant others. But if a child gets sick or an elderly parent falls ill, that spinning plate may need more attention than the one(s) involving work. It's a constant process of keeping the plates spinning at a point where they aren't wobbling. But they may not necessarily be spinning at the same speed in balance and harmony either. In today's fast-paced world, that may be the best we can hope to achieve in terms of balance.

Economic boom

Salaries have gone up. Wall Street and the Feds tell us that productivity has also increased, and so has the standard of living. A 40-hour work week is a distant memory. People are earning more but enjoying life less. Look at these statistics from *The New York Times* (September 5, 1999):

- American workers spend an average of 44 hours per week working. (This is a 3.5-hour increase since 1977.)
- Americans work 350 hours (or almost nine full work weeks) more per year than Europeans.
- Europeans get three to five weeks standard vacation time. Americans are given an average of 19 vacation and holiday days. Germans get 42 days.

Balancing programs

Many employers are developing work/life initiatives to help indispensable employees address the complexities of managing work, family, and personal lives with internal and external resources, information, support, and programs. They are also assisting them in being more productive at work and at home, encouraging them to look at every stage of life and all lifestyles.

Non-workaholic environments

To attract and keep indispensable employees, consider constructing a non-workaholic environment. Remember, "face time" does not always correlate to greater productivity. Such a strategy can help you to:

- Attract and retain top talent.
- Reduce absenteeism and tardiness.
- Reduce anxiety, stress, and distraction.
- Reduce turnover.
- Heighten morale and productivity.
- Enhance your public image.

Watch for workaholic behavior

Watch for these behaviors, which can lead to a decrease in your employees' productivity:

- Their job has been "all consuming."
- They show up for work on holidays and weekends.
- They always take work home.
- They call in while on vacation.
- They can't say no to projects, assignments, etc.

A shifting work ethic

In the past it was easy to separate our private and professional lives. Today it's more complex. Where does work end and leisure time begin? Professional life creeps into personal life easily in a world of laptops, e-mail, fax machines, cell phones, pagers, and voice mail. Employers are concocting a variety of programs to help indispensable employees maintain sanity at home and at work. Here are a few examples of what organizations are providing:

- Dependent care (before- and after-school care on-site or near site).
- Consultation, referral, and resource services (for child-care and eldercare).
- Sick child, summer, and holiday programs.
- Family education and support.
- Concierge services (such as dry cleaning, travel, tickets to concerts, etc.).
- Pet health insurance.
- Wellness programs.
- Employee assistance programs.
- A lactation room.
- Parent resource libraries.
- Adoption aid.

Straight from the expert's lips:

"We strive to create an environment that is sensitive to the work/life balance issues that face us today. For many employees, it is no longer acceptable to work an average of 50–60 hours per week to the detriment of one's personal life. Issues may surface that necessitate flexibility during the course of the workday to accommodate personal needs. To that end, Tufts Health Plan offers a variety of flexible work arrangements that allow staff the latitude to meet the responsibilities of their jobs and also the demands of everyday life. As a result, we find that our employees appreciate the flexibility, and thus tend to work harder and stay longer."

—Lyn Rosenstein, Vice President,
Human Resources, Tufts Health Plan

- Take-home meals.
- Financial planning.
- Gyms.
- Personal trainers.
- Massages.
- Managers' compensation tied to work/life effectiveness.
- Phase-back programs for new moms.
- Regular employee surveys.
- Task forces on balancing worklife.
- Pre-tax set asides for childcare and eldercare.
- Alternative work options (telecommuting, flextime, and compressed work weeks).
- Leave for new parents (mothers *and* fathers).
- Manager training.

Chapter 18

Crafting a Recruitment and Retention Action Plan

A permanent approach to your organization's labor shortage requires a comprehensive analysis of your projected labor needs. Assess crucial information such as the demographic composition and qualifications of your organization's current workforce, the anticipated turnover rate, and any expected position openings. Then devise a well-constructed labor forecasting plan that outlines how you'll keep the steady stream of applicants and staff to handle your organization's growing labor needs.

Analyze your employee demographic profile

A lasting solution to your labor shortage problem requires an understanding of your current workforce and a detailed analysis of what your labor needs will be over the next three years. Answer the following questions:

- What does your current workforce look like now?
- How does it break down by race, age, sex, and necessary qualifications?
- What is your turnover rate?

- Where is turnover a particular issue and why?
- What staff in what positions do you forecast you will need over the next three years?

(See Chapter 5 for more information.)

Recruitment techniques

Successful recruitment is the lifeblood of every organization. Utilizing your forecasted labor needs, establish where your organization's past recruitment dollars were best spent and where they should be spent in the future. Determine whether a traditional, nontraditional, or a mixture of recruitment techniques will net the best results for your organization.

Evaluate the effectiveness of the hiring process

An applicant's first impression of your organization comes from the hiring process. Understanding how applicants perceive this process is critical. Do they believe the process is expedient? Do they feel well-informed of their status during the entire interview process? Are key people included? Are all members of your employment search committees educated in interviewing skills and employment law? Do supervisors and managers feel that new hire matches are successful? If you've answered no to any of these questions, work to improve what you're doing.

Refine the hiring process

You need to know how long it takes to offer a job and whether that varies significantly depending on the kind of position. In addition, you must examine whether your company feels it is selecting the right staff for the right jobs. Is your selection process effective? If you were to ask your supervisors six months after a staff member had been hired if they were pleased with their selection, what would their response be?

Future Management Issues

As you plan to continue to recruit and retain indispensable employees, consider these future strategic issues for managers and how you will handle them:

- Planning for labor shortages (succession planning and forecasting).
- Articulating the changing employee/employer contract.
- Incorporating the contingency workforce/ telecommuters.
- Helping organizations manage diversity/ globalization issues.
- Incorporating office ergonomics that are compatible with teamwork and a contingency workforce.
- Moving workers from specialists to generalists.
- Managing consultants and outsourced functions.
- Instilling an attitude of lifelong learning just to keep a job.
- Rewarding performance without necessarily providing job advancement.

- Getting HR staff to transfer knowledge and become more strategic partners.
- Assisting organizations to become more flexible and help employees balance work, family, and personal life.
- Dealing with benefits for the older workers (retirement, eldercare, healthcare, etc.).
- Becoming an employer of substance and choice and developing workers' skills.
- Getting managers to become mentors and career coaches while realizing that employees will fly from the nest.
- Building a global workforce and understanding the needs of domestic and international workers.
- Cultivating school-to-work partnerships.
- Developing special relationships with temporary agencies, search firms, communities, and professional associations.

Skills managers need to survive in the new millennium

- Listening, oral, and written skills.
- Interpersonal skills.
- Computer skills.
- Negotiation, mediation, and consulting.
- Diversity.
- Customer service.
- Financial acumen.
- Project management.
- Team-building.
- Leadership.
- Networking/ability to form strategic alliances.
- Strategic planning.
- International knowledge of world events.
- Human resources management.
- Time management.
- Change management.

Final thoughts

Throughout this book, we've talked about the unprecedented, revolutionary times in which we live. Hiring and keeping IEs is a daunting, but not insurmountable, task. It is my hope that this book has provided you with some practical, interesting, and even radical ideas to help you conquer this workforce revolution. As you tackle the talent war, please keep this poem (one of my favorites) in mind. I believe it summarizes what all of our hard work boils down to when all is said and done. Best of luck to you in hiring and keeping your organization's most valuable resource: your IEs.

•••

Success

"To laugh often and much
To win the respect of intelligent people and the affection of children
To earn the appreciation of honest critics
and endure the betrayal of false friends
To appreciate beauty
To find the best in others
To leave the world a bit better, whether by a healthy child,
a garden patch or redeemed social condition
To know even one life has breathed easier because you have lived
That is to have succeeded."

—Ralph Waldo Emerson

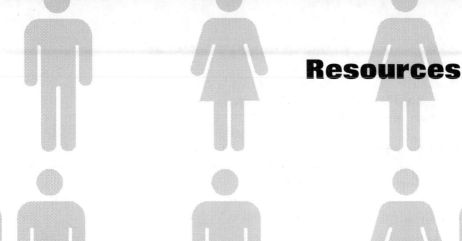

Resources

Books

Breaking Through: The Making of Minority Executives in America
by David A. Thomas and John J. Gabarro
(Harvard Business School, 1999)

CareerXRoads
by Gerry Crispin and Mark Mehler
(Jist Works, 2000)

Finding and Keeping Great Employees
by Jim Harris and Joan Brannick, Ph.D.
(AMACOM, 1999)

Love 'Em or Lose 'Em: Getting Good People to Stay
by Beverly L. Kaye and Sharon Jordan-Evans
(Berrett-Koehler, 1999)

The 100 Best Companies to Work for in America
by Robert Levering and Milton Moskowitz
(Plume, 1994)

1001 Ways to Reward Employees
by Bob Nelson
(Workman, 1994)

Workforce 2000: Work and Workers in the Twenty-First Century
by William B. Johnstone
(Hudson Institute, 1987)

Workforce 2020: Work and Workers in the 21ˢᵗ Century
by Richard W. Judy and Carol D'Amico
(Hudson Institute, 1997)

Web sites

Stats.bls.gov/news.release/ecopor.table7.htm
(Information by O*Net: The Occupational Information Network of the U.S. Department of Labor.)

www.pcepd.gov
(The President's Committee on Employment of People with Disabilities.)

fortune.com/careers
(Advice on finding and keeping jobs.)

www.rainmakerthinking.com
(Bruce Tulgan's free newsletter has good ideas for managing Generation X.)

fortune.com/archive.html
(For lists of America's most admired companies and best companies to work for.)

Company Web sites
with employment sections:

www.capitalone.com

www.cisco.com

www.compaq.com

www.eddiebauer.com

www.fidelity.com

www.ibm.com

www.partners.org

www.tacobell.com

Census

Consult the U.S. Census 2000 for information about population demographics, including information on race, gender, population migration patterns, etc.

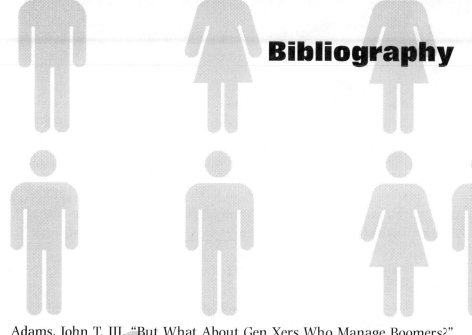

Bibliography

Adams, John T. III. "But What About Gen Xers Who Manage Boomers?" *HR Magazine,* December 1999.

Adams, Marc. "The Stream of Labor Slows to a Trickle." *HR Magazine,* October 1998.

——. "Building a Rainbow, One Stripe at a Time." *HR Magazine,* August 1998, Vol. 43, Issue 9.

Alch, Mark L. "Get Ready for the Net Generation." *Training and Development,* February 2000.

Armas, Genaro. "US Survey Shows Rise in Foreign-Born." *Boston Globe,* 3 January 2001.

Benson, Roland. *"Cultural Diversity in Health Care is Part of Good Customer Service."* South Florida Business Journal, *4 July 1997.*

Blanchard, Ken and Spencer Johnson. *The One Minute Manager.* New York: William Morrow & Company, Inc., 1982.

Boles, Richard Nelson. *What Color is your Parachute (2001 Edition).* Berkley, Toronto: Ten Speed Press, 2001.

Brady, Diane. "Uncle Sam Wants You...to Have Fun." *Business Week,* 2 February 2000.

Bruner, Richard W. "It's All in the Mix, Say Industry 'Diversity' Programs." *Electronic News,* July 21, 1997.

Building the Business Case for Workplace Flexibility. Report No. 1154. 1996.

Case, Tony. "Remember Newsroom Diversity?" *Editor & Publisher,* February 22, 1997.

Casison, Jeanie. "Young and In Charge." *Incentive*, December 1999.

Catlette, Bill and Richard Hadden. *Contented Cows Give Better Milk.* Germantown, Tenn.: Saltillo Press, 1998.

Chapa, Julie. "Recruiting Hispanic College Graduates." *Hispanic*, March 1998.

Chideya, Farai. *The Color of Our Future.* New York: William Morrow & Company, Inc., 1999.

Colvin, Geoffrey. "Changing of the Guard: GE Succession." *Fortune*, 22 January 2001.

Contreras, Maggie. "The Diversity Drive." *Hispanic*, June 1994.

Digh, Patricia. "The Next Challenge: Holding People Accountable." *HR Magazine*, October 1998.

——. "Race Matters." *Mosaics*, September/October 1998 (SHRM Diversity Program).

Diversity: Business Rational and Strategies Report No.1083. 1994.

"The Diversity Myth: True Multiethnic Countries are Concentrated in Just a Few Areas." *American Demographics Magazine*, June 1998.

Ebenkamp, Becky. "Couch & Potatoes." *Brandweek* 10 April 2000.

Fein, Ester B. "Language Barriers Are Hindering Health Care," *New York Times*, 23 November 1997, late edition.

Fields Associates, Inc. *The XYZs of How to Become More Diverse: Making Diversity an Organizational and Personal Priority.* 1998. (Video)

Freeman, Laurie. "Burnett Striving for Relevance in Communications." *Advertising Age*, 17 February 1997.

Fyock, Catherine. "Finding the Gold in the Graying of America." *HR Magazine*, February 1994.

Gendron, Marie. "Keys to Retaining Your Best Managers in a Tight Job Market." *Harvard Management Update*, June 1998.

Harris, Christy. "Study Finds Success in Recruiting Hispanics." *Federal Times*, 5 May 1997.

Imperato, Gina. "35 Ways to Land a Job Online." *Fast Company* 16 August 1998.

Jennings, Andrea. "Hiring Generation X." *Journal of Accountancy*, February 2000.

Jennings, Marianne. "What's Behind the Growing Generation Gap?" *USA Today Magazine*, November 1999.

Kavanaugh, Kathryn H. and Patricia H. Kennedy. *Promoting Cultural Diversity: Strategies for Health Care Professionals.* Newbury Park, Calif.: Sage Publications, 1992.

Kaye, Beverly and Sharon Jordan Evans. *Love 'em or Lose 'em-Getting Good People to Stay.* San Francisco: Berrett-Koehler Publishers, Inc., 1999.

Kennedy, Marilyn Moats. "Managing the Deliberately Mute." *Physician Executive,* Jan/Feb 2000.

Levering, Robert and Milton Moskowitz. "The 100 Best Companies to Work For." *Fortune,* 22 January 2001.

Locke, Don C. Increasing Multicultural Understanding: A Comprehensive Model. *Thousand Oaks, Calif.: Sage Publications, 1998.*

Losyk, Bob. "Using Right Approach Works with Gen Xers." *Business Journal Serving South Florida (Miami-Dade Edition),* 14 January 2000.

Mulling, Emory. "Best Companies Employ Novel Retention Methods." *Austin Business Journal,* 3 March 2000.

National Business and Disabilities Council. *(www.business-disability.com)*

Nucifora, Alf. "After Boomers and Xs, Here come Ys." *Nashville Business Journal,* 21 April 2000.

President's Committee on Employment of People with Disabilities. (*www50.pcepd.gov/pcepd*)

Quigley, Kelly. "Diversity for Survival's Sake." *Business Journal Serving Greater Milwaukee,* 26 June 1998.

Reingold, Jennifer. "Why Your Workers Might Jump Ship." *Business Week,* 1 March 1999.

Retention Management: Strategies, Practices, Trends. Saratoga, New York: American Management Association, 1997.

Rodriguez, Cindy. "Sun Belt Gains Seen in 2000 in census Data." *Boston Globe,* 28 December 2000.

Rowe, Mary P. "Fostering Diversity." *Program Manager,* March/April 1995.

Ruch, Will. "How to Keep Gen X Employees from Becoming X-Employees." *Training & Development,* April 2000.

"SHRM Releases New Survey of Diversity Programs." *Mosaics,* July/August 1998 (SHRM Diversity Program).

Smith, Bob. "Recruitment Insights for Strategic Workforce Diversity." *HR Focus,* January 1994.

Smith, J. Walker and Ann Cluman. *Rocking the Ages: The Yankelovich Report on Generational Marketing.* New York: HarperBusiness, 1997.

Stein, M.L. "New Diversity." *Editor & Publisher,* 14 June 1997.

Svehla, Trisha A. and Glen C. Crosier. *Managing the Mosaic.* Chicago: American Hospital Publishing, Inc., 1994.

Terry-Azios, Diana. "Kraft Employee Council Unites Hispanics." *Hispanic*, March 1998.

Tulgan, Bruce. *Managing Generation X.* Merritt Company, 1997.

Ulrich, Bob. "Generation "Why." *Modern Tire Dealer*, March 2000.

Wah, Louisa. "Managing Gen Xers Strategically." *Management Review*, March 2000.

Wallsten, Kevin. "Diversity Pays Off in Big Sales for Toyota Dealership." *Workforce*, September 1998.

Washburn, Earl. "The Five Generations." *Physician Executive*, Jan/Feb 2000.

Waterman, Jr., Robert H., Judith A. Waterman, and Betsy A. Collard. "Toward a Resilient Work Force." *Harvard Business Review* July/August 1994.

Wilke, Michael. "IBM Recruitment Ads to Appear in 'Advocate.' *Advertising Age*, November 25, 1996, Vol. 67, Issue 48.

Woodward, Nancy Hatch. "The Coming of the X Managers." *HR Magazine*, March 1999, Vol. 44, Issue 3.